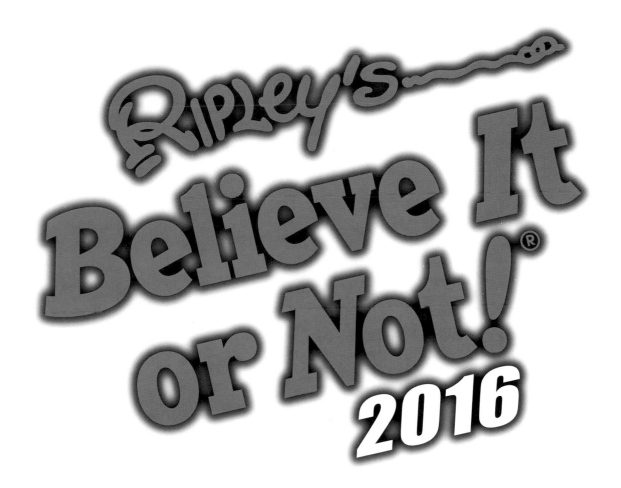

PUBLISHING

Executive VP Norm Deska
VP, Exhibits & Archives Edward Meyer

Publisher Anne Marshall

Editorial Director Rebecca Miles
Senior Researcher & Picture Manager James Proud
Project Editor Charlotte Howell
Editorial Assistant Dominic Lill
Text Geoff Tibballs
Additional Text James Proud, Dominic Lill
Editors Judy Barratt, Peter Mavrikis, Sally McFall
Factchecker Alex Bazlinton
Indexer Hilary Bird

Art Director Sam South
Senior Designer Michelle Foster
Design Dynamo Design
Reprographics Juice Creative
Cover Artwork Chris Ransom
Cover Consultation Emily Ellis, Mabel South

Copyright © 2015 by Ripley Entertainment, Inc.

First published in Great Britain in 2015 by
Random House Books
Random House, 20 Vauxhall Bridge Road,
London SW1V 2SA

www.randomhouse.co.uk

Addresses for companies within The Random House
Group Limited can be found at:
www.randomhouse.co.uk/offices.htm

The Random House Group Limited Reg. No. 954009

ISBN: 9781847947529
10 9 8 7 6 5 4 3 2 1

The Random House Group Limited supports The
Forest Stewardship Council (FSC®), the leading
international forest certification organisation. Our
books carrying the FSC label are printed on FSC®
certified paper. FSC is the only forest certification
scheme endorsed by the leading environmental
organisations, including Greenpeace. Our paper
procurement policy can be found at www.
randomhouse.co.uk/environment.

A CIP catalogue record for this book is
available from the British Library

Printed in China

PUBLISHER'S NOTE
While every effort has been made to verify
the accuracy of the entries in this book,
the Publishers cannot be held responsible
for any errors contained in the work. They
would be glad to receive any information
from readers.

WARNING
Some of the stunts and activities in this book
are undertaken by experts and should not
be attempted by anyone without adequate
training and supervision.

Ripley's Believe It or Not!

EYE-POPPING ODDITIES 2016

CONTENTS

152

ROBERT RIPLEY'S ENDURING LEGACY

Robert Ripley—artist, author, explorer, radio host, television and movie personality, and the man who coined one of the most famous phrases in the English language, "Believe It or Not!"—died more than 65 years ago. However, he is still very relevant in our media-driven world as the founder of reality TV and social media as we know it today.

From his first Believe It or Not! cartoon at *The New York Globe* in 1918 until his death in 1949, Robert Ripley created a legacy that still has meaning and relevance today. By shining a light on the weird and wonderful people, places and things he discovered around the world, Ripley showed us that being unique is something all humans have in common, and something to be pro...

As poi...
2015 ...
aw...
R...
D...

This incredible, never-before-seen color photo of Robert Ripley was taken during his expedition to Panama in 1939.

While working on the PBS biography, our researchers unearthed many rare photos of the 1940 New York Odditorium and its unusual performers, as well as new pictures of Ripley with his wife Beatrice and original photographs with his closest confidant during the 1940s, the wonderfully talented Li Ling Ai, who was not only the first person to win an Oscar for a documentary film (1941's *Kukan*), but also the first woman in America to host a weekly television show when she took the helm of the original Ripley's Believe It or Not! series after his death in 1949.

As the Ripley archive grows, so does the man's legend. Our fans' continuing desire to be part of our vast realm of "oddities" is proved by the many great photos and stories readers just like you have provided for this book.

Robert Ripley and his beloved friend and colleague, Li Ling Ai.

Here, Robert Ripley is being greeted by Panamanian indigenous people in 1939, the first year full color photography was readily available.

THE HUNT FOR THE
ODD, UNUSUAL
AND
UNBELIEVABLE

Readers like you have always been a tremendous help in building our Believe It or Not! collection. We're constantly searching for new facts, photos, news and videos to add to our cartoon and books—and we need YOUR help! Send in a photo or a source to help us verify your submission, and your ideas just might be in our next book. Bookmark our website—www.ripleys.com—to stay up-to-date on our latest contests and outreach programs.

RIPLEY'S BIZARRE BUYING BAZAAR

This violin was brought to the Ripley's Bizarre Buying Bazaar. It may very well be an actual Stradivarius!

Last year, the *Ripley's Bizarre Buying Bazaar*, our traveling acquisitions road show, visited five national locations: Key West, Florida; Phoenix, Arizona; Panama City Beach, Florida; Peoria, Illinois; and Seattle, Washington. We invited anyone and everyone to bring us their oddities for an official Ripley *odd-praisal* and the opportunity to sell their unbelievable treasures to us for inclusion in our permanent Ripley collection.

We saw everything from Prohibition whiskey, to antique hair wreaths, to a priceless ivory German medieval bubonic plague prevention flea catcher. We even saw what may have been an ultra-rare Stradivarius violin—possibly one of only 650 in the world!

We'll hit the road again soon to visit more locations, so visit our website, www.ripleys.com, to find a stop near you.

UNUSUAL MAIL

We at Ripley's HQ love to give things away—especially Ripley books! For last year's Unusual Mail Contest, fans were invited to send anything to us—*literally anything*—for a chance to win books from our vast library of titles. The only rule was that all submissions had to be received intact by regular post (no couriers), with *no wrapping or packaging of any sort!* The address and the stamps had to be placed directly on the object mailed.

We received inventive submissions from 27 different states and five different countries. Some entries were simple: postcards, playing cards, as well as small objects like toothbrushes and fridge magnets. However, our big winners all thought big AND strange!

This life-sized rag doll was one of the largest entries we received.

This beautiful fan was one of the more unusual submissions. Note the postage stamps along the bottom handle.

This traffic cone was one of the more inventive submissions to Ripley's Unusual Mail Contest.

STRANGE SHOPPING

Wherever we go, we get asked, "What is the weirdest, strangest, best thing you have acquired lately?" The answer of course is subjective, but there are always a few worthy standouts. Made of recycled metal, this life-sized Tyrannosaurus rex was created by artist John Lopez and is one of the latest Ripley's acquisitions.

EYE-POPPING ODDITIES

It's not always clear how a book gets its title, but this volume should be self-explanatory. We believe all of our amazing stories—and especially our astounding photos of these individuals with a talent for voluntary eyeball propulsion—might literally cause your eyes to pop right out of your head.

Way back in 1928, Robert Ripley first learned about voluntary eyeball propulsion when he met a Cuban eye popper named Avelino Perez Matos of the Baracoa District of Santiago de Cuba. After featuring Avelino in his Believe It or Not! newspaper feature on August 3, 1929, Ripley decided to make him a featured performer in the very first Odditorium, to be held at the 1933 Chicago World's Fair. As the curtain went up in Illinois at the Century of Progress World's Fair, Avelino stole the show and was forever nicknamed, "The Human Eye Popper."

Since then, we have found a small handful of other people who can also pop their eyes out of their sockets—some one eye only, some one at a time, some both at once, and all incredible to behold. We think you'll agree that, however they do it, the results are definitely eye-popping!

Jalisa Thompson, a former cashier at our Atlantic City Odditorium, was herself an eye popper! She traveled to several Ripley's locations, demonstrating her unique skill.

Ripley's EXPLAINS

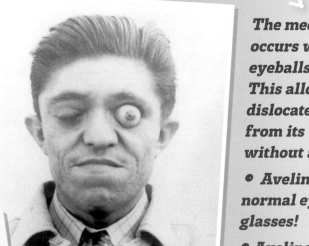

1939 photos of Avelino Perez Matos taken at the New York World's Fair.

The medical condition that occurs when humans "pop" their eyeballs is called exophthalmos. This allows the person to dislocate and relocate the eye from its "orbit," or socket, at will without any discomfort or effort.

● Avelino and Jalisa both had normal eyesight—neither wore glasses!

● Avelino could pop his eyes a full 9 millimeters and hold them out for several minutes!

R
Ripley's Believe It or Not!®
www.ripleys.com/books
EYE POPPERS

Brothers Hugh (left) and Antonio Francis (right) of Essex, England, show that eye poppers can run in the family!

Jorge Ivan Latorre Robles can't believe he's in this year's annual—turn to pages 116–117 to see what else he can do!

ALL NEW!

Ripley's Believe It or Not!

Ripley's
Believe It or Not!®
EYE-POPPING ODDITIES

○ Man pulls truck with nose
○ Meet Burma's sacred hairy family
○ Girl cries stone tears
○ Cow farts blow up building
And many more crazy stories...

IT'S EARTH-SHATTERING!

EYE POPPERS OF THE WORLD UNITE!

If you're an eye popper, we'd love to know! Send us your videos or photos—we may reach out to you for an exciting opportunity.

Visit www.ripleys.com/eyepopping for more information.

01

BELIEVE IT!

FIREWORKS SUIT

Colin Furze, a plumber and inventor from Lincolnshire, England, built his own inflatable "Iron Man" suit that allowed him to stand inside a huge fireworks display.

Although he had giant rockets attached to his suit, turning him into a human firework, and nearly $1,000 of fireworks went off all around him, the homemade armor enabled him to emerge from the display without a single burn or a even scratch.

Daredevil Colin, who has previously built a 55 mph (88 km/h) toilet and a moped that fired 15-ft-long (4.5-m) flames from the back, used a process called hydroforming, which employs water pressure to bend and inflate steel sheets, so that the steel armor fitted snugly around his body.

"Being able to stand inside a firework display is an experience I will not forget," he said afterward. "Seeing a lit rocket going off just six feet from your face is pretty epic."

Colin modeled the torso and limb armor piece by piece, then welded the parts together.

Once he was inside the robot-like suit, his steel helmet was bolted on, leaving Perspex-covered eye slits so that he could see.

HE'S NOT SAFE

BEDPAN COLLECTOR

For 25 years Eric Eakin has been building up a collection of more than 250 bedpans—in porcelain, metal, glass and even recycled newspaper—which he keeps in the basement of his home in Bay Village, Ohio. The oldest pan dates from the 19th century and the smallest, designed for a dollhouse, is less than ½ in (1.2 cm) long. His collection includes beautifully decorated bedpans with Native American imagery, another in the shape of a guitar with barbed wire strings and a novelty item with a little Richard Nixon head inside.

SPARKLING WREATH Finnish floral designer Pasi Jokinen-Carter created a Christmas wreath studded with more than 40 diamonds and rubies—that went on sale for nearly $5 million. The wreath would last only 12 days before the flowers wilted, but the precious stones could be turned into a bespoke piece of jewelry.

BODY POWER Inspired by the fact that at any given moment the human body produces energy equivalent to a 100-watt lightbulb, 16-year-old Ann Makosinski from Victoria, British Columbia, has invented a flashlight that is powered solely by body heat. Requiring no batteries, it powers as soon as it is held in the hand.

BIONIC KANGAROO Global engineering firm Festo has created a robot that exactly mimics the hopping jumps of a kangaroo. Bionic Kangaroo weighs just 15 lb (7 kg) and stands only 3 ft 3 in (1 m) tall, but it can jump 1 ft 4 in (40 cm) vertically and 2 ft 8 in (80 cm) horizontally.

FLYING PIGS Farmer Sying P'an set up a zip wire as a means to stop his pigs running off whenever he takes them to market in Weinan, China. He created a series of harnesses and pulleys to transport the 220-lb (100-kg) pigs through the air from his own truck straight into the truck of their new owner without allowing their trotters to even touch the ground.

CRASH LANDINGS In 1937, street sweeper Joseph Figlock was cleaning an alley in Detroit, Michigan, when a baby boy fell from a fourth-story window and landed on Joseph's head and shoulders. The collision broke the baby's fall and saved his life. A year later, Figlock was sweeping out another alley when two-year-old David Thomas fell from a fourth-story window and landed safely on him.

YOUR UPLOADS

THUMBS UP

Paws, a cat owned by Billy Rice of Atwater, California, has extra toes that are separated from the rest so that it looks as though he has thumbs. He has quickly learned to adapt to his unusual condition and uses his "thumbs" to reach inside food containers for his favorite whipped cream.

Employ Me

Unemployed university graduate Adam Pacitti spent his last £500 ($750) on renting a huge billboard in London, England, begging for a job. He also set up a website, employadam.com, and the resulting publicity helped him receive more than 60 firm offers. Once he had landed a job with a top media company, he spent his first paycheck on another billboard to say thank you.

EXPENSIVE BED A battered and chipped ceramic bowl that an elderly couple from Essex, England, regularly allowed their pet cat to sleep in sold for £108,000 ($170,000) in 2014 after it turned out to be a Chinese Ming dynasty piece dating back to the 15th century.

NUMBER ONE Currency collector Billy Baeder of Royersford, Pennsylvania, owns a $10 bill that is worth $500,000. The rare 1933 silver certificate bears the serial number A00000001A, making it probably the most valuable U.S. bill printed since 1929, when notes were shrunk to their current size.

GAME OPTION In Taiwan, drunk drivers are given the option of playing games of Mahjong with the elderly instead of paying a fine.

MISSING PERSON A model drone helped authorities locate an 82-year-old man who had been missing for three days. When Guillermo DeVenecia disappeared near Fitchburg, Wisconsin, police dogs and helicopters scoured the area to no avail. When David Lesh, who was in the area visiting his girlfriend's family, offered the services of his drone, however, rescuers spotted the pensioner in a corner of a bean field in less than 20 minutes.

LIVING PROOF Sixty-eight-year-old Jean-Marie Sevrain was forced to obtain a letter from his doctor certifying that he was still alive after the French health service had refused to pay his medical expenses on the grounds that he was dead. When he applied for a $30 refund after renewing a prescription, he was informed that he was not entitled to one because, according to health service records, he had died four years earlier.

ZOMBIE SNAKE Chef Peng Fan died when he was bitten by the severed head of a snake he was cooking at a restaurant in Guangdong, China. Twenty minutes after decapitating the Indochinese spitting cobra, he went to throw the head in the bin when it suddenly injected him with its deadly venom.

CANINE MAYOR Voters in Cormorant, Minnesota, elected a seven-year-old dog, Duke, as the town's mayor in 2014. He was given five hours of grooming as a reward.

TAKING THE PLUNGE Jessy Schild and Ingo Mueller from Freiburg, Germany, got married on board an airplane at an altitude of 16,000 ft (4,875 m) before skydiving to the ground with the priest, best man and bridesmaid. The newlyweds sealed their union with a midair kiss during freefall.

DELAYED MEDALS Ninety-three-year-old Tom Harrison, of Salt Lake City, Utah, received seven military medals in 2011—more than 60 years after his service in World War II.

STRANGE WEAPON A man was charged with trying to rob a convenience store in Fort Smith, Arkansas, in April 2012 while armed with a pair of hot dog tongs.

TRAIN SMASH In April 2012, a 31-year-old man from Pewaukee, Wisconsin, was found wandering around Canadian Pacific railroad tracks, unaware that he had just been hit by a 76-car freight train traveling at 48 mph (77 km/h).

PEN PALS Forty-one years after losing touch with her French pen pal Yvette Metay, Sue Ellis, from Staffordshire, England, found that they were living just 1 mi (1.6 km) apart. The girls had been randomly paired together as pen pals at their respective schools and visited and wrote to each other until 1973. Then, four decades later, Sue spotted her old friend in a local store and discovered that Yvette had moved from France in the 1980s, settling in Staffordshire in 2013.

SAME FIRE When 20-year-old Lunenburg, Massachusetts, firefighter Matt Benoit attended his first call—a house blaze in nearby Fitchburg—the first person he met there was his mother. Leominster Fire Lt. Audra Brown was exiting the house as Benoit arrived, mother and son having responded to the same fire from different fire departments.

WOOLY AVALANCHE

While Pete Oswald was skiing on Hector Mountain on New Zealand's South Island, he saw what appeared to be a mini avalanche snowballing toward him—but then realized it was an injured sheep.

He managed to carry the 88-lb (40-kg) animal safely down the mountain on his skis before releasing it.

WEDDING GIFT Mary and Ivor Waite from the West Midlands, England, are still using a vacuum cleaner made in 1925 that also paints, grinds coffee and minces meat and has never broken down. The German Piccolo appliance was a 1976 wedding gift from Ivor's aunt.

KIND GESTURE After Carol and Willie Fowler's daughter Tamara called off her wedding in Atlanta, Georgia, rather than let all the food go to waste, the couple invited 200 of the city's homeless people to a four-course meal.

NEAR MISS While Sarah Kaiser loaded her supermarket shopping in the trunk of her car in Dusseldorf, Germany, her five-year-old son David climbed into the driver's seat and sent the car rolling across the car park towards the River Rhine. It eventually came to rest with its front wheels hanging precariously over the edge of the harbor.

SINGING FISH A break-in at a bait and tackle store in Rochester, Minnesota, was foiled by a singing fish. The wall-mounted novelty bass, called "Big Mouth Billy," sings "Take Me to the River" whenever the door is opened, and the noise was enough to scare off the intruder before he could take anything.

EXTREME EMBALMING As part of the new craze of extreme embalming, the centrepiece of the wake of New Orleans socialite Mickey Easterling, who died in April 2014 at age 83, was her body propped up on a bench wearing a cocktail gown and pink feather boa and holding a cigarette and champagne glass.

DIFFERENT YEARS Lindsay Salgueiro of Toronto, Ontario, gave birth to twin girls— but they were born in different years. Gabriella arrived at 11.52 p.m. on December 31, 2013, and her younger sister Sophia was delivered 38 seconds after midnight, so has a birth date of January 1, 2014.

LATE POST A nine-page letter written in 1931 by Miriam McMichael of Houlton, Maine, to her mother Dollena 150 mi (240 km) away in Pittsfield was finally delivered in 2014—83 years later. Both women have since died and ironically in the letter Miriam apologized for not writing sooner.

STORYBOOK ENDING A book given to an Australian girl by her father found its way back to her after 66 years and a journey around the world. When Betty Fowkes of Melbourne was 11, her father gave her the book, titled *Magic Australia*, and had inscribed in it: "To Betty, from Daddy, Christmas 1944." She lost the book in a house move four years later, but then in 2014 she heard the author's name mentioned on a radio broadcast and asked her daughter, Liz Crooks, to search for a copy online. Ms. Crooks randomly selected a copy from New York's Austin Book Shop— and when it arrived it was Betty's original, complete with her father's inscription.

SKATEBOARDING COP Joel Zwicky, an officer with the Green Bay Police Department, Wisconsin, patrols the streets on a skateboard with red and blue LED lights. The skateboard enables him to access more areas than in a car and is quicker than traveling on foot.

WRONG BIRTHDAY Shortly before turning 100 years old, Evelyn Frost of Staffordshire, England, discovered she had been celebrating her birthday on the wrong date her whole life. When she applied for her birth certificate to register for the traditional 100th birthday letter from the Queen, she found that it listed her date of birth as April 16, 1914, not April 17 as she had always thought.

FAIRY TALE HOUSE

Artist Mary Rose Young has decorated her three-bedroom cottage in Gloucestershire, England, so that it resembles a full-size dolls' house. The unique interior has bright, clashing colors, and is adorned with vibrant pottery pieces that she makes in her workshop. She has also sold her pottery to the likes of Ozzy Osbourne, Demi Moore and Lady Gaga. Mary calls the cottage "an Alice in Wonderland sweet shop for adults."

FITTING FAREWELL Instead of a hearse, U.S. Navy veteran Ronald Bloss Sr. of Mount Wolf, Pennsylvania, was taken to his grave in a motorboat. He loved spending time on rivers and, in accordance with his wishes, his casket was loaded onto a small boat and trailer and pulled to the cemetery by a pickup truck driven by one of his sons.

GOD MYSTERY A New York City man claims that a credit-rating agency refuses to acknowledge that he has a financial history because his first name is God. Russian native God Gazarov, who owns a Brighton Beach jewelry store, is named after his grandfather.

Rocking Wake

For her wake at a funeral home in San Juan, Puerto Rico, the body of 80-year-old Georgina Chervony Lloren was clothed in her wedding dress from her second marriage and seated in her favorite red-cushioned rocking chair. Her daughter Miriam said her mother specified that was how she envisioned her wake.

KOO KOO THE BIRD GIRL

Koo Koo the Bird Girl, blind and toothless, with her small head, thin face and beaky nose, was a well-known character on the circus sideshow circuit in the early 20th century.

Koo Koo's act, completed with fluffy feathers and oversized chicken feet, consisted of dancing strangely and acting the fool. She was born Minnie Woolsey in Georgia in 1880, and became a fixture for many years in the Ringling Brothers Circus sideshow. In 1932, her unique appearance earned her a role in the Hollywood movie *Freaks*, featuring an ensemble cast of bizarre sideshow workers, and she was performing as the "Cuckoo Girl" at the World Circus Side Show at Coney Island, New York, into the 1940s. Unlike many of her outlandish colleagues, Minnie was quiet and reserved away from the stage and did not draw attention to herself until dressed in her feathers. It's likely that Woolsey suffered from a type of dwarfism called Seckel syndrome, also known as "bird-headed" dwarfism.

DINING WITH DEATH

Customers at the New Lucky restaurant in Ahmedabad, India, drink tea surrounded by human graves—because it is built in the middle of an old Muslim cemetery. It was originally opened in the 1950s as a tea stall outside the cemetery, but the business expanded until it encircled about a dozen of the graves. Rather than disturb the graves, owner Krishnan Kutti Nair decided to build tables around the coffins, which he had enclosed with iron gates.

WASTING TIME Students at the University of Pennsylvania can take a degree course titled "Wasting Time on the Internet." Offered by the Department of English, the course partly requires students to "stare at the screen for three hours, only interacting through chat rooms, bots, social media and listservs."

ROOKIE PASSWORD Master computer hacker Jeremy Hammond, once the FBI's most wanted cyber criminal, is serving a ten-year prison sentence because his password was surprisingly easy to guess. He was convicted in 2013 of infiltrating dozens of U.S. government websites after detectives raiding his home obtained the incriminating evidence from his laptop by quickly working out his password—the name of his pet cat, Chewy, followed by 123.

CEMETERY RACE To encourage more people to buy plots there, Springdale Cemetery in Peoria, Illinois, staged a 5K race and hired actors to dress up as well-known people who have been buried in the cemetery since it opened in 1857.

OFFICE BEACH Using a carpet of sand, as well as speakers and a 3-D projector, the Japanese company Bizreach re-created a tropical beach in the reception area of their Tokyo office in the hope of persuading employees and potential clients that it is a fun place to work.

TWIN SHERIFFS In November 2014, twin brothers Rob and John Snaza were elected sheriffs in neighboring southwest Washington counties. Voters elected Rob to become sheriff of Lewis County while John was re-elected sheriff of Thurston County.

↥ YOUR UPLOADS

FOUR-EYED MOUSE

Katheryn Hung sent Ripley's this picture of an incredible four-eyed mouse that she spotted several times while she was on vacation in Destin, Florida. When she first saw it, she thought it was carrying a baby mouse, but later realized it was a strange mutant.

OLD PANTS A pair of pants discovered in a cemetery in Xinjiang, China, is believed to have been worn by a horseman 3,300 years ago. Stripped from a mummy, the pants were made of three pieces of cloth—two for legs and one for the crotch. Nomads in Xinjiang originally wore pants just consisting of two legs that were fastened to the waist with strings. It was only later that crotches were sewn on to the legs.

HOSPITAL WEDDING When Kimberly Elgin from Galloway, Ohio, was stricken with appendicitis on the eve of her planned South Carolina beach wedding to Travis Smith, the ceremony had to take place instead at Waccamaw Community Hospital near Myrtle Beach—with the bride wearing a mint-green hospital gown and walking down an aisle made of bed sheets.

BIRD BOMBS Before releasing 10,000 pigeons for 2014 National Day celebrations in Beijing, Chinese officials examined the butts of every bird in case any one of them was carrying a bomb.

FIRST AND LAST The first and last British soldiers to die in World War I, Privates John Parr and George Ellison, are both buried in St. Symphorien cemetery, in France, and face each other only yards apart.

FLESH SEATS British furniture designer Gigi Barker has devised a range of flesh-colored leather sofas and chairs that look and feel like human skin. She started by tracing the outline of a man's midriff before modeling it in clay and then impregnating the leather with pheromones and aftershave to make it seem more human.

LICENSE TO STUDY In 1990, 15-year-old student James Bond sat for his school examinations at Argoed High School, North Wales—and his examination paper reference number was 007.

CERAMIC
INFLATABLES

Pennsylvania artist Brett Kern creates ceramic models that look exactly like inflatable toys.

He is able to copy the precise wrinkles and shapes of inexpensive air-filled dinosaurs, rabbits and astronauts, but his ceramic versions sell for up to $800. The series of artworks was inspired by an inflatable dinosaur he was given as a child.

HUMAN PENDULUM

Top animal trainer, Frank "Cheerful" Gardner, is seen here with one of the elephants that toured with the Hagenbeck-Wallace Circus in 1931.

Luckily, this isn't a vicious attack, but Cheerful's signature act—a trick known as the "head carry," or "human pendulum," in which the elephant would carry his trainer around the circus tent. It was said that a rival trainer once tried the same trick and ended up in hospital with a fractured skull. Cheerful was known as the "Dean" of elephant trainers, and looked after herds for several different circuses in a career that spanned decades. He proudly stated, "Elephants are the smartest and most lovable animals on earth," and that he had never been injured in his work.

CHEERFUL GARDNER

BELIEVE IT!

HANDCUFF DAY February 20 is National Handcuff Day in the U.S.A.—in honor of George A. Carney's revolutionary lightweight adjustable handcuff, which he patented on that date in 1912.

BRIDGE THEFT Thieves stole a footbridge weighing 5,000 lb (2,270 kg) from a property in Detroit, Michigan. The 40-ft (12-m) structure was later found undamaged 20 mi (32 km) away in Belleville, Michigan.

DECEPTION TACTIC Colonel William Washington forced the surrender of more than 100 British loyalists during the American War of Independence without firing a shot, by painting a log to look like a cannon—a so-called "Quaker Gun."

BAD START The U.S. Secret Service, tasked with protecting the President, was created by Abraham Lincoln on the day he was assassinated.

GREAT SURVIVOR Violet Jessop, an Irish stewardess who survived the sinking of the *Titanic* in 1912, also lived through disasters involving her two sister ships—the sinking of the *Britannic* in 1916 and the collision of the *Olympic* with H.M.S. *Hawke* in 1911. A total of more than 1,500 people died in the three incidents.

STRAW DRAW Charles Piazza won a 2014 tied election for alderman in Waveland, Mississippi, by drawing the longer of two straws. Back in 2002, he had lost another tied Mississippi election on the toss of a coin. Local law calls for tied elections to be decided by a game of chance.

SAME BIRD British birdwatcher Dave Clifton caught the same small bird twice in a few weeks—at locations 1,500 mi (2,400 km) apart. On vacation in Portugal, he netted a tiny blackcap and when he looked at the identification ring on its leg he realized it was the very bird that he had previously caught near his home in Staffordshire, England.

SUBWAY WEDDING Hector Irakliotis and Tatyana Sandler spent so much of their courtship on the New York City subway that they decided to marry there. A chaplain performed the ceremony on the N train as it crossed from Brooklyn into Manhattan, and their fellow passengers applauded as the couple were pronounced man and wife.

CHRISTMAS WOE Twin sisters Lorraine and Levinia Christmas decided on the spur of the moment to deliver presents to one another's houses on Christmas Eve 1994. The country road between their villages in Norfolk, England, was treacherously icy and the 31-year-old sisters were involved in a head-on crash—with each other.

BED TEST Andrew Iwanicki from Los Angeles, California, was paid $18,000 by NASA to lie in bed for three months straight. He lays on a tilting bed at the NASA Flight Analog Research Unit in Houston, Texas, so that scientists could study the effects space has on bone and muscle.

FORGER'S NIGHTMARE The face of English composer Sir Edward Elgar was chosen to appear on the British £20 note for more than a decade because his distinctive, bushy mustache was difficult for would-be forgers to copy.

↑ YOUR UPLOADS

EXTRA TOES
Kirstin Mercer of Orangeville, Ontario, Canada, sent Ripley's this picture of her cat Lilli who was born with 32 toes. Cats are normally born with 18 toes, so Lilli, who has a condition called polydactyly (or "many fingers"), boasts nearly twice as many.

Exploding Whale

In these images courtesy of Newsflare, after marine biologist Bjarni Mikkelsen cut open a huge sperm whale that had died after becoming trapped in a narrow channel in the Faroe Islands, its corpse suddenly exploded, spewing guts and internal organs all over him. The 45-ft-long (14-m) whale had been dead for two days and in that time bacteria inside the carcass had been producing methane gas as part of the decomposition process. Unable to escape, the gas steadily built up and finally exploded as soon as the whale's skin was pierced.

OLD NOTE While out walking on a beach near his home in Houhora, New Zealand, Geoff Flood stumbled across a bottle sitting in the sand—and inside was a 76-year-old note dated March 17, 1936, sent from an address in Leederville, Western Australia.

TV STATIC The static on an untuned television set is partly caused by photon radiation left by the Big Bang 14 billion years ago.

COMPUTER ERROR A computer error meant that grandparents Nigel and Linda Brotherton from Lancashire, England, received an electrical bill for £500 million ($850 million) and were told by their energy supplier that if they failed to pay it their monthly direct debit payment would go up from £87 ($148) to £53.5 million ($91 million).

GOAT DUNG

Artist and goat breeder Patrick Page-Sutter built this life-size sculpture of a goat entirely from pellets of goat dung collected on the family ranch in Natalia, Texas.

WATER GUN

Alex Bygrave of London, England, spent 50 hours molding together 55 separate parts of everyday objects to make a Gatling-style water gun with six barrels, a 2.64-gal (10-l) water tank, and a firing range of 40 ft (12 m). The spare parts he used included plumbing pipes, a walking pole handle for the pump and a windshield wiper to provide the gun's rotary motion.

JOB CHAOS Police in Stockholm, Sweden, had to disperse an angry crowd of job hunters outside an employment office after it called thousands of people for a recruitment meeting by mistake. The email should have gone out to around 1,000 unemployed individuals, but instead went to 61,000—all the registered job hunters in the city.

GOOD SAMARITAN Glen James, a homeless man from Boston, Massachusetts, returned a backpack he had found containing $42,000 to its rightful owner and was rewarded for his honesty. A complete stranger living more than 500 mi (800 km) away in Virginia set up an online fund and raised $150,000 to help Glen overcome his plight.

CRYSTAL BLAZE A house fire in London, England, was caused by a crystal doorknob. Sunlight refracted through the doorknob and reflected onto a nearby dressing gown, setting it on fire.

HOMEMADE STAMPS For three years, Angus McDonagh of Somerset, England, posted letters for free by using homemade stamps featuring his own face. He outfoxed Royal Mail by sending more than 100 letters using stamp designs that he printed on his home computer. Many showed his face in a side profile with a comic eye patch or weird hat, while at Christmas he created some of himself sporting a white Santa beard.

FORTUNE COOKIE Seventy-five-year-old Emma Duvoll of New York City, won a $2 million lottery prize after playing the numbers she found in a fortune cookie. She bought the winning ticket after dining at a Chinese restaurant in Greenwich Village.

PERFECT JOB A specialist pharmacist at the Royal Cornwall Hospital in Truro, Cornwall, England, is listed as Mr. A. Pothecary. Andrew Pothecary first thought about studying medicine because he had a suitable name and, although he has enjoyed a successful career, he believes he may have been turned down for some jobs by employers who thought the name on the application form was a joke.

MISSING RING Elizabeth Clark of Granite Falls, Washington, was reunited with her 1953 university class ring 60 years after she'd lost it, when it was found in a dried-up West Texas lake. She lost her Howard Payne University class ring in 1954 in Lake Nasworthy near San Angelo, and despite a lengthy search it remained undetected until, following years of drought, it revealed itself in the lake bed in March 2014. Elizabeth identified it by her initials inside the band.

BIG WEDDING When a Sri Lankan couple, Nisansala and Nalin, got married in Colombo in 2013, they walked down the aisle with 126 bridesmaids, 25 best men, 20 pageboys and 23 flower girls.

DREAM MONITOR San Diego, California, company iWinks has invented a headband that can help people control their dreams. The Aurora measures brain activity and plays lights and sounds during REM (rapid eye movement) sleep to help people become aware they are dreaming even though they are still asleep. The idea is that this will enable them to take control of their sleeping brain and direct the course of their dreams.

DRAFT MOTION Eminent scientist Isaac Newton (1642–1727) was elected as an M.P. (Member of Parilament) to represent Cambridge University in 1689 and 1701, but the only time he spoke in Parliament was to ask for a window to be closed because of a draft.

PLANT HAUL Thieves stole 10,000 carnivorous Venus flytrap plants, worth a total of $65,000, from greenhouses at a farm near Wilmington, North Carolina.

PHONE SHIELD A gas station clerk in Winter Garden, Florida, was saved from a robber's bullet by his cell phone. He didn't realize the phone had stopped the bullet until he took the shattered device from his shirt pocket.

FAMILY BIRTHDAY Joshua Strnad of Ingersoll, Ontario, tells Ripley's that his fiancée, Sarah Mailloux, their daughter Olivia and son Elijah were all born on March 9—in 1992, 2011 and 2012 respectively. Joshua's own birthday is exactly a week earlier than Sarah's, as he was born on March 2, 1990.

HARD TO SWALLOW

Doctors in Chhattisgarh, India, removed 431 coins, 197 fishnet pellets, 19 bicycle chain bolts and three keys from a man's stomach. The haul weighed over 13 lb (6 kg).

A woman in Thailand was found to have 199 nails in her stomach—some as long as 3 in (7.5 cm).

A 10-lb (4.5-kg) hairball was found in the stomach of a Chicago teenager who suffered from trichophagia, a habit of eating her own hair.

A 52-year-old woman in Rotterdam, the Netherlands, had 78 items of metal cutlery removed from her stomach.

Doctors in Hunan Province, China, discovered a 2-in-long (5-cm) thermometer in a woman's lung that she had swallowed 44 years earlier.

A 38-year-old woman from Galati, Romania, accidentally swallowed her boyfriend's false teeth during a passionate kiss.

A 62-year-old man in Cholet, France, swallowed 350 coins, an assortment of necklaces and several needles with a combined weight of 12 lb (5.5 kg).

Fridge Magnets

After studying this hospital X-ray, surgeons removed 42 tiny magnets from the stomach of a 16-month-old boy who had swallowed them at his home in Chelyabinsk, Russia. The child's mother had become alarmed when she noticed that all of the fridge alphabet magnets had gone missing after her son was alone in the kitchen for a few minutes.

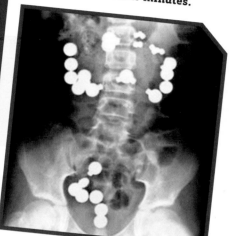

Artist Lucy Sparrow from Bath, England, created a life-size grocery store in which every one of the 4,000 items was made of felt.

It took her seven months and more than 250,000 stitches to make the display, which included fish sticks, cans of Spam, newspapers, toilet rolls, a cash register and a pricing gun—all made from felt.

HONEYMOON PRANK

Newlyweds Jamie and Emily Pharro returned home from their honeymoon to find their friends had covered the entire ground floor of their house in Lincolnshire, England, with 14,000 Post-It® notes. The yellow notes were stuck in neat rows to the walls, floors, furniture, cupboards and the TV, and took 2½ hours to remove.

FART MACHINE Plumber and inventor Colin Furze from Lincolnshire, England, built a 16-ft-high (5-m) "fart machine," transported it to Kent and aimed it at France to see whether it could be heard 21 mi (33 km) away across the English Channel. People in France reported hearing a "faint rumble" from the machine, which consisted of a giant pulse jet engine housed in a pair of specially constructed buttocks.

DOG SPIDER Polish prankster Sylwester Wardega dressed his dog Chica in a giant furry spider costume and then used a hidden camera to film people's reactions as the eight-legged monster sprang into action. The video was watched 22 million times on YouTube in just two days, which works out at nearly 130 views per second!

THE STING A thief in Leeds, England, was caught after he accidentally disturbed a nest of angry wasps while stopping to urinate in a bush during his getaway. Jamie Brown had made off with a £200 ($300) fish tank from a store, but was caught by police officers who saw him crying in pain after being repeatedly stung by the insects. He spent six hours in agony in a hospital before appearing in court.

PERSONALITY CHANGE After suffering a stroke, a 49-year-old Brazilian man underwent a complete personality change and developed "pathological generosity," where he could not help giving money away to strangers.

WHAT A MUG! On the day he was freed from jail, Andrew Graham broke into a hair salon in Leicester, England, and escaped with more than $9,000 (£6,000) worth of equipment, but he accidentally left behind his prison papers, including his mugshot.

Painted Snails

To prevent snails being stepped on, Swedish artist Stefan Siverud decorates their shells in bright designs, including a red and yellow McDonald's logo and a vivid blue shark. He uses non-toxic paint so that the "pimped" mollusks come to no harm and then he releases them back into his garden.

DUMMY FAMILY Suzanne Heintz from Englewood, Colorado, has lived with a family of mannequins for more than 14 years and has traveled 10,000 mi (16,000 km) around the world with them. For an art project she takes pictures of herself at various locations with her plastic "husband" Chauncey, a clothing-store dummy, and a plastic teen "daughter" Mary-Margaret as if they were a real family.

BIGFOOT LAW It is legal in Texas to kill Bigfoot if you can find him because he is not technically an endangered species.

NAME CHANGE Melanie Ann Convery and her husband Neal James Coughlin from Holyoke, Massachusetts, successfully petitioned a court to change both of their middle names to "Seamonster."

Ripley's—
Believe It or Not!®
www.ripleys.com/books
BELIEVE IT!

FROG IN THROAT

This jungle perch caught by fisherman Angus James near Townsville in Queensland, Australia, literally had a frog in its throat.

When James opened the fish's mouth, he saw a live green tree frog staring back at him. He said: "As I was pulling my lure from the fish to release it back into the water, I noticed two little eyes looking back at me from inside the fish's mouth. The frog then leaped straight past my head onto the nearest tree. It was one of the coolest things I have seen in my life. This is one lucky frog!"

02

Skull Cups

A ritual bowl called a kapala, used by Indian Hindus and Buddhists in Tibet, is made from a human skull. The skulls are usually collected at burial sites before being ornately carved or mounted with precious jewels or silver. There are two types of kapala—those that use the whole skull and those that use only the skull cap or top half of the cranium. They often serve as vessels for holding food or wine, but some followers also allegedly drink blood from skull caps.

ELEPHANT TOMBSTONE A 5.5-ft-tall (1.7-m), 7-ft-long (2.1-m), life-sized tombstone in the shape of a baby elephant stands on the grave of circus owner William F. Duggan in Moultrie, Georgia. The real elephant—Nancy—that inspired the tombstone was Duggan's favorite, and followed him to the hospital on the day he died in 1950.

DOUBLE STRIKE Casey Wagner, a 31-year-old rodeo clown, miraculously survived after being struck by lightning twice on the same day. He was taking part in a car race at Saint Jo, Texas, on October 26, 2013, when the first bolt hit him while he was taking shelter under a tree. Seconds later, he was struck again and felt the electricity surge up through his right boot and into his body, dropping him to his knees. Although he lost the feeling in his arm and leg for a few days, he made a full recovery.

BLUE LAVA Kawah Ijen, a volcanic sulfur mine on the island of East Java, Indonesia, produces blue lava. The 660-ft-deep (200-m) active crater is home to a deadly turquoise-blue lake made up of almost pure sulfuric acid, which would kill anyone who fell in. By day, the hot molten sulfur that flows from the edge of the lake appears bright red, but at night it gives off an eerie blue light with flames that can reach up to 16 ft (5 m) high.

CHILD CHARMERS

Children among the 600-strong nomadic Vadi tribe in western India begin charming cobras from just a few feet away at the age of just two. It is the start of ten years of training—the boys charm the snakes with flutes while the girls handle and care for the reptiles. After capture, the normally deadly cobras are fed a herbal mixture which supposedly makes their venom ineffective. Snake charming has been banned by the Indian government since 1991, but there are still around 800,000 snake charmers in the country and the Vadi are determined to maintain the tradition.

BURNING ↘ TONGUE

Camphor—a highly flammable substance— burns brightly on the tongue of a devotee at the Ganga Dhaaraa Hindu festival in Trinidad.

The annual ceremony mirrors a much larger religious celebration, which is attended by hundreds of thousands of pilgrims, held on India's Ganges River.

HOTEL MOVE Over a nine-day period in 1888, the 6,000-ton Brighton Beach Hotel in New York was dragged 600 ft (180 m) away from an eroding shoreline by six steam locomotives.

LARGE LEAF While walking with his family, four-year-old Tommy Lindsey of Mount Vernon, Washington, found a maple leaf that measured more than 2 ft (61 cm) from stem to tip and more than 21 in (53 cm) wide, making it almost as big as him.

BLOODY THEME Haw Par Villa, a Chinese mythology theme park in Singapore, has more than 1,000 gruesome scenes, including the Ten Courts of Hell, which showcase blood-curdling punishments for minor misdemeanors. Exhibits depict the fleshy heart being torn out of a woman for being ungrateful, a young girl being flung by the Devil into a hill of knives, and an executioner pulling the intestines from a man tied to a pole because the victim had cheated during exams.

NATURE LESSON Gan Lin, the wife of a wealthy businessman from Chongqing, China, rented an entire mountain at a cost of more than $5,000 a month just so that her daughter Yin could learn about nature.

HARD CELL The Victorian Oxford Prison in England has been converted into a $300-a-night hotel, complete with the original 3-in-thick (7.5-cm) steel doors, bars on the non-opening windows and stark images of prison life adorning the walls.

FINGER JEWELRY The Angu people of Papua New Guinea wear the smoked fingers, hands and breastbones of dead relatives as jewelry.

CAVE HOTEL

UNDERSEA BEDROOM A hotel in Zanzibar, Tanzania, has a suite that floats in the sea with an underwater bedroom so that guests can watch fish swimming by. The suite is anchored above a coral reef 820 ft (250 m) off the coast and it costs $1,500 for a couple to stay there for one night.

Visitors to Farmington, New Mexico, can stay in a cave guesthouse within vertical sandstone cliffs located 300 ft (90 m) above the La Plata river valley. With its entrance set in the cliff face, the 1,700-sq-ft (149 sq-m) Kokopelli's Cave was originally built for geologist and owner Bruce Black to use as an office, but is now a bed-and-breakfast hotel, complete with bedroom, kitchen, dining area and bathroom with jacuzzi. The temperature inside stays at about 70°F (21°C) all year round.

ROCK SLIDE A landslide at a copper mine outside Salt Lake City, Utah, in April 2013 sent 165 million tons of rock, dirt and debris crashing at speeds of 100 mph (160 km/h) into a nearly mile-deep pit with such force that it triggered 16 small earthquakes. The avalanche, which loosened enough material to bury New York's Central Park in 66 ft (20 m) of debris, is thought to be the largest non-volcanic slide in modern North American history.

DRAGON BLOOD The dragon blood tree of the Amazon gets its name from its blood-red sap, which is used by native tribes as a dye, and has been developed as a medicine to treat diarrhea and some skin conditions.

FOG DRINKERS Giant redwood trees, which can be more than 300 ft (91 m) tall, receive 40 percent of their moisture from fog at the top of their branches.

DUMPSTER HOME Californian designer Gregory Kloehn has converted a $2,000-dumpster in Brooklyn, New York, into a fully functional home, complete with a bathroom, bed, sun deck and electrically powered kitchen. He installed a 6-gal (22.7-l) tank on the roof to provide drinking water, carved a door on the side of the dumpster for access and added wheels to the base in order to create a mobile home.

SPELLING ERROR The Colorado Rockies baseball team handed out 15,000 jerseys to fans with the name of their star player, Troy Tulowitzki, spelled incorrectly.

FLAG ERROR The flag of the Turks and Caicos Islands, a British colony in the Caribbean, mistakenly featured an igloo for 100 years because a British flag maker mistook piles of salt in a sketch for an igloo.

BIG FREEZE With an outside temperature of −20°F (−29°C) and a wind chill of −49°F (−45°C), it was cold enough in Dubuque, Iowa, in January 2014 to be able to freeze a wet T-shirt solid in under one minute.

PLASTIC BRIDGE Stretching nearly 25 ft (7.6 m), the Onion Ditch Bridge in West Liberty, Ohio, is made from 120,000 lb (54,431 kg) of recycled plastic, including old detergent bottles and car dashboards. Although it cost $250,000 to build, its projected 150-year life span is more than three times longer than conventional materials such as concrete or steel.

Liquid Lunch

There is never any need to ask for water with your meal at this jungle restaurant in San Pablo City in the Philippines, because the dining tables are located right at the foot of the man-made Labasin Falls. While customers eat at the Waterfalls Restaurant at Villa Escudero, the clear spring water from the falls runs over their feet, and between courses they can cool down by standing directly under the cascade.

Actual waterfall!

UNDERSEA WATERFALL A waterfall lies miles beneath the North Atlantic Ocean in the Denmark Strait between Greenland and Iceland and drops 11,500 ft (3,506 m)—more than three times the height of Angel Falls in Venezuela, which is generally considered to be the world's highest waterfall. The amount of water the Denmark Strait Cataract carries is estimated at 175 million cubic ft per second (5 million cubic m per second)—equivalent to nearly 2,000 Niagara Falls at their peak flow. It is formed by water of different temperatures meeting along an underwater ridge—the cooler water flows downward, creating the underwater waterfall.

WATERMELON DROP The town of Vincennes, Indiana, rings in the New Year with its annual Watermelon Drop where 14 real watermelons are placed in an 18-ft (5.5-m), 500-lb (227-kg) steel-and-foam artificial watermelon and hoisted 100 ft (30 m) into the air. At the stroke of midnight, a trapdoor in the bottom of the giant watermelon opens and the fruit inside drop to the "splatform" below.

NO MORTAR Amazingly, there is no mortar holding together the 555-ft-tall (170-m) Washington Monument—the marble bricks are kept intact by gravity and friction alone.

Crazy climber!

TALL ↗ STORY

This giant sequoia tree called "The President" in California's Sequoia National Park is 3,200 years old, has two billion leaves and stands 247 ft (74 m) tall.

The tree is so big that to show it all *National Geographic* magazine needed 126 individual photographs pieced together in a five-page foldout.

MOLE MAN Known as "The Mole Man," Manuel Barrantes spent ten years digging an underground home in Perez Zeledon, Costa Rica, by hand, using picks and shovels. His subterranean house, "Topolandia," has more than 4,300 sq ft (400 sq m) of tunnels, the largest over 52 ft (16 m) deep. The walls of the tunnels are decorated with hand-carved sculptures of dinosaurs and the bedrooms contain beds made of stone. He says the house offers him protection against global warming and earthquakes.

CLAY HOUSE Architect Octavio Mendoza has spent 14 years building his house in Villa de Leyva, Colombia, entirely from clay. Named Casa Terracotta, it is also known locally as "Flintstone House," and even has furniture, beds and kitchen utensils made from clay.

PAINT JOB Every seven years, 25 painters spend 18 months repainting the 1,063-ft-high (324-m) Eiffel Tower in Paris with 60 tons of brown paint. The tower, which was painted yellow at the start of the 20th century, is now coated in three shades of brown, which get lighter with elevation to emphasize the structure's silhouette against the Parisian sky.

CAMERA CAFÉ A coffee shop in Yangpyeong County, South Korea, is built in the shape of a vintage camera. The Dreamy Camera Café was built by photography enthusiast Park Sung-hwan and has two floors, the first of which is decorated with miniature cameras. Even the toilet paper is made to look like a film reel.

Local Bigwig

Chichester Cathedral in West Sussex, England, boasts a modern gargoyle depicting former barrister and cathedral chapter clerk Clifford Hodgetts, complete with wig, glasses and an appropriately placed spout to carry excess rainwater off the roof and away from the walls.

GARGOYLES

Smiling Face

Nora Sly from Gloucestershire, England, has an image of her smiling face carved as a gargoyle into a stone tower on the roof of St. Mary's Church, Cowley. Local people voted unanimously for the honor to go to the retired secretary, who has been a church regular for over 60 years and has lived in the village all her life. "I was astounded," she said, "but I did not feel the carving was all that flattering!"

Stone Tribute

David Rice, who worked as a stonemason at Wells Cathedral in Somerset, England, for half a century, is immortalized in the framework of the building in the form of a stone gargoyle.

Ripley's Believe It or Not!®
www.ripleys.com/books
WORLD

Royal Gargoyles

The church tower of St. John the Divine in Kennington, London, features stone gargoyles of Queen Elizabeth II, Prince Charles (seen here) and a young William, Duke of Cambridge.

Evil Vision

When Washington National Cathedral held a decorative sculpture competition for children in the 1980s, a drawing of Darth Vader by Christopher Rader from Kearney, Nebraska, was so impressive that it was sculpted and carved as a gargoyle high up on the building's northwest tower.

Alien Monster

A gargoyle that was added to the 13th-century Paisley Abbey in Scotland in the 1990s looks just like the monster from the movie *Alien*.

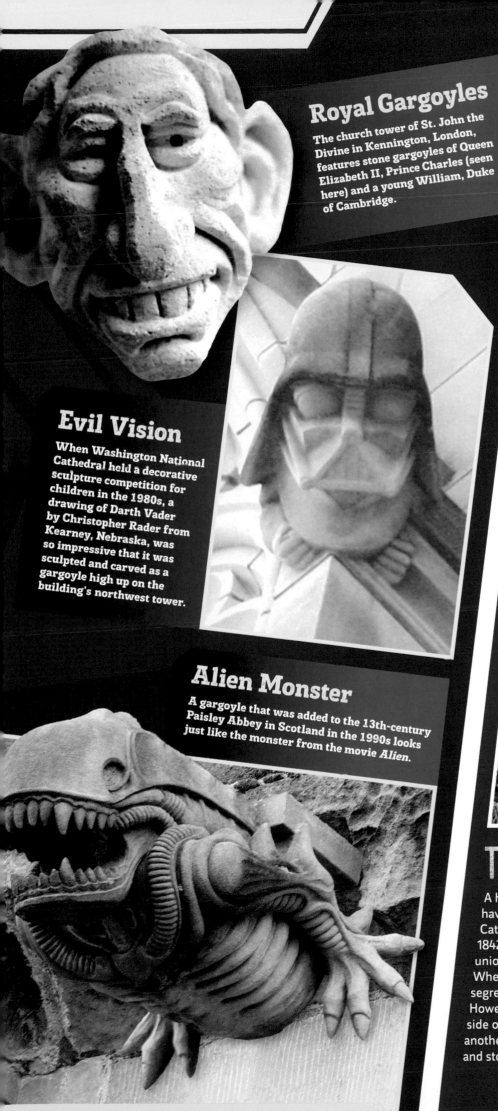

TOGETHER FOREVER

A husband and wife in Roermond, the Netherlands, have been holding hands for more than 120 years. A Catholic noblewoman married a Protestant Colonel in 1842 causing a religious and social scandal, but their union lasted nearly 40 years, until the colonel died. When his widow passed away eight years later, religious segregation meant they couldn't be buried together. However, she had ordered a monument to be built on one side of the cemetery wall, where she was laid to rest, and another on the other side of the wall for her husband, and stone hands join the couple together forever.

UPSIDE-DOWN HOUSE

This house in Moscow, Russia, has not been hurled around by a tornado—it was deliberately built upside-down for an exhibition. It even has an upside-down Mini car installed in a garage, and an upside-down dog and kennel. Meanwhile inside the house, tables, chairs, beds and kitchen appliances seem to defy gravity by hanging from the ceiling.

BANNED LETTERS Turkey banned the use of the letters Q, W and X in names and public notices from 1928 until 2013. The laws had been introduced to help Turkey's transition from the Arabic alphabet to the Latin one. However, the letters continued to appear in the minority Kurdish language and in 2005, 20 Kurds were fined $74 for holding up placards containing the letters Q and W at a New Year's celebration.

FAKED DEATH Alexey Bykov from Omsk, Russia, faked his own death so that he could propose to his girlfriend. He hired a movie director, stuntmen, make-up artists and even a scriptwriter to stage a bogus car crash, which was so convincing that when Irena Kolokov arrived at the scene and was told he was dead, she broke down in tears. Convinced that she really loved him, Bykov then jumped to his feet and proposed, still covered in fake blood. She said yes!

YARD SALE An annual yard sale known as the "127 Corridor Sale" stretches from Addison, Michigan, to Gadsden, Alabama—a distance of 690 mi (1,110 km). Mostly following the route of Highway 127, it travels through six states—Michigan, Ohio, Kentucky, Tennessee, Georgia and Alabama—and boasts thousands of vendors along the way.

ROOF BOOTH There is a phone booth on the roof of the two-story Lincoln City Hall, Illinois. It was installed in the 1960s as a weather station so that watchers could use the phone to warn of bad weather and it now attracts inquisitive tourists from all over the world.

PARKER'S PISTOL Two guns found on the bodies of notorious Depression-era gangsters Bonnie Parker and Clyde Barrow after they were killed by a posse in 1934 sold at auction in Nashua, New Hampshire, in 2012, for a total of $504,000. Bonnie's .38-caliber Detective Special, which she had taped to her thigh when she died, fetched a gun-slinging $264,000, while Clyde's 1911 Colt .45 semi-automatic went for a bullet-busting $240,000.

TUMBLING TOWER The 47-story, 612-ft-tall (187-m) Singer Tower in New York City—the world's tallest building when it was constructed in 1908—was also the tallest to be demolished when it was pulled down by its owner in 1967.

BALL FACTORY Every football used in the NFL since 1955 has been made in the same Wilson factory in Ada, Ohio, which produces 4,000 balls per day.

POO SCULPTURE

American artist Paul McCarthy built this 51-ft-high (15-m) inflatable poop—the size of a house—as an art installation.

Complex Pile has been exhibited all over the world. In 2008, a sudden gust of wind cut it loose from its moorings outside a modern art museum in Bern, Switzerland, and sent it soaring through the air before it landed 600 ft (180 m) away on the grounds of an orphanage.

MOUNTAIN MISERY The 2,600-ft-high (800-m) Mount Disappointment in Victoria, Australia, was named in 1824 by explorers Hamilton Hume and William Hovell who were prevented from crossing it by dense undergrowth.

HOME MOVIES Movie fan Paul Slim from the West Midlands, England, has spent £15,000 ($25,000) converting his garden shed into a 20-seat cinema, complete with 119-inch (3-m) screen, 3-D projector, surround sound system and his collection of 3,000 DVDs.

BOARD GAME In the Czech Republic sport of *woodkopf*, a pair of combatants wear 6-ft-6-in-long (2-m) wooden boards on their head. Each uses his board to try and knock off his opponent's board without his own falling off. The player who knocks down an opponent's board twice in succession is the winner. Each board weighs up to 8.8 lb (4 kg) and only plank-to-plank contact is allowed.

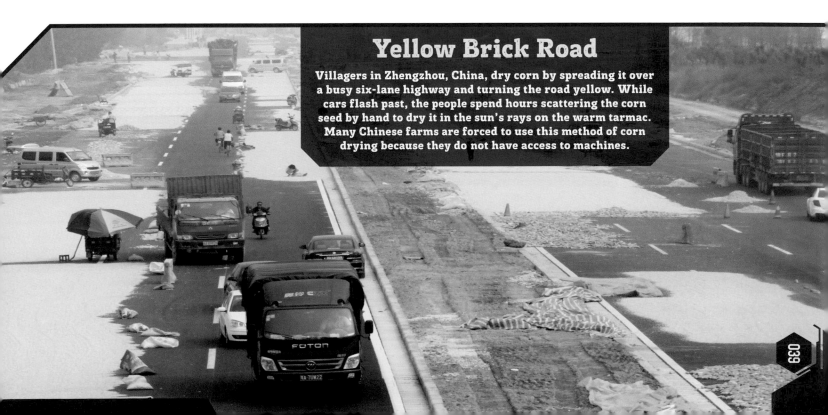

Yellow Brick Road

Villagers in Zhengzhou, China, dry corn by spreading it over a busy six-lane highway and turning the road yellow. While cars flash past, the people spend hours scattering the corn seed by hand to dry it in the sun's rays on the warm tarmac. Many Chinese farms are forced to use this method of corn drying because they do not have access to machines.

SHARP PRACTICE

At the annual Phuket Vegetarian Festival in Thailand, devotees have needles pierced through their arms, legs, back and even their face as a way of bringing good luck to the community. The ritualized mutilation is performed while the recipient is placed in a trancelike state at a local Buddhist shrine.

POND HOCKEY Every January, 250 teams and nearly 2,000 skaters from across North America descend on Lake Nokomis in Minneapolis, Minnesota, for the U.S. Pond Hockey Championships. Staged on 25 man-made rinks on the frozen lake, the teams compete for the Golden Shovel, pond hockey's answer to the Stanley Cup. The games are four-a-side with no goalies and the players call the penalties. The referees only keep track of the score.

SALTY SEA California's largest lake is located in the middle of its biggest desert. The 362-sq-mi (940-sq-km) Salton Sea in the Colorado Desert was formed after the Colorado River flooded in 1905. Its surface is 220 ft (67 m) below sea level and its water is 30 percent saltier than the Pacific, meaning that very few species of fish can survive there.

STEEP STREET Baldwin Street in Dunedin, New Zealand, has a gradient of almost 1 in 3 ft (1 in 2.86 m) at its steepest point—a 35 percent gradient—making it the steepest residential street in the world. The street rises from 98 ft (30 m) above sea level at its base to 330 ft (100 m) above sea level at its top over a distance of just 1,150 ft (350 m). The steeper upper reaches are surfaced in concrete for fear that asphalt would flow down the hill on a warm day. Each year, hundreds of competitors take part in the Baldwin Street Gutbuster race, where they have to run from the bottom of the street to the top, and down again. The fastest time recorded is under 2 minutes.

LAZY OLYMPICS Montenegro, a country that prides itself on its slow pace of life, stages an annual Lazy Olympics where the only event involves lying in the shade of an oak tree near Breznik for as long as possible. Vladan Bajalica won the inaugural event in 2013 by lazing under the tree for 32 hours. Any competitor who appears to be putting too much effort into relaxing is disqualified.

MARATHON MONKS The Tendai Buddhist monks of Enryakuji, a 1,200-year-old temple complex in the foothills of Mount Hiei, Japan, take part in the Sennichi Kaihogyo, or Thousand Day Challenge, a seven-year endurance test that involves walking a distance equivalent to circling the globe. Wearing white robes and flimsy straw sandals, the monks must visit 250 sites on Mount Hiei during their long pilgrimage, covering a distance equal to 1,000 marathons. They even continue walking at night, carrying lanterns to guide their way. The challenge is so arduous that since the tradition began in 1585, only 50 monks have completed it, and many have died en route.

BLOTTO GROTTO Richard Pim of Herefordshire, England, created a garden shed out of 5,000 old wine bottles. He calls the glass dome, which measures 19 ft (5.8 m) wide and 11 ft (3.4 m) high, the Blotto Grotto.

GRAND BOWL The Inazawa Grand Bowl in Japan is a bowling alley with 116 lanes. Opened in 1972, the bowl spans 91,500 sq ft (8,500 sq m) across the lanes with no supporting beams and can accommodate nearly 700 bowlers at any one time.

FAST FLOW The men's room urinal at the Madonna Inn at San Luis Obispo, California, features an 8-ft (2.4-m) waterfall.

IN THE DRINK On an expedition to find evidence of the Loch Ness monster, U.S. research teams found thousands of golf balls sent sailing by locals and visitors practicing their driving skills on the loch.

Pipe Rooms

A low-cost hotel in Henan, China, has around 15 rooms constructed from old industrial concrete pipes. Each section of pipe is decorated on the outside with street art, while the interior caters for two people and has air conditioning, soundproofing, a restroom and a double bed.

ICE CAVE

This incredible ice cave in the Kamchatka Peninsula of eastern Russia measures nearly 0.6 mi (1 km) long and was formed by a hot spring gushing from the nearby Mutnovsky volcano and carving its way through the glaciers.

As these glaciers have been melting in recent years, the roof of the cave is now thin enough to allow sunlight to penetrate and create colorful illuminations inside.

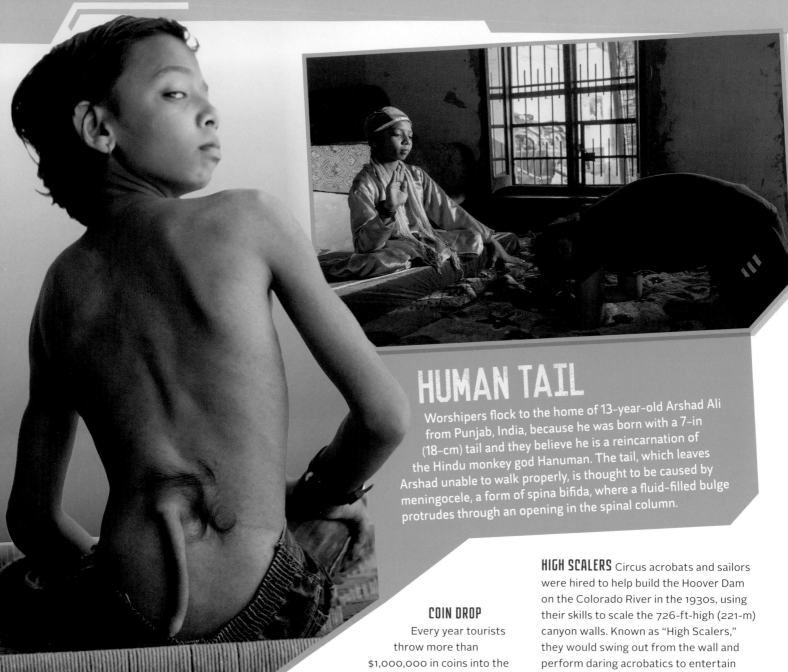

HUMAN TAIL

Worshipers flock to the home of 13-year-old Arshad Ali from Punjab, India, because he was born with a 7-in (18-cm) tail and they believe he is a reincarnation of the Hindu monkey god Hanuman. The tail, which leaves Arshad unable to walk properly, is thought to be caused by meningocele, a form of spina bifida, where a fluid–filled bulge protrudes through an opening in the spinal column.

HIGH SCALERS
Circus acrobats and sailors were hired to help build the Hoover Dam on the Colorado River in the 1930s, using their skills to scale the 726-ft-high (221-m) canyon walls. Known as "High Scalers," they would swing out from the wall and perform daring acrobatics to entertain the men below during work breaks. One worker, Louis Fagan of Jonesboro, Arkansas, was dubbed "The Human Pendulum" for his ability to swing both colleagues and cases of dynamite across the canyon while dangling at the end of a rope 200 ft (60 m) long.

COIN DROP
Every year tourists throw more than $1,000,000 in coins into the famous Trevi Fountain in Rome, Italy. All the money goes to a charity that helps the city's needy.

FLORAL VILLAGE
Villagers in Zalipie, Poland, paint the exterior of their houses not in a single color, but in a variety of bright floral patterns. Popular since the 19th century, even chicken coops, trash bins, dog kennels, wells and the village bridge are traditionally painted with vibrant flower decorations.

WEE MEASUREMENT
A *poronkusema*, which is a unit of measurement used by the Sami people of Finland, is based on the distance a reindeer can travel before it needs to urinate. It was once used to equate to a distance of around 4.5 mi (7.24 km) but now describes something that is simply far away.

HEMORRHOID FESTIVAL
The Kunigami Shrine in Japan's Tochigi prefecture is home to an annual festival dedicated to preventing and curing hemorrhoids. Visitors point their backsides at a large, egg-shaped washing stone at the center of the shrine in recognition of an ancient hemorrhoid cure, which required sufferers to wash their backsides in a nearby river and to eat eggs.

RED-HOT RESULTS
Matt Simpson, 43, grows the hottest chillies in the United Kingdom—by shouting at them! He believes the chillies' heat is produced as a defense mechanisms against predators, and the results of his ruckus is the "Katie"—which measures an eye-watering 1,590,000 Scoville units.

→ AUSTRALIAN METEOROLOGIST CLEMENT WRAGGE (1852-1922) WAS THE FIRST TO NAME HURRICANES—CALLING THEM AFTER POLITICIANS HE DISLIKED.

DIVINE PEAKS
As the twin peaks of the Boma mountain in Chhattisgarh, India, are said to resemble female breasts, it is considered a sacred place—and local villagers fine anybody caught setting foot on the mountain the sum of 500 rupees ($8).

HEPIDERMIS EDITION
Harvard University's Houghton Library contains countless curiosities—including skin among its stacks. A nineteenth century copy of *Arsène Houssaye's Des destinées de l'ame* is bound in the human skin of an unclaimed female mental patient who had died of a stroke.

SMALLEST MOUNTAIN Although Mount Villingili, a small hill on the fifth tee of the only golf course on the Maldives, stands just 16 ¾ ft (5.1 m) above sea level, it is enough to make it the highest point on the low-lying Indian Ocean archipelago.

CABIN DAY Every year in June, Michigan celebrates Log Cabin Day. It was proposed by the Log Cabin Society and the Bad Axe Historical Society in 1986 to promote the preservation of log cabins and was approved by the state legislature three years later.

MYSTERY FIRES Since 2004 there have been hundreds of cases of spontaneous combustion in the Sicilian village of Canneto di Caronia, including cars, chairs, clothes, mattresses, vacuum cleaners, fridges and switched-off cell phones. Even a water pipe once burst into flames, while the same mirror caught fire three times in 35 hours.

SHELL GROTTO A grotto in Margate, Kent, England contains over 4.5 million sea shells arranged in beautiful mosaics that cover the walls and roof over an area of 2,000 sq ft (186 m²). While the grotto was discovered in 1835, nobody knows who created it.

SKYPE RULER Togbe Ngoryifia runs a car repair garage in Frankfurt, Germany, but is also an African king with 200,000 subjects whom he rules via Skype. He became King Banash of the Hohoe people in southeast Ghana in 1987, after being named as the successor to his grandfather. His father and older brother were not permitted to rule because they are left-handed, a sign of dishonesty among the Hohoe.

UNDERGROUND CITY Seattle has a mysterious "underground city" in which many streets and storefronts, damaged in the Great Seattle Fire of 1889, exist below street level.

VOLCANO HOAX As an elaborate April Fool's Day hoax in 1974, prankster Oliver "Porky" Bickar hired a helicopter to drop hundreds of tires into the crater of Mount Edgecumbe, a dormant Alaskan volcano, and then set them on fire to try and trick local people into believing that the rising plume of black smoke meant the volcano was active again.

CREMATION RIDE A ghoulish ride at the Window of the World theme park in Shenzhen, China, aims to replicate the experience of being cremated! Passengers on the 4D Death Simulator lie down in a coffin before being pushed into a furnace where temperatures reach a sweltering 104°F (40°C). Although they are removed soon after, many say it feels like being burned alive.

HOUSE MOVE When Walter Thornton-Smith decided to move from Essex to Surrey, England, in 1912, he arranged for his home, a 400-year-old Tudor mansion, to be transported brick by brick more than 70 mi (112 km) to its new location. Every part of the 12-bedroom Cedar Court was numbered so that it could be re-assembled as before.

FIRE FIGHT

At the annual Mesabatan Api fire fight in Gianyar, Bali, bare-chested young men pick up blazing coconut husks with their bare hands before swinging and hurling them at each other's bodies.

The centuries-old Hindu tradition symbolizes the purification of the body, but often leaves the participants battle-scarred with nasty burns that have to be treated with a mixture of turmeric and coconut oil.

ROCKET MAN

Huang Yuzhan, a farmer from Guangdong Province, China, has built an enormous replica space shuttle and rocket, complete with boosters on either side, on the roof of his house. It took him over a year to fulfill a childhood dream by building the 23-ft-high (7-m) rocket and 12.4-ft-high (3.8-m) shuttle, which tower spectacularly over his neighbors' homes.

DIRT PYRAMID The 1,000-year-old Dirt Pyramid of the ancient city of Cahokia, built by Native Americans in modern Illinois, covers 14 acres (5.7 ha) and was the largest building by volume in the U.S.A. at that time.

GOLDEN SEWERS A small group of men earn a living in Dhaka, Bangladesh, by panning the city's sewers for gold. Tiny specks of gold are often accidentally brushed into the open sewers that run alongside the narrow streets of the city's historic gold bazaar.

ONLY ONE People in North Korea are banned from having the same name as the country's leader, Kim Jong-un. Anyone already born with that name was ordered to get a new name and authorities were also told to reject all registrations of newborn babies called Kim Jong-un.

SOLEMN VOW After jubilant Austrian generals celebrated victory over Hungary in 1849 by clinking glasses and drinking beer, Hungarians vowed not to clink glasses for the next 150 years.

DOORLESS VILLAGE None of the 300 houses in Shani Shingnapur, a village in Maharashtra, India, have doors. Villagers say that a local deity once told them they do not need doors because he will always protect them. Some households do erect loose door panels at night to keep out wild animals.

MAGIC LAKE Medicine Lake, a 4-mi-long (6.4-km) body of water in Jasper National Park, Alberta, disappears completely every winter. In summer it fills with water as melting glaciers from the surrounding mountains meet with the Maligne River, but because the lake is located on top of a series of sinkholes, the water eventually drains from the bottom like a bathtub that has no plug. Although 6,340 gal (24,000 l) of water seep out of the lake every second, the phenomenon takes several weeks to drain.

BIG BUG The giant blue termite sculpture on the roof of the Big Blue Bug Solutions building in Providence, Rhode Island, is 58 ft (18 m) long and 9 ft (2.7 m) tall—nearly 1,000 times the size of a real termite. Called Nibbles Woodaway, it is made of steel and fiberglass and weighs 4,000 lb (1,816 kg).

HIGH LIFE A cable car suspended 9,000 ft (2,740 m) above sea level near the summit of Mt. Sommet de la Saulire in the French Alps has been transformed into a luxury two-bed hotel room. Guests are ferried up the mountain by snowmobile before checking into their room, which is then winched up for the night to the highest point in the region.

DELAYED SNOW Weather patterns in the U.K. mean that statistically there is always a higher chance of a white Easter than a white Christmas.

TWO DESIGNS Oregon's state flag features a picture of a beaver on its reverse side and is the only U.S. state flag to carry two different designs.

TWIN TESTS Twins Steve and Matt Rudram from Norfolk, England, took their driving tests at 11:11 a.m. on consecutive days and both passed with seven minor errors, two of which were identical.

NAVEL ATTACK Parents in Japan will often warn their children to cover their stomachs during a storm because local superstition claims that Raijin, the god of thunder and lightning, eats the belly buttons of children.

⬆ YOUR UPLOADS

TREE FACE

Janet Potter sent Ripley's this amazing picture of a maple tree near her home in Malone, New York, with a large burl that resembles either the face of one of the Seven Dwarfs or Edvard Munch's famous painting *The Scream*.

MYSTERY PARCEL A sealed package was left unopened for 99 years and 363 days in Otta, Norway. The mysterious parcel was sealed in 1912 by the town's then mayor and bore the inscription "Can open in 2012." When it was finally opened amid great anticipation, it was found to contain just a few letters from the U.S.A., some newspapers and a discussion about a military memorial.

ACID RAIN Scientists studying rocks in Italy have discovered that rain as acidic as vinegar fell on Earth 250 million years ago. The acid rain was caused by sulfur dioxide spewing from a series of deadly volcanic eruptions.

WATER WALL Internal waves beneath the Tasman Sea off Australia can be 1,000 ft (300 m) tall. The waves often travel 1,400 km (870 mi) in just 4 days to hit the southeast coast of Tasmania.

ONE ROOF Ninety percent of the 200 residents of Whittier, Alaska, live under one roof in a 14-story condominium called Begich Towers. In addition to residential apartments, the building houses a police station, health clinic, convenience store, post office, laundromat, church and bed and breakfast. The local school is located nearby in a separate building that is accessed by an underground tunnel.

LOST FOREST Buried underwater off the coast of Norfolk, England, is a 10,000-year-old prehistoric forest, including fallen oak trees with branches over 25 ft (7.6 m) long.

WRONG TARGET Boise City, Oklahoma, was the only continental U.S. town to be bombed during World War II. On the night of July 5, 1943, a B-17 bomber based at Dalhart Army Air Base in Texas dropped six practice bombs on the sleeping city, leaving craters in the streets. The pilots had mistaken the city lights for their intended target 30 mi (48 km) away.

HUGE HAILSTONES ↓

EXTREME WEATHER

- A blistering temperature of 134°F (56.7°C) was recorded at Death Valley, California, on July 10, 1913.

- At Vostok Station, Antarctica, the temperature plunged to –128.56°F (– 89.2°C) on July 21, 1983.

- 71.9 in (1,825 mm) of rain fell in just 24 hours at Foc-Foc on the Indian Ocean island of La Réunion on January 7–8, 1966.

- 93 ft 6 in (28.5 m) of snow fell in one year on Mount Rainier, Washington, between February 19, 1971, and February 18, 1972.

- A snowflake 15 in (38 cm) in diameter landed at Fort Keogh, Montana, on January 28, 1887.

- A hailstone 8 in (20 cm) in diameter fell at Vivian, South Dakota, on July 23, 2010.

- A huge hailstone that fell during a storm in Gopalganj, Bangladesh, on April 14, 1986, weighed 2 lb 4 oz (1.02 kg), the heaviest ever recorded.

- When a tornado hit the suburbs of Oklahoma City on May 3, 1999, the wind reached a speed of 302 mph (486 km/h).

- There was not a single drop of rain in Arica, Chile, for more than 14 years between October 1903 and January 1918—a total of 173 months.

Hailstones the size of tennis balls battered the town of Bray, Nebraska, on June 3, 2014, ripping large chunks out of houses, wrecking cars and injuring 20 people.

The 90 mph (144 km/h) storm brought hailstones as wide as 4¼ in (10.6 cm).

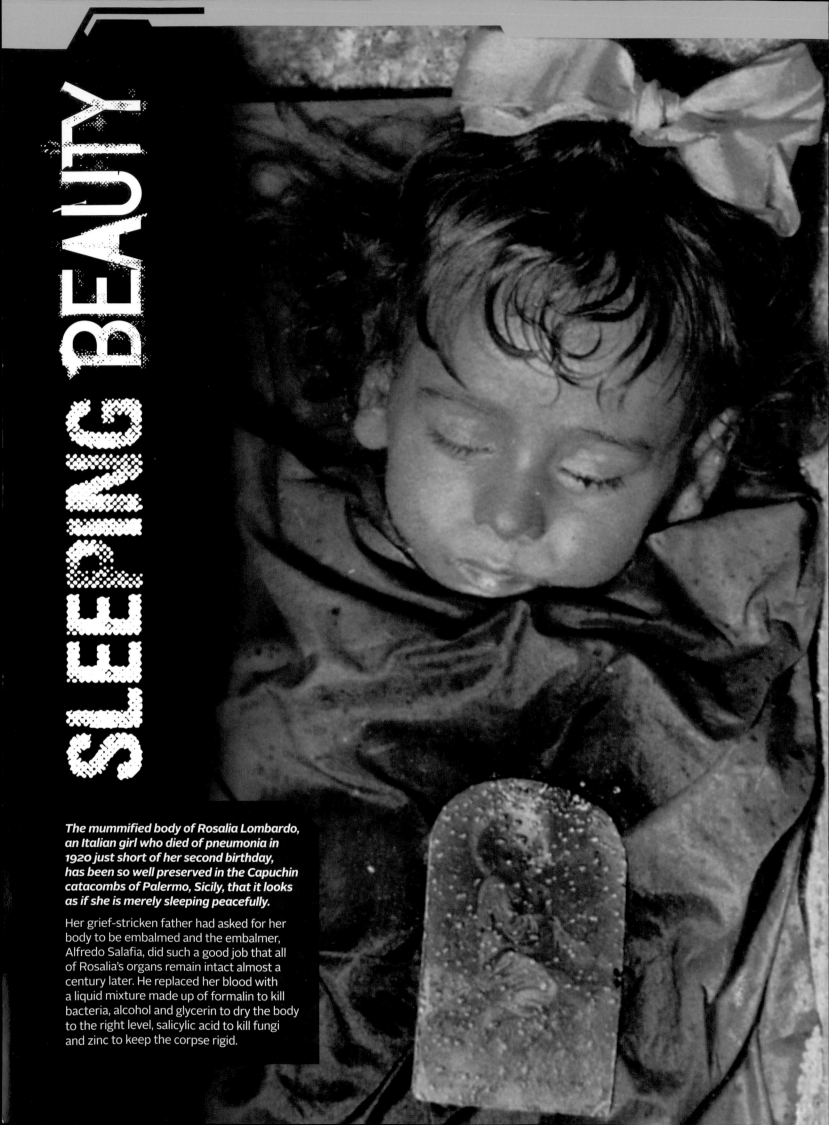

SLEEPING BEAUTY

The mummified body of Rosalia Lombardo, an Italian girl who died of pneumonia in 1920 just short of her second birthday, has been so well preserved in the Capuchin catacombs of Palermo, Sicily, that it looks as if she is merely sleeping peacefully.

Her grief-stricken father had asked for her body to be embalmed and the embalmer, Alfredo Salafia, did such a good job that all of Rosalia's organs remain intact almost a century later. He replaced her blood with a liquid mixture made up of formalin to kill bacteria, alcohol and glycerin to dry the body to the right level, salicylic acid to kill fungi and zinc to keep the corpse rigid.

CARS SWALLOWED In February 2014, a gaping sinkhole 40 ft (12 m) wide and 30 ft (9 m) deep opened beneath the National Corvette Museum in Bowling Green, Kentucky, swallowing eight iconic American cars.

CHRISTMAS LIGHTS David Richards illuminated his family home in Canberra, Australia, in 2013 with 502,165 Christmas lights connected by more than 31 mi (50 km) of wire. A local power company donated over $2,000 to pay for electricity to keep them lit for a month.

CRANE HOTEL An industrial dockside crane perched high above the ground in Harlingen, the Netherlands, has been converted into a luxury, $389-a-night hotel. Elevators take guests up to the living quarters, which are located in the crane's old machine room. From there, guests can climb a ladder to access a balcony.

POISON FLOWER The Alutiiq people of Alaska once hunted using weapons tipped with poison made from larkspur-leaf and monkshood flowers, a dose of which is powerful enough to paralyze a 40-ton humpback whale.

MELON MASK Passengers on China's Beijing Metro in 2015 were unnerved by a man wearing a hollowed-out watermelon on his head. Apart from his melon mask, which had cut-out stars for eyes and a hole for his mouth, the stranger was normally dressed and just sat quietly on the train.

ONE-COP SHOP A police station in Trafalgar Square, London, is so small there is space for only one officer. Built in 1926 to allow the police to keep an eye on demonstrators, the tiny building was equipped with a telephone connected to Scotland Yard, but is now used instead as a broom closet for local council cleaners.

FAMILY PHOTO A photograph of Apollo 16 astronaut Charlie Duke and his family has been sitting on the surface of the Moon for more than 40 years. A message on the back of the photo reads: "This is the family of Astronaut Duke from Planet Earth. Landed on the Moon, April 1972."

BIG FOOT The Statue of Liberty has a 35-ft (10.6-m) waistline and wears size 879 shoes on her 25-ft-long (7.6-m) feet.

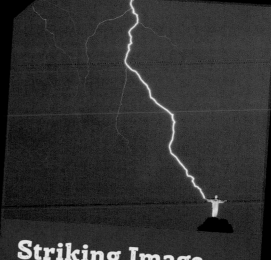

Striking Image

The 125-ft-high (38-m) statue of Christ the Redeemer, which stands on a mountaintop overlooking Rio de Janeiro, Brazil, was struck by a powerful lightning bolt on the night of January 16, 2014, that chipped the statue's right thumb. The previous month, the middle finger of the same hand was chipped during another storm.

STONE'S THROW Athletes taking part in the Unspunnenstein competition in Interlaken, Switzerland, lift a giant stone that weighs 184 lb (83.5 kg) over their head and throw it as far as possible. Strongman Markus Maire once managed to throw it a distance of 13 ft 6 in (4.1 m). Believe it or not, the stone has twice been stolen!

SWOLLEN SHOULDERS

At Italy's 1,500-year-old Festival of Lilies, teams of men must carry 82-ft-high (25-m), 2,000-lb (900-kg) wooden structures on their shoulders through the streets of Nola, near Naples, with children and musicians often climbing onto the platforms to make them even heavier. As a result these cullatori, or "cradlers," develop horrific swollen calluses on their shoulders, but far from keeping their injuries hidden, they proudly display them as a symbol of religious devotion.

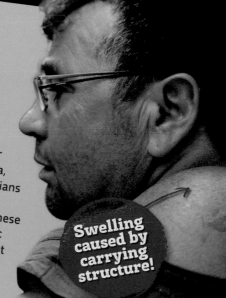

Swelling caused by carrying structure!

047

GOLDEN GUMBOOT Towering over the town of Tully in Queensland, Australia, is a 26-ft-high (7.9-m) golden gumboot, a symbol of the area's high rainfall. The dimensions of the fiberglass boot, which has an internal spiral staircase leading to a viewing platform at the top, represent the record 311 in (7,900 mm) of rain that fell on the town in 1950.

VOLCANIC ERUPTION Lake Taupo on New Zealand's North Island was formed by a supervolcanic eruption 26,000 years ago. The dust from the eruption would have been visible as far away as modern-day China.

PRISON COMPETITION The Prison World Cup for soccer-playing inmates of different nationalities is held every four years at the Klong Prem Prison in Thailand.

HIGH TEE The Extreme 19th hole at the Legend Golf and Safari Resort in Limpopo Province, South Africa, is only accessible by helicopter. The tee for the par-3 hole is perched high on a cliff on Hanglip Mountain and is 394 yd (360 m) above the green, which is shaped like the outline of Africa.

VALUABLE STAMP An 1856 British Guiana One-Cent Magenta postage stamp sold at an auction in New York in 2014 for $9.5 million, making it the world's most valuable stamp.

DESERT DIP ↗

This swimming pool is hidden away deep in the Mojave Desert—and can be found only by means of a lengthy treasure hunt. The secret pool was built by Austrian artist Alfredo Barsuglia, but anyone wishing to use it must first go to the MAK Center for Art and Architecture in Los Angeles, California, to collect the keys and the G.P.S. coordinates detailing its exact location.

Quake Ramp

A skateboarder uses a section of buckled road tarmac as a makeshift ramp in the aftermath of a 6.1 magnitude earthquake that hit the San Francisco Bay area in Napa, California, on August 24, 2014.

HUMONGOUS FUNGUS A single 2,400-year-old honey mushroom in the Malheur National Forest, Oregon, is believed to be the world's largest living organism, covering 2,200 acres (890 ha). Most of its bulk lies underground, out of sight, but it is estimated to weigh up to 35,000 tons— 350 times the weight of an adult blue whale.

UNLUCKY FIND On Friday June 13, 2014, miners in Russia's Irkutsk region found a nugget of gold that they nicknamed "the devil's ear" because of its shape. When weighed, the nugget tipped the scales at 6,664 grams—666 supposedly being the devil's number.

WATER CONTAMINATED The 38-million-gal (173-million-l) Mount Tabor Reservoir in Portland, Oregon, was drained in 2014 after CCTV cameras captured a teen urinating into it. The reservoir provides drinking water to the city's population of 600,000.

TOILET TOUR American Rachel Erickson conducts regular tours of the most interesting toilets in London, England. The tour, which lasts several hours, begins at the aptly named Waterloo Station and ends with a visit to underground toilets that were once frequented by writer Oscar Wilde, but which have now been converted into a cocktail bar.

R Ripley's Believe It or Not!®
www.ripleys.com/books
WORLD

TAR AN FAR

Digital art collective Projector Club incorporated 3D projection mapping techniques to turn an entire Scottish farm tartan, in a project commissioned by event company mclcreate.

They used state-of-the-art technology to create a spectacular light display that transformed the barns and log cabins of Leyden Farm, West Lothian, by night.

TITANIC SHED John Siggins from Derbyshire, England, has converted his 18 x 12 ft (5.5 x 3.6 m) garden shed into a replica of a first-class cabin on the *Titanic*. After being given a genuine blanket worn by a *Titanic* survivor on the fateful night the ship sank in 1912, he began fitting the shed out with other *Titanic* artifacts and items from its sister ship the *Olympic*, including chairs, light fittings, silverware, table linen and china tea sets that he had acquired over 25 years. With beautiful wood panels on the walls, the shed is so luxurious that John and his wife Audrey eat Christmas dinner there.

MALE MONOPOLY The European country of Liechtenstein did not give women the right to vote or run for office until 1984.

BURNING BIRDS Thousands of birds have been bursting into flames over California's Mojave Desert, apparently as a result of intensely focused rays of sunlight from a solar energy plant. The plant uses more than 300,000 mirrors to power homes, but wildlife experts say the birds are scorched to death as they fly near the panels. In the middle of the day, they have counted a bird being incinerated every 2 minutes.

CHILD BRIDES As part of a lesson on family life, a kindergarten in Zhengzhou, China, "married" more than 100 toddlers. The brides and grooms—all aged between three and six years old and wearing wedding dresses and suits—had to choose their partner before exchanging rings and making vows in front of a registrar. Their parents were assured that the ceremony was not legally binding.

A CUT ABOVE For more than 25 years, retired hair stylist Anthony Cymerys (also known as Joe the Barber) has been offering homeless people in Hartford, Connecticut, free haircuts in exchange for hugs. Every Wednesday, the wooden benches in Bushnell Park are packed with homeless people waiting for a relaxing trim and shave from Joe, who uses a car battery to power his clippers.

Dull and Boring

This signpost welcomes visitors to the small Scottish town of Dull, which, since 2012, has been paired with Boring, Oregon, in a joint initiative to boost tourism by playing on their names. The towns host annual Dull and Boring celebrations, featuring a bagpipe player and a barbershop quartet.

Welcome to **DULL** Paired with Boring, Oregon, USA
Drive Safely

Highland Safaris

FIRE JUMPERS

A young Georgian man leaps over a blazing bonfire at the Chiakokonoba folk festival in Tbilisi—a ritual that is claimed to purify the jumper's soul of evil spirits. The dangerous tradition has put at least a dozen jumpers in hospitals with burns in recent years.

LIVING ROCKS The Romanian village of Costesti is home to strange rocks called *trovants* that can balloon 1,000 times in size when it rains. Trovants are balls of sand that appeared on Earth following powerful earthquakes six million years ago and they grow when they come into contact with water. Stones as small as 0.03 in (0.8 mm) can swell up to 26 ft (8 m). Scientists believe that beneath their outer shell, the stones have a high mineral content and when the surface becomes wet the minerals spread and the sand expands under pressure.

ROOM TO ROAM The biggest piece of property in Australia, the Anna Creek cattle station in South Australia, covers 9,400 sq mi (24,000 sq km), which is larger than the entire country of Israel.

Salt Ponds

A salt mine in Maras, Peru, which has been in operation for more than 800 years, dating back to before the time of the Incas, consists of 4,500 ponds covering an area of 3.7 acres (15,000 sq m) on the side of a steep mountain. The salt water emerges from a nearby spring from where it is directed by a network of channels into the ponds. There, the water evaporates in the hot, dry air to form salt crystals, which the miners are then able to collect.

TREE CLIMBING Since 1976, contestants have participated in the International Tree Climbing Championships, tackling trees up to 50 ft (15 m) high. Held in different locations around the U.S.A. each year, events include the speed climb, the secured footlock, and the aerial rescue, when one climber has to lower another safely to the ground. Different scoring systems operate for men and women and climbers use a variety of techniques and safety equipment.

WORLD TOUR By age 24, James Asquith of Hertfordshire, England, had visited every one of the world's 196 internationally recognized countries. Starting with Vietnam while he was a student in 2008, he funded his £125,000 ($190,000) adventure by taking jobs in bars and hostels as he traveled. He spent five months in North America, getting to 27 states including Hawaii and Alaska.

ELECTION FRAUD In 1927, the Liberian President Charles King was accused of fraud after he was re-elected by 230,000 votes—in a country with fewer than 15,000 registered voters. He resigned in 1930.

GIANT PADDLE A huge paddle at Mark Teasdale's farm in Parson, British Columbia, measures 60 ft (18 m) long, 9 ft (2.8 m) high and weighs 5,300 lb (2,400 kg). Made from one western red cedar log, the paddle took ten days to build and is 13 times the size of a standard oar.

WOVEN MASK ↑

This Asmat tribesman in Western New Guinea wears a striking death mask made from intricately woven plant fibers.

The mask is part of a costume worn at a funeral ritual in which the living dress as recently deceased relatives. Each elaborate outfit can take months to create, and carries the name of a dead individual whose spirit is thought to haunt the tribe. Brightly colored headdresses are seen as status symbols among the tribe and are often decorated with feathers and furs. Rarely photographed, the Asmat are known as fearsome warriors said to have killed Michael C. Rockefeller, son of New York governor Nelson Rockefeller, when he swam into their territory in 1961.

TREE TUNNEL

Overgrown trees have formed a beautiful 1.86-mi (3-km) green tunnel along a railway track in Klevan, Ukraine. Visitors regularly walk along the "Tunnel of Love," even though the track is still used by trains up to three times a day to transport wood to a nearby factory.

Working train track!

APRON MUSEUM Carolyn Terry of Iuka, Mississippi, is the owner and curator of the world's only apron museum. She has collected more than 3,000 aprons, some dating from the 1860s.

TREKKIE MANSION When entrepreneur Marc Bell bought an eight-bedroom mansion in Boca Raton, Florida, he converted the 2,000-sq-ft (185-sq-m) ballroom into an arcade with more than 60 games, and in another room built an exact replica of the bridge of the Starship Enterprise from *Star Trek*.

PINK MOSQUE Built for Ramadan 2014, the Masjid Dimaukom, a mosque in Datu Saudi Ampatuan, the Philippines, has its entire exterior painted bright pink. The color was chosen because it symbolizes peace and love.

MISSPELLED SIGNS

In 2010, workmen painted **SHCOOL** in big white letters on the road leading to Southern Guilford High School, North Carolina.

A sign erected in 2009 on Interstate 39 near Rothschild and Schofield, Wisconsin, spelled only one word correctly—"exit." It read:

"Exit 185 Buisness 51 Rothschield Schofeild."

In 2002, California highway department employees painted the warning sign **CRUVE** in large white letters near a bend in the road.

In 2003, highway workers in Richmond, California, painted a warning sign in 4-ft-high (1.2-m) letters on the road, which read **BMUP.** While doing this, they had erected a sign saying **SLOW MEN WORKING.**

Spelling Mistake

Workmen in Bristol, England, blundered by painting BUP STOP instead of BUS STOP in large yellow letters on the road during street repairs in August 2014!

ARCHAIC LAWS Until 2014, it was illegal in India to fly kites or balloons without police permission because they were classified as aircraft. It was also a criminal offense to unearth and keep treasure worth more than 10 rupees (19 cents)—and in the state of Andhra Pradesh all car inspectors were required by law to have clean teeth.

GUIDING ROCK The 486-ton granite boulder that gives its name to the coastal city of White Rock, British Columbia, originally acquired its white coating from layers of seabird excrement. This made the rock stand out so much from the surrounding landscape that 19th-century sailors used it as a beacon to guide their way.

WIZARD ROOMS The Georgian House Hotel in London, England, offers guests the chance to stay in Hogwarts-themed bedrooms that are designed to look like Harry Potter's fictional dorm room. The hotel's two Wizard Chambers feature four-poster beds, cauldrons, potion bottles and spell books.

TOURIST TRAP More than 8 million people—equal to the entire population of Switzerland—visited the Great Wall of China in a single day in October 2014.

BULLET BLOCKER A Modesto, California, store clerk was saved when armed robbers shot him—the wallet in his back pocket stopped the bullet from hitting his butt!

HIROSHIMA SURVIVOR A bonsai tree survived the atomic bomb that devastated the Japanese city of Hiroshima in 1945—even though it stood less than 2 mi (3.2 km) from where the bomb exploded. First planted in 1625, the ornamental white pine was presented to the American people in 1976 as a gift for the U.S.'s Bicentennial celebrations.

TOUGH MAZE A corn maze built for Halloween each year since 2007 by brothers Matt and Mark Cooley in Dixon, California, is so difficult to navigate that lost visitors have been forced to call 911 for help in getting out. The maze consists of up to 5 mi (8 km) of hand-cut twisting paths.

GLOBETROTTING BUNNY Travel Bunny, a toy rabbit owned by Peter Franc of Melbourne, Australia, traveled with him to 24 countries, posing at such iconic locations as Italy's Leaning Tower of Pisa, the Petronas Twin Towers in Malaysia and Stonehenge, England. He even went diving with Peter on Australia's Great Barrier Reef.

MOVIE MOTOR Movie fan Brian O'Neill of Sussex, England, spent two years and thousands of pounds creating a replica of the silver Delorean car from the 1980s' *Back to the Future* trilogy. He even wears a wig and white coat to dress up as the character Doc Brown while driving the car.

HOT SPRINGS Geothermal springs in Laugarvatn, Iceland, can reach temperatures of 50°C (122°F)—so hot that bread can be baked in the surrounding earth. In steam rooms built above these springs, guests can hear and smell the boiling water beneath.

ISLAND KINGDOM Portuguese art teacher Renato Barros bought a small rocky island in Funchal Harbour on the Atlantic Ocean island of Madeira for $31,000 and established his own kingdom there, inhabited by only himself and his family. He named the island the Principality of the Pontinha and declared himself Prince Renato II. He generates his own electricity via solar panel and a little windmill, and even holds a special Pontinha passport.

RAINBOW ←HOUSE

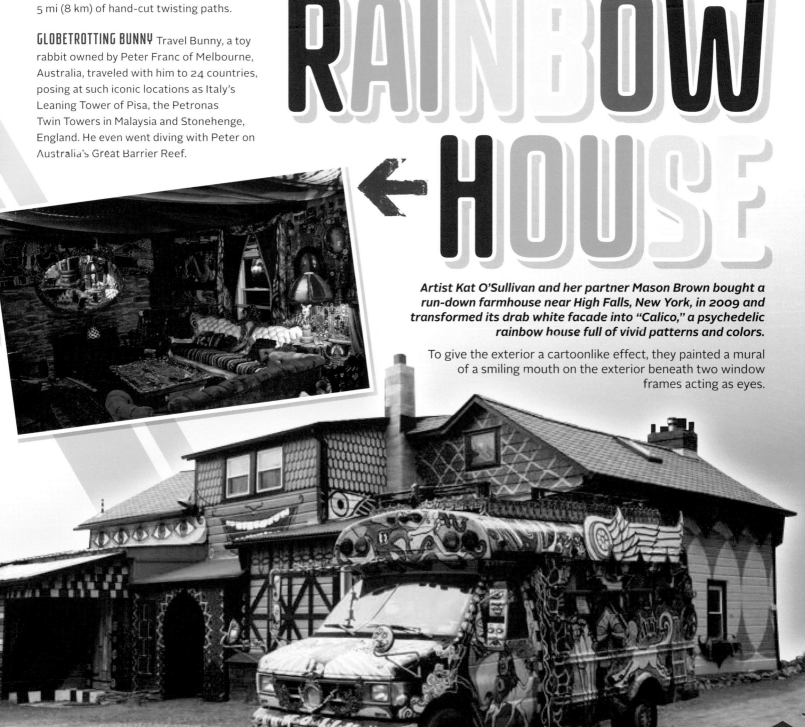

Artist Kat O'Sullivan and her partner Mason Brown bought a run-down farmhouse near High Falls, New York, in 2009 and transformed its drab white facade into "Calico," a psychedelic rainbow house full of vivid patterns and colors.

To give the exterior a cartoonlike effect, they painted a mural of a smiling mouth on the exterior beneath two window frames acting as eyes.

TORNADO FIRE

Janae Copelin photographed this spectacular "tornado fire" as a funnel of flame twisted into the sky while a farmer was burning his field in Chillicothe, Missouri. Sometimes called a "fire devil," the natural phenomenon occurs when strong winds whip a fire upward, and funnels can reach nearly 100 ft (30 m) high. This funnel lasted only a couple of minutes, but Janae described it as the coolest/scariest thing she had ever seen.

HAY STORM Over a period of four days in June 2014, huge clumps of hay fell from high altitudes over large parts of the western U.K.—including Devon and Lancashire, which are more than 200 mi (320 km) apart. Dry grass was seen falling from clear blue skies on windless days, covering cars, roads and gardens in a thick layer.

Ripley's EXPLAINS

The hay had probably been cut by farmers during the preceding spell of warm weather and been lifted by convection, where the ground heats the air above it, causing the air to rise. The hay was then carried along by warm thermals. As the hay rose high into the sky, the cooler air caused the thermals to break down and the grass fell back to earth.

REVERSING FALLS The Reversing Falls of Saint John in New Brunswick, Canada, flow in different directions according to the time of day. The change in direction is produced by a series of underwater ledges combined with surges from the powerful local tides, which can cause water levels to vary by 50 ft (16 m)—the same height as a five-story building—from low to high tide.

REPLICA COLON A hotel located on an island near Antwerp, Belgium, is designed to resemble a giant human colon. Made of wood, foam and fiberglass, the Hotel CasAnus follows the contours of the digestive system, starting with the tongue, continuing through the stomach, then the small and large intestines, and ending with the anus. It was originally created by Dutch designer Joep van Lieshout as an artwork, but has been converted into one-bedroom living quarters, allowing guests to curl up in a replica butthole.

DISAPPEARING SUMMIT When Mount St. Helens in Washington State erupted in 1980, the angry volcano spewed about 540 million tons of ash over an area of more than 22,000 sq mi (57,000 sq km). It caused such a huge landslide that the mountain's summit was reduced by 1,300 ft (400 m).

DOUBLE TREE Known locally as "Bialbero di Casorzo" or the "Double Tree of Casorzo," a strange tree in Casorzo, Italy, consists of a cherry tree growing on top of a mulberry tree. It is thought that a bird might have dropped a cherry seed on top of the mulberry tree and then the seed grew roots through the hollow trunk to reach the soil below.

TOO DIM The Statue of Liberty became the U.S.A.'s first electric lighthouse in 1886. It was decommissioned in 1902 because it was not bright enough.

SHORTEST HIGHWAY I-97 is the shortest 2-digit interstate highway in the contiguous U.S.A. It is only 17 mi (27 km) long and lies entirely in Anne Arundel County, Maryland.

BUSY CROSSING Every day of the year, about one million people walk on the Shibuya pedestrian crossing outside Shibuya railway station in Tokyo, Japan. At its busiest, in half an hour enough people use the crossing to fill a 45,000-seat sports stadium.

OVERNIGHT OASIS A large 60-ft-deep (18-m) lake suddenly appeared in the Tunisian desert in July 2014. One minute the area was sand, the next it was a turquoise body of water dubbed Lac de Gafsa in honor of the nearest town. The lake is believed to have been caused by a rupture in the rock above the local water table.

Ripley's Believe It or Not!®
www.ripleys.com/books
WORLD

← ## Roof Garden

Zhang Biqing spent six years building a rock-covered rooftop villa decorated with trees and bushes on top of a 26-story apartment block in Beijing, China. At around 8,600 sq ft (800 sq m) in area, it had to be demolished for fear that its weight might cause the entire building to collapse.

UNDERGROUND TRAMPS Workers in Gwynedd, North Wales, spent 4,500 hours transforming an old slate cavern to house three huge underground trampolines. The Bounce Below trampolines are 60 ft (18 m) wide and linked by 60-ft-long (18-m) slides. The top one is suspended 180 ft (54 m) above the floor of the cavern.

MISSOURI MOVE During the American Civil War (1861–1865), Marshall, in the state of Texas, was the capital city of the state of Missouri. A major Confederate city, Marshall became the headquarters of Missouri's Confederate government-in-exile.

RAIN DAY The town of Waynesburg, Pennsylvania, holds an annual Rain Day festival—complete with a Miss Rain Day pageant—on July 29 to recognize the fact that it has rained here on that date 114 times in the past 141 years.

DOG WEDDING

An 18-year-old girl called Mangli Munda married a dog in Jharkhand, India, in 2014 after village elders told her that the union would ward off a curse.

More than 50 guests attended the elaborate Hindu wedding ceremony, and the canine groom, a stray named Sheru, arrived in a chauffeur-driven car. The dog wedding is not legally binding, leaving Munda free to marry a human in the future.

Dense Island

The tiny Caribbean island of Santa Cruz del Islote, off the coast of Colombia, covers just fewer than 3 acres (0.012 sq km), but up to 1,200 people live there. There are 90 houses, two shops, one restaurant and a school, covering virtually every inch of the island. As there is no room for a cemetery, Islote's dead have to be buried on a neighboring island.

STORM LAKE A lightning storm occurs up to 160 nights each year in exactly the same spot over the mouth of the Catatumbo River where it empties into Lake Maracaibo, Venezuela. The violent storm unleashes lightning that can last for 10 hours. It generates 1.2 million lightning strikes annually and, as it is visible from as far away as 250 mi (400 km).

RAT CATCHERS The Canadian province of Alberta has been rat-free for over half a century thanks to a 5,822 sq mi (15,080 sq km) rat control buffer zone along the vulnerable eastern border—a zone that remains staffed by eight professional rat catchers.

EARTH SLOWING The rotation of planet Earth is slowing down by 0.002 seconds per century, meaning that in 180 million years' time, Earth days will be 25 hours long.

TONGUE TWISTER Muckanaghederdauhaulia is the name of a small village in County Galway, Ireland. It means "piggery between two brines."

BRIDAL COFFIN

During their Valentine's Day wedding ceremony at a temple near Bangkok, Thailand, groom Tanapatpurin Samangnitit and his bride Sunantaluk Kongkoon chose to lie down in a pink-lined coffin. They were one of seven couples to lie in the coffin that day in the belief that doing so would bring them good luck.

WACKY WEDDINGS

● In Scotland, friends and relatives carry out a tradition called blackening where they take the bride- or bridegroom-to-be and pour substances like tar, dead fish, eggs, mud and curdled milk over them in a bid to ward off evil spirits.

● Newlyweds from the Tidong people of northern Borneo are not allowed to go to the toilet after their wedding for 72 hours as it will bring bad luck. Their families spy on them and feed them only small amounts of food and water.

● In Korea, the groom's friends beat his feet with a fish on his wedding night to boost his stamina.

● At a Maasai wedding in Kenya, the father of the bride blesses his daughter by spitting on her head and breasts. She then leaves the village with her husband and dare not look back for fear of being turned to stone.

● After a Greek wedding, the bride throws a pomegranate at a door covered with honey. If the fruit seeds stick to the door, it is a sign that the couple will have many children.

● Among the Tujia in China, the bride must cry for one hour every day in the month leading up to the wedding. Gradually the other women in the family also join in for what is seen as an expression of joy as they all cry in different tones.

HORSE HAIRCUT

As part of a 400-year-old Spanish festival, several hundred wild horses are rounded up and wrestled to the ground each year so that they can have their manes and tails trimmed.

The "Shearing of the Beasts" is carried out over four days in the village of Sebucedo by aloitadores, *or fighters, who herd the animals down from the mountains and then work in teams of three to overpower them.*

DEAD BATS More than 100,000 bats fell dead from the sky during a heatwave that engulfed Queensland, Australia, in January 2014. With the animals unable to cope with temperatures over 109°F (43°C), trees and the ground were littered with bat bodies and the stench of rotting carcasses filled large towns and parts of the city of Brisbane.

TIME TRAVEL People in the Spanish border town of Sanlucar de Guadiana can cross to neighboring Portugal by zip wire—and travel forward in time. Passengers ride at 45 mph (72 km/h) down the ½-mi (0.8-km) gradient spanning the Guadiana River, which separates Spain from the Portuguese town of Alcoutim. Although the journey lasts barely a minute, it crosses a time zone so that they arrive in Portugal about 1 hour before they left.

SEE-SAW The British Isles are slowly rising in the north and sinking in the south—by about 2 in (5 cm) a century—owing to the melting of northern ice since the last Ice age 20,000 years ago.

WATER RELEASE Each year, a large oak tree can release 1,000-bathtubs-worth of water from its leaves into the atmosphere.

HIGH TEMPERATURES A 541-ft-high (165-m) digital thermometer was fitted to an industrial chimney in Puxi Expo Park in Shanghai, China, in June 2014. As well as displaying the temperature, the Expo Thermometer—the highest meteorological signal tower in the world—has a top that changes color at night in accordance with weather conditions. White represents good weather and purple means that the weather is going to be bad.

FORGOTTEN BOOK Finding a long-forgotten library book that he had borrowed from Taunton School, Somerset, England, 66 years earlier, Sir James Tidmarsh returned it in 2015—along with $2,300 to cover the fine. He discovered the copy of *Ashenden* by W. Somerset Maugham at his home.

DEERLY DEPARTED In February 2012, the Russian town of Naryan-Mar built a memorial to 6,000 reindeer and their herders who served in the Soviet Army, transporting ammunition, orders and wounded soldiers, in World War II.

GARBAGE DUMP The Jardim Gramacho dump outside Rio de Janeiro, Brazil, covered an area of 14 million sq ft (1.3 million sq m)—the equivalent of 244 American football fields—and was piled with garbage 300 ft (90 m) high. It received 9,000 tons of garbage a day, but closed in 2012, after 34 years.

MAYBE MONARCHY When Jeremiah Heaton's daughter Emily asked in 2014 if she could be a real princess, he created a kingdom for her by laying claim to an unused 800-square-mile swath of desert in the African region of Bir Tawil, calling it the "Kingdom of North Sudan"—and naming her its princess! The Abingdon, VA., natives are currently seeking recognition of the claim from authorities.

Salt Cathederal

Believe it or not, this beautiful cathedral not only lies 443 ft (135 m) underground, it is made entirely of salt—including the chandeliers. Miners at the 800-year-old Wieliczka Salt Mine in southern Poland have labored through the centuries carving dozens of religious statues, three chapels and a cathedral out of rock salt. The ornate chandeliers were made from rock salt that was dissolved and then reconstituted with the impurities taken out to give it the appearance of glass. The mine stretches for 178 mi (287 km) and also has its own underground lake.

BEAR NECESSITY People in Churchill, Manitoba, Canada, leave their cars and sometimes their houses unlocked in case pedestrians need to make a quick escape from polar bears.

STREET CATCH Jake Sawyer, 16, used his bare hands to catch a huge 40 lb (18 kg) carp in a flooded street in North Royalton, Ohio. Heavy rain on May 12, 2014, had caused flash flooding, and the 3-ft-long (0.9-m) fish probably swam out of a nearby pond as the waters rose.

SHRINKING EARTH The Earth loses weight by 50,000 tons every year as hydrogen and helium gases leave the atmosphere because they are too light for gravity to keep them around. Even so, it will take trillions of years to deplete Earth's supply of hydrogen.

FISHING FRENZY

At the sound of a gunshot, up to 35,000 fishermen, teamed in pairs, jump into Nigeria's muddy Matan Fada River for the annual Argungu Fishing Festival. One fisher carries gourds for flotation, while the other wields large nets, although some fishermen prefer to catch the fish with their bare hands. Fish weighing 145 lb (66 kg) have been caught within the 1-hour time limit and the winning team receives a prize of $7,500 and a new bus.

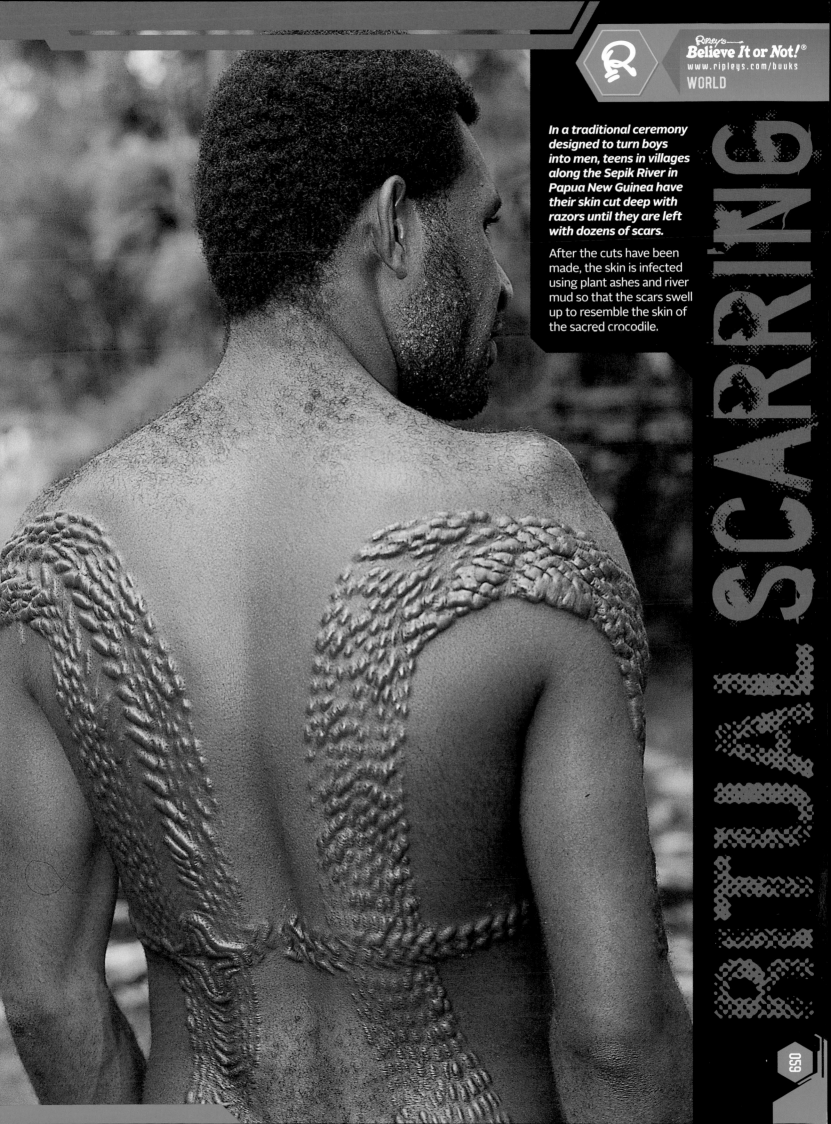

RITUAL SCARRING

In a traditional ceremony designed to turn boys into men, teens in villages along the Sepik River in Papua New Guinea have their skin cut deep with razors until they are left with dozens of scars.

After the cuts have been made, the skin is infected using plant ashes and river mud so that the scars swell up to resemble the skin of the sacred crocodile.

ANIMALS

MEGA MIGRATIONS

40 billion African migratory locusts can form a swarm covering 11,000 sq ft (1,000 sq km) and eat 80,000 tons of vegetation per day—enough food to feed a million people.

120 million red crabs migrate to the seashore to mate every fall on Christmas Island in the Indian Ocean.

As many as **60 million** monarch butterflies fly from Canada to the California coast and Mexico every November for the winter.

30 million sockeye salmon migrate to Canada's Fraser River in the annual salmon run.

8 million straw-colored fruit bats fly 2,000 mi (3,200 km) from the Republic of the Congo to Zambia from October to December to feed on their favorite delicacy, the musuku fruit.

1.5 million wildebeest stampede through Kenya's Mara River each year in search of greener pastures.

RAY SCHOOL

Schools of Munk's devil rays can number tens of thousands of fish and cover an area of over 32,000 sq ft (3,000 sq m)—more than half the size of a football field.

This aerial view was taken over the Sea of Cortez, off Baja California, Mexico. Scientists are mystified as to why the fish, which often somersault out of the water, gather in such large numbers.

CLAM CALAMITY By counting the number of rings on the inside of the shell, scientists have calculated that a deep-sea clam discovered alive off the coast of Iceland in 2006 was 507 years old, meaning that it was born seven years after Christopher Columbus discovered America. Sadly, in removing it from its ocean home and putting it in a freezer for further study, the scientists accidentally killed what could have been the world's oldest-living sea creature.

SURROGATE MOTHER When Dina Alves adopted two orphaned baby armadillos in the Brazilian town of Guaporema, her pet dog Faisca became so attached to the new arrivals that she began producing her own milk to nurse them.

CLEVER COLLIE Chaser, a border collie belonging to John W. Pilley of Spartanburg, South Carolina, knows more than 1,000 different word commands. It took John, a professor of psychology, three years to teach Chaser the names of 1,022 different toys, one by one. Each time, he got her to fetch the toy and then repeated its name to reinforce the understanding.

PREGNANCY TEST In the 1950s the African clawed frog was used as a pregnancy test on humans. A woman's urine was injected into a frog, and if the frog produced eggs, the woman was declared pregnant.

ROAMING FISH A 3-ft-long (1-m) sturgeon that escaped from an aquatic center in Hampshire, England, during floods in February 2014 was found alive and well in a puddle at a car wash one mile away.

CUDDLE CLONE

Working from submitted photographs, Louisville, Kentucky, online retailer Cuddle Clones offers custom-made, exact stuffed replicas of pets for people who want to present their furry best friends with life-sized plush pet "clones." Founded in 2009, the company spends between eight to ten weeks creating the lifelike likenesses of dogs, cats, birds, lizards, and other pets—such as Stan, a schnauzer in Toronto, Canada (pictured right), and his carbon copy Cuddle Clone.

PATRIOTIC CAT Margo, a cat owned by Oleg Bouboulin of Yekaterinburg, Russia, stands to attention like a soldier whenever the Russian national anthem is played. She stands on her back legs without moving a muscle and even seems to know when the anthem is about to end because she relaxes as the final notes are played.

AGENT SWAN An Egyptian man arrested a swan and took it to a police station because he thought the bird was a spy. He became suspicious when he noticed the swan was carrying an electronic device, but it turned out to be a wildlife-tracking instrument.

FIERY SHRIMP *Acanthephyra purpurea*, the fire-breathing shrimp, blinds and distracts its would-be predators by spewing out a blue-glowing bacterial cloud.

HARMFUL ARMS A mysterious plague has been causing starfish to tear themselves to pieces. An afflicted starfish's arms crawl in opposite directions until their bodies are pulled apart—and, unlike healthy starfish, diseased specimens are not able to regenerate.

SILK THREAD The silk used to form a silkworm's cocoon is actually hardened saliva that has been secreted from its mouth, and it can unravel into a single thread up to 1 mi (1.6 km) long.

CLEAN CAT Natasha, a six-month-old Siberian forest cat owned by Daryl Humdy of Oakland, California, survived a 40-minute cycle inside a running washing machine after climbing in with a load of laundry.

DOLPHIN PROPOSAL

Alex Rigby of Merseyside, England, used a dolphin to deliver his marriage proposal to girlfriend Debbie Preston. She was in the water at Discovery Cove in Orlando, Florida, on a family vacation when the dolphin swam toward her pushing a buoy that said: "Debbie, will you marry me?"

HEROIC CAT When a savage dog attacked four-year-old Jeremy Triantafilo and tried to drag him from his bicycle outside his home in Bakersfield, California, the boy was saved by his cat Tara, who intervened and chased the dog away. Tara was rewarded for her bravery by being invited to "throw out" the first pitch at Bakersfield Blaze's baseball game against the Lancaster Jethawks.

SIX-CLAWED LOBSTER A mutant six-clawed lobster was caught off the coast of Massachusetts in 2013. Donated to the Maine State Aquarium in West Boothbay Harbor, 4-lb (1.8-kg) Lola has a normal claw on one side, but instead of a singular claw on the other, she has five claws arranged like a hand. The extra claws are either a genetic mutation or an unusual re-growth from a damaged or lost claw.

Extra Legs

In the mid 1990s, hundreds of frogs in ponds across the U.S.A. and Canada developed extra legs. Some frogs had as many as a dozen! The condition was caused by a parasitic flatworm, *Ribeiroia*, which can invade the bodies of tadpoles. The parasites bury themselves in the tiny buds that eventually grow into the hind legs, resulting in the developing leg either being missing or malformed.

SEE-THROUGH SHRIMP New Zealand fisherman Stewart Fraser scooped up a strange, translucent creature swimming near the ocean's surface some 40 mi (64 km) north of the Karikari Peninsula. It was later identified as a salpa maggiore, a marine invertebrate that moves by pumping water through its gelatinous body. It is also able to create a clone of itself.

BONE CRUSHER *Trichobatrachus robustus*, a breed of frog found in Cameroon, breaks its own bones to produce claws when it feels threatened. At rest, its claws, which are found on the hind feet only, are nestled inside a mass of connective tissue, but if the frog comes under attack the claws puncture their way out of the amphibian's toe pads to form a lethal weapon.

TWO-TONE LAMB A lamb named Battenberg was born with black markings on one side of his face and white on the other—and while his front right and back left legs are black, the other two legs are white. His distinctive coloring helped save his life by ensuring that he was spotted in deep snow shortly after he was born in the Brecon Beacons National Park in Wales.

BAT CAVE A cave near San Antonio, Texas, is home to 10 million Mexican free-tailed bats, crammed together on the walls at 400 bats per sq ft (4,300 per sq m).

SPOILED SHELLS Fewer than 500 of Madagascar's ploughshare tortoises are living in the wild, prompting some conservationists to deface the animals' beautiful shells in order to reduce their value to poachers.

SHARK DIVER Hawaiian freediver Ocean Ramsey swims and rides with great white sharks up to 17-ft-long (5.2-m) in order to prove they are nothing like the terrifying maneater from the movie *Jaws*. She travels the globe in search of sharks and has swam with over 30 species.

LONG → WHISKERS

Whiskers, a two-year-old black and white cat at an animal center in Somerset, England, gets her name from her huge whiskers that stretch 12 in (30 cm) from tip to tip—and they're still growing.

Extended facial hair obviously runs in the family because when she gave birth to a litter of kittens they, too, had very long whiskers.

FISH DRUGGED The slow-moving geographic cone snail, which lives off the coast of Australia, drugs fish to catch and eat them. The snail releases a toxic cloud containing insulin, which causes the fish's blood-sugar levels to plummet and puts it in a coma.

STRETCH JELLY Although its body is sometimes only about 6 ft (1.8 m) long, the lion's mane jellyfish has tentacles that can grow up to 120 ft (37 m), making it longer than the length of a blue whale.

TALENTED FISH Ilana Bram of Poughkeepsie, New York , spent two months training her pet cichlid fish Erasmus to play soccer in his tank with a miniature ball. The talented fish can also weave his way through a slalom course and perform a limbo dance.

SEE-THROUGH FISH

The head of the Pacific barreleye fish is covered with a transparent shield, like the glass canopy of a jet fighter plane, which helps it to see better in the dark ocean depths where it lives. It also has rotating eyes, allowing it to look up through the shield at potential prey, as well as to look forward. Believe it or not, the eyes are not the indentations above its mouth (these are the equivalent of nostrils), but the huge green tubular, barrel-shaped objects, which give the fish its name.

CHICK DISGUISE Chicks of the cinereous mourner bird, which lives in the Amazon, scare off predators by mimicking the appearance of poisonous hairy moth larvae. Whereas the adult birds have dull gray plumage, the juveniles grow vivid orange spiky feathers and, when disturbed, move their head from side to side just like a caterpillar.

SIZE MATTERS The female blanket octopus can be 40,000 times heavier and 100 times larger than its male mate—the equivalent to a human standing next to a walnut. Whereas the female can reach 6.6 ft (2 m) long and weigh 22 lb (10 kg), the male often measures just 0.9 in (2.4 cm) and weighs no more than .009 oz (0.25 g).

JELLYFISH SWARM
Thousands of blue blubber jellyfish washed up on a beach near Brisbane, Australia, in January 2015. When at sea the swarm stretched for over 160 ft (50 m), covering an area equal to nearly 10 tennis courts.

HUNGRY HIPPOS Although they are thought of as herbivores, hippos occasionally eat each other when food is scarce.

DARK HOME Scientists have discovered fish living beneath 2,430-ft-thick (740-m) ice in the Antarctic. They live in a 33-ft-deep (10-m) area between the ice and the ocean floor sustained by energy from the Earth's core.

RIPLEY'S RESEARCH

The barreleye fish was first described in 1939 but it was almost 70 years later that Bruce Robison and Kim Reisenbichler of the Monterey Bay Aquarium Research Institute discovered that it had eyes that could rotate within the transparent shield of its head. They made the discovery after studying the fish at depths of 2,600 ft (800 m) off the coast of Central California and successfully bringing a live specimen to the surface to observe it in a tank for several hours.

HOME FOR PAW-SIONERS Since 2001, England's Lincolnshire Trust for Cats retirement home has offered older cats a safe place to "retire" and enjoy a happy life should their owners die or become unable to care for them. The Trust and feline-friendly retirement home was set up by 65-year-old Jain Hills, who realized that older cats were often turned away by pet shelters because it is difficult to find them new homes.

SINISTER SKULL The pink underwing moth caterpillar of Australasia has sinister face markings on its head that look uncannily like a human skull and which enable it to scare off predators.

Ripley's Believe It or Not!®
www.ripleys.com/books
ANIMALS

DRASTIC MEASURES After mating, the male coin spider bites off its own genitals so that it is more agile and better able to keep rival males away from the female. As an extra precaution, it also uses the severed genitals to block the route to the female's reproductive organs.

Snake's HEAD

In order to deter predators, the moth caterpillar **Hemeroplanes triptolemus** *can transform itself in seconds so that its body looks just like the head of a poisonous green viper snake.*

KILLER CROC After a 20-ft-long (6-m) crocodile ate his pregnant wife, distraught fisherman Mubarak Batambuze, of Kibuye village, Uganda, spent his savings on a spear and killed the 2,200-lb (1,000-kg) reptile.

FAMOUS FAN Wilson, a 29-in-tall (74-cm) pony owned by Sarah Kessler, is the Seattle Seahawks' most famous fan—and even has his mane and tail painted in the NFL team's colors with nontoxic, washable paint.

STALKING CROC New Zealand kayaker Ryan Blair was trapped on Governor Island off the coast of Western Australia for two weeks by a giant crocodile that he thought would eat him if he tried to escape. Having been taken to the remote location by boat, Blair had intended to kayak the 2½ mi (4 km) back to the mainland, but every time he tried to paddle away, the 20-ft-long (6-m) crocodile stalked him, forcing him to return to the island. Desperate for water, he finally managed to shine a light to alert a rescuer.

IN A SPIN Chica, a guinea pig belonging to Marilyn Jones from New Plymouth, New Zealand, emerged unscathed after accidentally spending 30 minutes inside a running laundry dryer on an intense cycle at temperatures of 160°F (71°C).

DOGGY DENIM Mel and Matt Westwood, from Melbourne, Australia, design custom-made denim jackets for dogs—from Chihuahuas to greyhounds—which they sell all over the world.

Tiny little hedgehog!

Surrogate Mother

Abandoned by its mother, a baby hedgehog in Russia faced a bleak future until it was nursed back to health by Sonya the cat, who lovingly kept the tiny animal warm and fed it along with her other kittens.

STRIPED POLECAT

Workmen on a road on the Shetland Islands, off the north coast of Scotland, gave this dead polecat, a relative of the mink, unusual markings when, instead of moving it out of their way, they painted a white line right over it as it lay squashed in the road.

GLOWING REINDEER Reindeer herders in Lapland, northern Finland, have given their livestock glow-in-the-dark antlers in a bid to stop them being hit by cars. The animals have been painted with fluorescent dyes to reduce the thousands of reindeer road deaths in Lapland each year.

JELLYFISH SHREDDERS Scientists in Korea have developed swimming robots that can destroy 880 lb (400 kg) of jellyfish in an hour. The Jellyfish Elimination Robotic Swarm (or JEROS) glides along the surface of the water at 4.6 mph (7.4 km/h) using cameras on board to detect any jellyfish. Submerged nets then suck up the creatures before a propeller shreds them to pieces. Jellyfish are a major problem in Korea, terrifying swimmers, clogging fishing nets and even causing nuclear reactors to shut down.

BEAVER DAMAGE A busy stretch of road in the Sverdlovsk region of Russia caved in because of a beaver dam. A pipe under the road had been blocked by the beavers, and the weight of water trying to get through the pipe caused the road to collapse, opening up a 13-ft-wide (4-m) hole.

POWER NAPS Swainson's thrushes, found in the Americas, sleep for just 10 seconds at a time. When they leave their wintering grounds in Mexico or South America, they travel at night and take hundreds of power naps en route. They are also able to sleep with one eye closed and rest half their brain, while the other eye remains open and the other half of the brain is alert to deal with threats from predators.

DEADLY VENOM Tim Friede has survived being bitten by more than 100 venomous snakes, including a lethal black mamba that can kill a person in under 20 minutes. He keeps dozens of the most poisonous snakes on Earth in the basement of his Milwaukee, Wisconsin, home, but says he has become immune to their bites after injecting himself with their diluted venom.

EGG REPAIR Finding a rare kakapo parrot egg that had been accidentally crushed by the mother bird, New Zealand ranger Jo Ledington repaired the egg with masking tape and glue—and the chick hatched successfully. There are only around 125 kakapos alive in the world today.

RACING SHEEP With the 2014 Tour de France race starting in Yorkshire, England, local farmer Keith Chapman used agricultural dye to spray his flock of sheep polka-dot pink, green and yellow to make it look as though they were wearing cycling jerseys.

SURPRISE PASSENGER After driving for more than 9 mi (15 km), Cameron Blaseotto of Canberra, Australia, heard something rummaging around under the hood of his car—and when he stopped to investigate he found that a female duck-billed platypus had hitched a ride.

SLIPPERY CUSTOMER Julius, a 16-ft-long (5-m) albino Burmese python belonging to American-born Jenner Miemietz, learned to open doors in her owner's German apartment by using her body weight to press down on the handles. She could also open the fridge door and drain the bathtub.

VINTAGE VENOM Poison from taipans, tiger snakes and death adders that was collected by scientists and stored at the University of Melbourne's Australian Venom Research Unit is still deadly—even though some of it is more than 80 years old.

SHARP HEARING Blue whales can hear each other over distance of 100 mi (160 km), but zoologists believe the whales used to communicate over distances of up to 1,000 mi (1,600 km) prior to the increase of human noise pollution in recent decades.

Cebu City Zoo in the Philippines offers visitors free massages from four giant Burmese pythons, weighing a combined 550 lb (250 kg).

The snakes are placed one at a time on top of the volunteers who lie down on a bamboo bed for the 15-minute massage. The pythons are each fed ten chickens beforehand to stop them from feeling hungry, preventing them squeezing anyone to death to make them their dinner.

DAINTY DOGGIE

Abandoned as a puppy three years ago in Shanghai, China, Xiaoniu the dog found a home—and a fashion designer—in her 62-year-old owner, Mr. Fang. This furry fashionista now brings a smile to all of her neighbors in their Pudong Zhengdajiayuan housing estate by wearing fabulous custom-made outfits Mr. Fang creates. These dog-tastic clothes are accessorized with everything from sunglasses and hair bows to Santa hats and backpacks. But Xiaoniu doesn't just strike a pose: this supermodel also struts UPRIGHT on her hind legs for up to an hour at a time!

WINTER WARMTH Shortly after a group of ring-tailed lemurs arrived at Tropiquaria Zoo in Somerset, England, staff noticed that the wall heater in the lemur enclosure was repeatedly turned up to maximum during winter. They found that on particularly cold nights the lemurs—named Devine, William, Katrina, Barry and Julien—were reaching into the heater cage and turning up the thermostat. When the weather warmed up, the lemurs left the thermostat alone.

BEER CARRIER Jana Salzman of Reykjavik, Iceland, has trained her collie Atlas to fetch cold cans of beer. The dog pulls a towel attached to the refrigerator door handle to open it and retrieve an ice-cold beer.

SUPER SUCKER The northern clingfish, found off the Pacific coast of North America, possesses such strong suction power that it can support 300 times its own body weight.

HAIRY HEROES New York City guide dogs Salty and Roselle were awarded a joint Dickin Medal, a British honor given by the People's Dispensary for Sick Animals, for loyally remaining at the side of their blind owners and courageously leading them down more than 70 floors of the World Trade Center and to a place of safety before the towers collapsed during the September 11, 2001 terrorist attack. Roselle, who had been sleeping under her owner's desk when one of the planes hit Tower 1, went on to be posthumously named American Hero Dog of the Year 2011 by the American Humane Society, and has a book written about her.

Snake Massage

CAT CANDIDATE

Morris, a black-and-white cat owned by Sergio Chamorro, ran for mayor in the Mexican city of Xalapa in 2014. Campaigning under the slogan "Tired of voting for rats? Vote for a cat," Morris received more than 130,000 likes on his Facebook page—far more than his human rivals—and received around 12,000 votes in the actual election, placing him fourth out of the 11 candidates.

MONKEY WHISPER Instead of making loud alarm calls when a distrusted stranger enters their territory, Cotton-top Tamarin Monkeys of Colombia often communicate with each other in hushed whispers.

BOVINE GAS A barn in Hesse, Germany, was badly damaged after a herd of 90 dairy cows passed so much gas that the resultant methane ignited and caused an explosion, which blew off the roof of the building.

Monster Poop

A 40-inch-long (1-m) alleged fossilized dinosaur poop, found in Washington State, sold for $8,500 in 2014. The monster coprolite—believed to be passed by an unknown species some 25 million years ago—was so long it had to be presented in four sections at the Beverly Hills auction.

40 INCHES LONG!

ALOHA, KITTY! The feline of a family moving from Virginia to Hawaii in 2014 was supposed to stay with relatives—but had other plans. The land and sea journey for the Barth family's belongings took more than a month, but when they opened a box, their beloved cat Memeow was inside—somehow having survived without food or water!

EAGLE HAS LANDED While Wendy Morrell was watching tennis on TV at her home in Dorset, England, a huge Russian Steppe Eagle with a 4-ft (1.2-m) wingspan suddenly flew in through the patio doors and perched on a cabinet. The escaped eagle, named Storm, was eventually coaxed down by a bird-of-prey expert who offered it a dead chick as a snack.

CHIMNEY ORDEAL Chloe, a pet rabbit owned by nine-year-old Natasha Cameron, was sucked up the chimney of the family house in Cheshire, England, by a sudden gust of wind. The rabbit was trapped up the chimney for three days before being rescued by fire crews.

DUNG MOUNTAIN A single elephant can produce 300 lb (136 kg) of dung—the weight of an average gorilla—in 24 hours.

SNAKE BALLS Each spring, more than 140,000 Red-sided Garter Snakes emerge from hibernation and turn an area near Narcisse, Manitoba, into a writhing mass of bodies. They form wriggling mating balls on the ground and in bushes and trees, often with as many as 50 males wrapping themselves around a solitary female. The snakes come from miles away to hibernate at the Narcisse Snake Dens—a series of sinkholes where tens of thousands of snakes are crammed into a space the size of a living room.

Ripley's
Believe It or Not!®
www.ripleys.com/books
ANIMALS

JAWS vs CLAWS

An 18-ft-long (5.5-m) saltwater crocodile, one of the most fearsome predators on Earth, was seen wrestling with a highly aggressive bull shark, clamping it in its jaws in the Adelaide River, northern Australia.

Usually, the shark would expect to be eaten alive, but this one may have got lucky because the croc, Brutus, is 80 years old and missing a front leg and most of his teeth.

SHARK ATTACK When a tiger shark took a bite out of his surfboard and knocked him into the ocean near Kilauea, Hawaii, 25-year-old Jeff Horton survived the attack by grabbing the shark's fin and repeatedly punching the fish in the eye until it finally spat out the surfboard and swam away.

CANINE PILOT When Graham Mountford of Bedfordshire, England, takes to the skies in his Cessna 210 Centurion light aircraft, his copilot is Callie, his chocolate Labrador dog. She has been flying since she was 12 weeks old and has clocked up more than 250 flying hours covering 50,000 mi (80,000 km).

DEEP BREATH The Nine-banded Armadillo, found in North, Central and South America, is able to cross rivers by holding its breath for up to six minutes while walking across the riverbed.

DOG SWALLOWS 43 SOCKS!

Veterinarians operating on a sick Great Dane in Portland, Oregon, were amazed to discover 43½ socks in the dog's stomach. The animal's owner knew he liked chewing socks, but had no idea he had actually been swallowing them. Once the socks were removed, the dog made a full recovery.

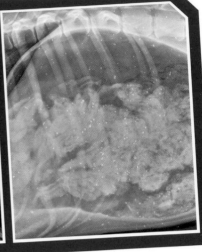

DETERMINED DOGGIE After being tossed a meatball, a stray dog refused to be left behind as a Swedish team trekked and kayaked through the grueling 430-mile (692-km) 2014 Adventure Racing World Championship in the Amazon jungle. Dubbed "Arthur," the intrepid canine accompanied the team to twelfth place—and a new home with Team Peak Performance leader Mikael Lindnord, who adopted him.

CRIME HAUL A dog that jumped into a pond in West Sussex, England, to fetch a stick came to the surface with a haul of stolen jewelry instead. Police divers discovered almost 1,000 stolen items, along with four handguns, a machete and a bayonet in the pond.

BEE SWARM A swarm of bees found in the ceiling of Frieda Turkmenilli's apartment in Queens, New York, consisted of a staggering 50,000 bees that had built 17 honeycombs.

TALENTED PUP Jiff, a tiny Pomeranian dog from Los Angeles, California, has become an online star thanks to his trick of being able to walk on just his front two paws. He can also walk on his hind legs, on three legs, and even backward in a semi-moonwalk. The skateboard-riding pup has his own Facebook, Twitter and Instagram profiles and has made several TV and movie appearances, as well as being in musician Katy Perry's "Dark Horse" video.

ODD COUPLE Roo, a two-legged Chihuahua, and Penny, an orphaned silky chicken, have become best friends at the Duluth Animal Hospital in Georgia after being rescued by hospital employee Alicia Williams. The dog, who gets around with the aid of a custom-made cart, sometimes runs the chicken over because he forgets how big his wheels are.

FOOT SUCKER The thorny devil lizard, which lives in the harsh deserts of Australia, drinks water through its feet. By using a series of tiny capillaries located between its scales, it can cover its entire body in 30 seconds.

STREAKING BACON

Piglet Chris P. Bacon was born without the use of his hind legs, so his new owner, Dr. Len Lucero of Sumterville, Florida, helped him get around by building a two-wheeled harness contraption using his son's K'Nex building set. The wheelchair attaches to the pig's body with a harness around his neck and rear and has wheels in place of his back legs. The device has turned the little pig into an online celebrity with his own Facebook and Twitter pages.

PENGUIN JUMPERS Volunteers with Knits for Nature, a program run by an Australian conservation group, knit sweaters for sick penguins that have been harmed by oil spills. The sweaters keep the birds warm, but they also prevent them trying to clean away the toxic oil with their beaks. Over the years, the group has come up with more than 300 different penguin sweater designs.

PET TRAILERS Inspired by vintage trailers of the 1940s, Judson Beaumont of Vancouver, British Columbia, has designed a range of miniature camper vans on wheels for pets, especially small dogs. The $800 mobile homes have a battery operated LED light and wireless speakers inside and can even be fitted with personalized license plates.

MONKEY SELFIE The U.S. Copyright Office has explicitly stated "a photograph taken by a monkey" cannot be copyrighted after ruling against photographer David Slater's application to copyright a photograph taken by an Indonesian macaque on his camera. In addition, animals cannot own copyrights of self portraits, including "a mural painted by an elephant."

FEARLESS RATS Rats infected by the *Toxoplasma gondii* parasite lose their fear of cats, meaning that cats are more likely to catch and eat them, continuing the life cycle of the parasite—inside the cat.

PET CONSOLE San Diego, California, entrepreneurs Dan Knudsen and Leo Trottier have designed a game console for dogs. CleverPet has three sensitive touch pads, which light up when touched and release food for the pet when hit in the correct order.

MUMMIFIED CAT While Andrew Hartley renovated the ceiling of an 18th-century house in North Yorkshire, England, a mummified cat fell on him. The cat was believed to be at least 100 years old and had probably been part of an old tradition where dead cats were put in the eaves and walls of properties to ward off evil spirits.

BEST FRIEND Seven-year-old Emily Bland from St. Albans, Hertfordshire, England, has a very special best friend—an orangutan called Rishi who lives at Myrtle Beach Safari Park, South Carolina. The pair first met as toddlers in 2008 when Emily gave Rishi a ride in her doll's stroller. The two youngsters have met up regularly since and have grown to form a strong bond like brother and sister.

STICKY SPOT Carol Brown sent Ripley's this incredible story about Toto, her parent's Siamese cat. Belonging to Dan Brazil of Lufkin, Texas, Toto survived for 90 days without food or water accidentally locked in a neighbor's storage room. He stayed alive by drinking condensation and licking the glue in the books that were kept there.

TRASH DIET A puppy survived nearly a month trapped in a locked car that had been impounded in a Kansas City, Missouri, lot. Despite having no water, the 12-week-old terrier and schnauzer mix, named Kia, survived by eating trash left in the car.

CAT BURGLER Norris, a two-year-old tabby cat owned by Richard and Sophie Windsor of Bristol, England, went on a four-month crime spree stealing food, towels, rubber gloves, dishcloths, baby clothes, underwear and a bath mat from neighbors' homes.

CLOTHES HORSE Jessica Clarke and Annie Brown from Pontypool, Wales, make $255 (£170) one-piece suits for horses—in a range of designs including polka dot, stars and leopard print! The equine onesies, which cover the entire body apart from nose, eyes, hooves and tail, were originally designed to protect the horse from allergies and skin conditions, but have also been snapped up by customers in the U.S. and Australia, who are keen to keep the animals' coats clean before a show.

FANCY FROG In an Indonesian rain forest, scientists have identified the first known frog out of the world's 6,455 species that gives birth to tadpoles instead of laying spawn. Herpetologist Jim McGuire grabbed a frog and discovered that it was a female with a dozen newborn tadpoles with her.

CLOSE SHAVE

Years of neglect had left Matt, an abandoned Persian cat, with a thick, tangled coat, so veterinarians in London, England, shaved it all off and placed the fur (with a set of cartoon eyes) next to him as he awoke on the operating table.

There was enough fur to fill two carrier bags and Matt was given a specially knitted jumper to wear until his own fur began to grow back.

Matt the cat

Matt's fur!

WASP INVASION

A swarm of 5,000 wasps built its nest on a bed in the spare room of a house in Hampshire, England, after the window had been left open. The nest measured 3 ft (0.9 m) wide and more than 1 ft (0.3 m) deep, and when finally discovered, the wasps had started chewing through the pillows and into the mattress.

LETHAL WEAPON The 2-in-long (5-cm) Asian Giant Hornet is such a ferocious predator that it will chase humans for up to 650 ft (200 m) at speeds of 25 mph (40 km/h) to leave bullet-sized sting holes in the skin. A plague of giant hornets stung 1,600 victims in China in the fall of 2013, killing at least 40 people. The sting is so potent that just a few giant hornets can wipe out a 30,000-strong honeybee colony in a couple of hours.

BUG'S LIFE Yuan Meixia of Fujian, China, keeps 100,000 cockroaches in her home. She breeds them, feeds them daily with fruit or sugary treats and keeps them warm in winter with a gas stove. Every two months, when they are ready to harvest, she drowns them, dries them in the sun and sells them to pharmaceutical companies who pay $130 per kilo for the bugs to use in medicines.

→ A PIGLET OWNED BY MR. TANG IN SICHUAN PROVINCE, CHINA, WAS BORN IN AUGUST 2014 WITH TWO EXTRA NONFUNCTIONING LEGS AND FOUR EXTRA TROTTERS. THE SEVEN OTHER PIGLETS IN THE LITTER WERE COMPLETELY NORMAL.

KOALA PASSENGER A koala bear tenaciously clung to a car grille for 55 mi (88 km) after being hit by the vehicle in Queensland, Australia. The family in the car realized they had acquired an extra passenger when they stopped at a service station—and, astonishingly, the four-year-old marsupial's only injury was a torn nail.

IT'S A GEEP! A baby animal named Butterfly, born at a petting zoo in Scottsdale, Arizona, in 2014, was half goat, half sheep—a geep. Butterfly's mother was a sheep, but the father was a pygmy goat, with the result that the newborn had a goat's head and the woolly body of a lamb.

SNAKE ISLAND Ilha de Queimada Grande, known as "Snake Island," located 20 mi (32 km) off the coast of Brazil, is home to thousands of highly venomous Golden Lancehead Vipers—as many as five per square yard—that are so dangerous that people are forbidden to land there. It is the only place in the world that is home to the deadly viper, whose potent venom can not only kill people but also melt human flesh.

FROG GRAB Roman Livane's pet frog Croak had to make a trip to the veterinarian after swallowing an engagement ring. Livane's girlfriend Kristina was playing with the ring at their home in Yekaterinburg, Russia, when the frog suddenly grabbed it and ate it. As the ring was too big to pass, vets used a special hook to pull it out of Croak's stomach.

HONEY THIEF When raiding hives for honey, the Death's-head Hawkmoth of Europe disguises itself by chemically mimicking the scent of bees. This calms the bees and allows the moth to enter the hive and steal honey without being stung.

Five-legged Cow

A five-legged cow, whose extra limb was attached to its neck, toured India for over eight months visiting six states and 15 major cities with its owner Laxman Bhosale of Solapur, Maharashtra. Hundreds of people turned out to see the cow wherever it stopped, and many believed that touching the extra limb would bring them good luck.

TWISTED FEET Kinkajous or "honey bears"—small, fruit-eating mammals that live in the rain forests of Central and South America—can twist their hind feet backward to climb trees. By rotating their feet, they can also run backward as fast as they can run forward, giving them a better chance of escaping predators such as jaguars and ocelots.

FLESH EATER The screwworm fly of South America breeds by laying flesh-eating maggot larvae in the open wounds, ears and eyes of mammals—including humans.

BIG EYES Each eye of the tarsier—a shy, nocturnal animal from Southeast Asia—is bigger than its brain. Its eyes are so large that they are unable to move in their sockets, but it has a flexible neck that allows it to swivel its head 180 degrees to look for predators.

SALIVA PRODUCE Dairy cows produce at least 26 gal (98 l) of saliva every day to help them chew their rough food.

MONSTER EARTHWORM

American naturalist Stephen Hopkins found this gigantic earthworm—5 ft (1.5 m) long and with a girth the size of a man's forearm—half-hidden under a rotten log in the foothills of the Sumaco Volcano in Ecuador.

HORSE WHISPERER

Self-taught Argentine horse trainer Martin Tatta persuades his five-year-old mare Primavera to roll on her back and allow him to sit on her stomach—just by tenderly talking to her, stroking her and making eye contact. The "Horse Whisperer," as he is known, forms a unique bond with his animals. In only a year he can tame unbroken horses and encourage them to join him in a series of acrobatic poses to the amazement of the thousands of tourists who come to witness his skills.

HEROIC PARROT When Rachel Mancino was attacked in a park in North London, England, she was saved by Wunsy, her African gray parrot who squawked and flapped her wings so loudly that the assailant fled. Wunsy always sits on Rachel's shoulder for their daily walk.

FOOD RUN Lilica, a stray dog in San Carlos, Brazil, makes a round-trip journey of 8 mi (13 km) every night to fetch food for the animals that live with her in a junkyard—another dog, a cat, a few chickens and a mule. Braving rush-hour traffic, she walks all the way to the home of a friendly woman who puts scraps out for her and then brings the food back to the yard where she shares it with her animal friends.

SLOW DEATH *Lingchi*—or slow slicing—was a form of execution in Imperial China, until it was banned in 1905. The condemned would have pieces slowly cut from their arms, legs and chest with a knife, until their limbs had been amputated. Then, finally, they would be decapitated or stabbed in the heart.

Floral Disguise

Native to the rain forests of Southeast Asia, the orchid mantis is the only living creature that poses as an exotic flower to lure its prey. With legs that closely resemble flower petals, it mimics orchids in both shape and color and its subterfuge is so convincing that it is even more attractive to flies and other small insects than the real blooms. The mantis can also change its color from pink to brown over a few days, depending on the prevailing humidity and light.

PIGEON TOWED Instead of flying from his nest in New York City to nearby New Jersey, Tony the pigeon preferred to take the ferry. Every morning for more than three years, the bird joined commuters on the 9 a.m. boat and rode back and forth for about two hours, briefly disembarking at each stop to search for crumbs before hopping back on board.

VOLCANIC NEST The endangered maleo bird, which lives on the Indonesian island of Sulawesi, uses the heat from volcanoes to help hatch its eggs. The adult does not sit on the eggs, but buries them in the soil or sand near volcanoes and relies on the heat from geothermal activity for incubation. When the chicks hatch they claw their way up to the surface and are immediately able to fly.

PEE TALK Crawfish communicate with each other by shooting streams of urine out of pores on the sides of their heads. Clusters of fan-like appendages direct the spout straight into the face of the other crawfish during a fight or during courtship. The urine contains hormone derivatives that give clues to the sprayer's current level of fitness and indicate whether or not that particular crawfish would make a fearsome adversary or a healthy mate.

ONE-EYED CHAMPION In 2014, Adventure de Kannan became the first one-eyed horse to win the Hickstead Derby, the most prestigious prize available in British showjumping and where horses are required to jump fences that are more than 5 ft (1.5 m) high and 6 ft 6 in (2 m) wide. The 14-year-old horse had his right eye removed the previous year following an infection.

PRIZED PLUMAGE The ancient Aztecs and Mayans valued the feathers of the colorful quetzal bird more than gold. The birds were considered sacred in both cultures, and the penalty for killing one was death.

TOXIC FLESH African spur-winged geese become so toxic after feeding on blister beetles that if a human were to consume the feasted bird's flesh, the result would be certain death.

STORY TIME While rescue animals at the Battersea Dogs and Cats Home in London, U.K., were waiting for new homes, a group of schoolchildren cheered them up by reading them stories. The staff at the rescue home say that the rhythmic sound of reading can help calm stressed animals.

TREE DISGUISE The nocturnal common potoo bird of South and Central America pretends to be a tree branch during the day. Perfectly camouflaged, it likes to sit completely still on a broken stump for its daytime rest. To prevent its bright yellow eyes alerting potential predators, it has thin notches in its eyelids that allow it to see even when its eyes are apparently closed.

LETHAL WEAPONS The great horned owl of North and South America has such powerful talons that it can kill and carry prey more than three times its own body weight—including cats and dogs.

CANINE JOCKEY Horse trainer Steve Jefferys has an unusual assistant at his equestrian center in Melbourne, Australia—his collie dog Hekan (short for "He can do anything.") The dog holds the horses as they are being saddled, takes them for walks on a leash, and, most incredible of all, even sits on their backs and rides them.

COMMUNAL NESTS

Huge haystack-like structures built on telephone poles in Southern Africa's Kalahari Desert are the nests of sociable weaver birds and each can accommodate as many as 400 birds at a time, including several different species!

Lovebirds, finches and pygmy falcons all nest alongside the weavers in up to 100 individual chambers. Meanwhile vultures, owls and eagles often roost on the nests' broad roofs. Built of sticks, grass and cotton, such nests can be 20 ft (6 m) high, 13 ft (4 m) wide, 7 ft (2 m) thick and weigh 2,000 lb (900 kg)—heavy enough to cause entire trees to collapse. The nests are so well constructed that some have remained occupied for 100 years.

SAVED BY ELVIS After her snowmobile broke down in the wilderness, 57-year-old Vivian Mayo of Cantwell, Alaska, survived three nights outdoors in winter temperatures as low as –20°F (–29°C) thanks to her small dog Elvis who, by cuddling up to her, helped her to preserve her body heat.

SPERM SAVERS Female guppy fish can become fertilized up to ten months after their male partner has died. Female guppies live eight times longer than males, and as they can store sperm inside their bodies, they are able to save it until the right time for fertilization. Older, larger females can carry the sperm of several dead males.

CHARCOAL CURE The red colobus monkeys of Zanzibar steal man-made charcoal to eat as an anti-toxic medicine to help relieve stomachaches.

SALTY SNEEZE Marine iguanas sneeze more than any other animal—as a way to expel excess salt and stop them becoming dehydrated. As their food is soaked in salt water from the sea, salt builds up in their bloodstream. Most of this salt collects in a special gland above the iguana's eyes, from which the animal can squeeze it out. The spray often falls back onto the iguana's head, where it quickly evaporates–leaving a crust that looks like a white wig.

BRAIN FOOD A giant squid's food passes through its brain before it reaches its stomach. As a result, it has to eat small morsels because anything too large might get caught in the brain and cause brain damage.

PAIN RELIEF Bino, an albino alligator at the Sao Paulo Aquarium, Brazil, had weekly 30-minute acupuncture sessions after he had lived for eight years with scoliosis, a condition that gave him a hunched back and left him unable to move two of his legs or to swish his tail. Before inserting up to a dozen needles into his back, veterinarian Daniela Cervaletti always made sure that Bino's jaws were taped shut.

→ **BIKANER, INDIA, STAGES AN ANNUAL CAMEL FESTIVAL, COMPLETE WITH CAMEL RACES, CAMEL DANCING AND A CONTEST FOR BEST CAMEL HAIRCUT.**

BIRTHDAY GUEST A 180-lb (82-kg) black bear crashed through the skylight of Alicia Bishop and Glenn Merrill's home in Juneau, Alaska, while they were preparing to celebrate their son Jackson's first birthday, and when the couple fled, the bear ate the party cupcakes!

GLADIATOR CAT For *Game of Thrones* fans, online shop Schnabuble sells cat battle armor that will give mice nightmares for years to come. The flexible scaled armor suit, which fits over the body of most adult cats and costs $500, is handmade from leather, has a terrifying line of dorsal spines and is adorned with nickel silver dome rivets.

SWINGING ASSASSIN The white-handed gibbon of southern Asia is so agile it sometimes plucks birds from the air to eat as it swings from tree to tree.

GRIZZLY SAMARITAN Vali, a grizzly bear at Budapest Zoo, Hungary, came to the rescue when it saw a crow drowning in the enclosure. The bear reached into the water, gently pulled out the bird with its mouth and left it poolside to recover.

RAT COPTER

Ripley's **REVISITED**

After reading in *Ripley's Dare To Look!* how Dutch artist Bart Jansen turned his cat into a radio-controlled model helicopter, 13-year-old Arnhem schoolboy Pepeijn Bruins asked Jansen and his inventor partner Arjen Beltman if they could do the same for his deceased pet rat, Ratjetoe. They stuffed the animal, attached three radio-controlled propellers and a computer to its body and gave it a new lease of life as a "rat copter"—the world's first flying rat.

INSIDE OUT

To illustrate the inner workings of animals, the Natural History Museum in London, England, staged an exhibition of almost 100 creatures inside out, including this dramatic shark showing the capillary blood vessel structures under its skin.

The exhibits were created by an anatomical process called plastination where resins preserve the organs and blood capillaries, and the surrounding tissue is dissolved with acid.

HAIR FLOSS Macaque monkeys living near a Buddhist temple in Lopburi, Thailand, pull out hair from the heads of human visitors and use it between their teeth as dental floss.

HEAVY HEART A blue whale's tongue can weigh as much as an adult elephant, while its heart can become as large as an automobile.

MAN BITES Fearing that it was about to attack him, Rai Singh, of Chhattisgarh, India, bit and killed a deadly blue krait snake as it slithered toward him in bed. Blue kraits are highly venomous and up to 80 percent of their victims die after suffering from progressive paralysis.

DENTURE SNATCH
A seagull swooped down and snatched 92-year-old Renee A'Bear's dentures after she had removed them to eat a biscuit outside a retirement home in East Sussex, England. Apparently unhappy with its loot, the seagull spat the false teeth out on the roof of a nearby building.

The Whole Hog

Fed on a regular diet of mealworms, a hedgehog at a rescue center in Fife, Scotland, saw her weight multiply six-fold in just seven months until she weighed more than double the average adult hedgehog and was so fat she was no longer able to curl up in a proper ball to protect herself. Named Edinburgh after the place where she was found, the hedgehog weighed 13 oz (370 g) when she arrived at the center, but rapidly ballooned to weigh a mighty 4 lb 13 oz (2.2 kg).

Lazy Frog

You've heard of Crazy Frog, well meet Lazy Frog! This frog could not be bothered to swim across a garden pond in Dorset, England, so it hitched a ride on a goldfish, clinging on with its webbed feet to make sure that it did not fall off. The goldfish repeatedly wriggled from side to side in an attempt to dislodge its amphibian jockey, but the frog refused to loosen its grip until it had reached its destination.

PATIENT OCTOPUS A female deep-sea octopus living off the coast of California was observed guarding her eggs for 53 months—nearly four-and-a-half years—until they hatched. During that time she was never seen to eat. Her vigilance marked the longest period of egg brooding ever recorded in the animal kingdom—most other octopuses take only a few months.

BIRDS BEWARE Crocodiles and alligators use sticks as lures to hunt birds. They gather sticks on their snouts and lie motionless in the water, and when a bird seeks a perch or tries to grab one of the sticks to make a nest, the reptile pounces.

WALKING FISH Scientists at McGill University in Canada discovered that some species of fish that are capable of walking can change their anatomy and learn to walk more efficiently if left out of water for long periods. After being kept permanently on land for less than a year, polypterus, an African fish with air-breathing lungs that allow it to walk on land to reach water, mastered the art of walking with its head up and its fins closer to its body. It also developed stronger and more elongated shoulders to support its body while walking.

NOISY BIRD During courtship the male nightjar, or nighthawk, attracts a mate with a distinctive chirping call that contains 1,900 notes per minute—that's more than 30 notes per second.

TWO TONGUES Bush babies have a second tongue under their main tongue, which they use to clean their teeth. Called a "grooming tongue," it is also used in conjunction with their front teeth to preen their fur.

POND DIP Rosie, a 12-week-old German shepherd puppy, landed in big trouble after driving both her owner and his car into a pond. John Costello of Canton, Massachusetts, had just got into his car and started the engine when Rosie excitedly jumped in, hit the gear shift and fell on top of the gas pedal, sending the car and its passengers careening into a nearby pond for an unscheduled swim.

SPIDER SCARE Consi and Richard Taylor and their two young children had to move out of their home in London, England, and into a hotel for three days after they discovered dozens of deadly baby Brazilian wandering spiders on a bunch of supermarket bananas.

DOLPHIN PLAYTIME Bottlenose dolphins have been known to take rides on the heads of humpback whales—just for fun.

AWESOME AMPHIBIAN

This little glass frog in Costa Rica certainly lives up to its name, and is using its transparent body to camouflage itself against a leaf to protect its precious eggs. Glass frogs lay their eggs out of water in order to steer clear of lurking predators and often choose leaves overhanging a stream so that when the tadpoles hatch, they drop directly into the water.

KILLER MANTIS

UNIQUE FISH While fishing off the coast of Costa Rica on March 11, 2014, New Yorker Karen Weaver reeled in the first-ever recorded case of an albino blue marlin. It took her 2 hours 45 minutes to land the 300-lb (136-kg) fish, which was later released back into the ocean.

WRESTLED GATOR Nine-year-old James Barney Jr. fought off an attack by a 9-ft-long (2.7-m), 400-lb (182-kg) alligator in Lake Tohopekaliga, Florida, with his bare hands. The alligator bit him three times on the backside and also left 30 tooth and claw marks on his back, stomach and legs, but he managed to pry its jaws open and force it to let go. Doctors found a tooth in one of the wounds and James now wears it as a necklace to remind him of his bravery.

HUMAN SHIELDS When under close observation by scientists, South African samango monkeys use the scientists as "human shields" to guard against predators such as leopards. Tests showed that the monkeys feel much safer eating on the ground if people are present.

SEX FACTOR The sex of the painted turtle, native to North America, is determined not by its genes, but by the weather outside when it is an embryo. Cold temperatures produce male painted turtles and hot temperatures produce females.

DOG POOL The Spanish town of La Roca del Valles has a special swimming pool just for dogs. The Resort Canino Can Jane is designed to be the right depth for all shapes and sizes of dogs and includes a doggie slide as well as extra tough inflatables for the dogs to play on.

FREE RIDE Randy, a seven-year-old African Gray parrot, escaped from owner Jean Hall's home in Cambridgeshire, England, and was found eight days later, 8 mi (12.87 km) away... perched on the back of a pony!

TORNADO TERROR Dexter, a six-month-old pit bull terrier, was rescued from beneath the rubble of an apartment in Washington, Illinois, nine days after it had been wrecked by a tornado. The building's roof and walls had been blown away, but, to the relief of his owner Jacob Montgomery, Dexter was found by a neighbor, who spotted the puppy's ears sticking up from beneath the debris. All the dog had had to eat and drink during his ordeal was snow—so, the neighbor lured him to safety with hot dogs.

This amazing photograph captures the moment that a praying mantis killed and ate a hummingbird!

Although it was not much bigger than its prey, the deadly insect—a master of camouflage—used its spiny left foreleg to impale the unsuspecting bird through the chest. After feasting on the bird, the mantis released its lifeless body. The whole scene was captured on camera in the yard of Richard L. Walkup in West Chester, Pennsylvania.

TIGHTROPE TERRIER

Melissa Millett from London, Ontario, Canada, sent Ripley's this picture of her five-year-old Boston terrier, Bella, who can walk 6 ft (1.8 m) along a narrow tightrope. She is so adept at tightrope walking that the family plans to construct a 30-ft-long (9-m) tightrope for her. Bella can also scooter and skateboard down ramps, ride a rocking horse, skip, and play basketball and the piano!

OSTRICH CHAOS An escaped ostrich caused rush-hour traffic chaos on roads in Kent, England, in January 2014 as it ran along a busy highway at speeds of 40 mph (64 km/h), running past at least 20 cars.

FREE CAT Russian bank Sherbank offers a free cat with every mortgage. Customers choose from one of ten breeds, but are not allowed to keep the animal for more than two hours—long enough for the cat to enter the property ahead of the owner, a good-luck tradition in Russia.

LIZARD CPR Sherrie Dolezal of Salem, Oregon, saved her pet bearded dragon Del Sol by giving him chest compressions and the kiss of life. Finding the three-year-old lizard floating face up and unconscious in his pool, she rubbed his belly, hung him upside down to clear water from his mouth and then breathed air past his teeth. Eventually, he opened his eyes and started to move.

CHIMP WEAPONS Chimpanzees in Senegal make sharpened spears with which to hunt bush babies. The chimp snaps off a thin branch, strips it of leaves and sharpens the tip with its teeth before stabbing it forcefully into the bush baby's hiding place. It then drags out the wounded animal and eats it.

DRUNK DOG Veterinarians in Melbourne, Australia, saved Charlie the Maltese terrier from certain death by getting him drunk in a 48-hour vodka binge. The dog was suffering from a serious case of ethylene glycol poisoning—a chemical commonly found in brake fluids—the only known antidote for which is alcohol. Via a tube placed through his nose to his stomach, Charlie was given successive doses of vodka over a two-day period. As he began to recover, his owner, Jacinta Rosewarne, reported that he was stumbling around like a drunk.

CAT ISLAND Tonawanda Island, a small 85-acre (35-ha) patch of land in the middle of the Niagara River in New York, has been overrun by hundreds of feral cats. The feline population boom has been caused by people dumping their unwanted cats and kittens on the island.

HYENA GUARD Having lost several animals to hyena attacks, Seyyid Abdishakur trained a wild male hyena to guard his farm in Ethiopia. The farmer took care never to slaughter a goat near the hyena for fear that it would see his livestock as a source of food and only ever gave it meat from a butcher. He fed it herbs to reduce its sex drive to prevent it looking for a mate.

Balancing Bunnies

In November 1946, *LIFE* magazine reported on these two acrobatic rabbits that walked on only their front paws. Mr. Walker and Junior were kept as pets by Reginald Freeman, a butcher from London, England. After Mr. Walker, the older rabbit, started getting around on just his front feet, Junior, who had been walking conventionally on all fours, copied him. The rabbits' spinal muscles were underdeveloped and so they found it easier to walk on two legs.

DEAD PETS

To help owners overcome the loss of their pets, photographer Emir Özşahin from Istanbul, Turkey, poses dead animals to make them look as if they are just sleeping peacefully.

He placed a cat corpse as if it were happily sunbathing in a chair with its paws up, and a dead dog so that it appeared to have gently fallen asleep while reading a book in the garden. He even uses specially made miniature clothes and pieces of furniture for his pictures, including a sweater for a guinea pig and a bed for a sparrow.

FIVE LEGS

Monica Beckner from Saint Joseph, Missouri, sent Ripley's this picture of her two-month-old pet rat Timmy, who was born with five legs. Monica reports that Timmy has no issues with his extra leg and walks around and plays with his brothers and sisters just like a regular rat.

SHARK TRANCE Divers Cameron Nimmo and Mickey Smith remove fish hooks from the jaws of 10-ft-long (3-m) silky sharks off the coast of Jupiter, Florida, by hypnotizing them. The pair can put the sharks into a trance for up to 15 minutes by holding them by the tail and twisting them upside down, paralyzing them in a state called tonic immobility.

SPACE PETS In a unique memorial, Celestis Inc., a company based in Houston, Texas, allows owners to launch their dead pets into space and even "set paw" on the moon. A rocket can carry part of the pet's cremated remains into space and back to Earth (cost $995); or the ashes can orbit Earth before re-entering the atmosphere and vaporizing like a shooting star ($4,995); or they can be taken all the way to the moon ($12,500).

WEDDING RING Five years after losing her diamond wedding ring, Lois Matykowski of Stevens Point, Wisconsin, was amazed to see her dog Tucker cough it up. The dog had just thrown up after swallowing a popsicle whole, and that probably dislodged the ring that had been inside his belly, perhaps for all that time.

SHELL SHOCK A tortoise that vanished for ten months was found alive after being dug up by a mechanical digger laying foundations for an extension to his owners' house in Cambridgeshire, England. Paul and Yvette White think Sydney burrowed down into their garden to hibernate in June 2012 after mistaking the unusually cool summer for winter.

TROPHY COLLECTION Waffle, a five-year-old Lakeland terrier, has sniffed out and collected almost 1,000 balls of all sizes from country walks near her home in Devon, England. She once brought home eight balls from a single walk and howls if her owner, Sarah Bennett, tries to throw any of them away.

CALMING CAT Milly Moo the family cat walks three-year-old William Dutton to and from nursery school every day to help him overcome his anxiety. She always joins William and his mother Victoria on the 13-minute walk to his school in Bedfordshire, England, and even knows when it is time to go and collect him.

FLYING COMPANION When American rock climber and BASE jumper Dean Potter decided to leap from the side of the 13,020-ft-high (3,969-m) Eiger mountain in Switzerland, his four-year-old Australian cattle dog Whisper joined him, strapped into a wingsuit bag, complete with dog goggles. With his pet bound to his back, the New Hampshire-raised adventurer hurtled toward the ground before safely deploying a parachute. Dean says that although Whisper has absolutely no fear of heights, she is terrified of vacuum cleaners.

GOLDFISH OP

George, a ten-year-old goldfish owned by Pip Joyce from Melbourne, Australia, underwent emergency surgery to remove a tumor from his head—and is now expected to live for another 20 years.

Veterinarian Tristan Rich sedated George in a bucket of water with anesthetic, performed a 45-minute operation, and then gave him injections of antibiotics and painkillers.

Ripley's Believe It or Not!®
www.ripleys.com/books
ANIMALS

BURPING MONKEYS To get rid of the excess methane and carbon dioxide that is a byproduct of digestion, leaf-eating African colobus monkeys often burp in each other's faces. The animals interpret the gesture as a sign of friendship.

PORCUPINE WHEELCHAIR A paraplegic porcupine at Brazil's Piracicaba Municipal Zoo has been given a new lease on life after a veterinarian fitted her with a $5 wheelchair made from plastic plumbing pipes. The miniature buggy has a sling to take the weight off the animal's lower body and wheels in place of its hind legs.

HEDGEHOG HUNTERS In Tudor England, people were encouraged to kill hedgehogs because it was believed that they suckled milk from cows at night.

JUMPING RAT The giant legs of the kangaroo rat of North America help it to leap ten times its own height and 30 times its own body length.

POTTY PET Luke Evans from Solihull, England, became so fed up with his nine-month-old cat Salem using a smelly litter tray that he trained the pet to use a human toilet instead. By offering cheese-flavored treats as a reward, it took Luke just a couple of months to train Salem to jump up on the toilet seat. "He can't use the flush yet," said Luke. "He needs more training for that!"

SEIZURE ALERT To warn of any impending seizure, epileptic Daniel Greene from Shelton, Washington, rides around town with his 5-ft-long (1.5-m) boa constrictor, Redrock, wrapped around his neck. When the snake senses that Daniel is about to have a seizure, it squeezes him more tightly, giving him a warning that allows him time to take his medication.

LOST EARS Luna, a white stray cat, had her ear tips cut off to prevent her getting cancer after she got sunburned on the streets of Kilmarnock, Scotland. Despite losing the blistered ears, her hearing is fine. White or pale cats are most vulnerable to sunlight because they have little pigment to protect them from harmful UVB waves.

GOLDEN BEETLE

The golden tortoise beetle (*Charidotella sexpunctata*), which is native to the Americas, can quickly change color from metallic gold to a ladybug-like orange with black spots, and back again. The color switch, which occurs during mating or when the beetle is disturbed, is an optical illusion. Tiny valves that control the moisture levels under the beetle's transparent shell cause a change in reflectivity to make the creature appear a different shade.

WEE WRIGGLER Mount Everest is home to a tiny black jumping spider that lives as high as 22,000 ft (6,700 m) above sea level—making it a candidate for the highest known permanent resident on Earth. *Euophrys omnisuperstes*, which means "standing above everything," is also known as the Himalayan jumping spider. The spider hides in crevices and feeds on frozen insects. Its food depends largely upon what is blown by the wind into the specific area.

Catch Snatch →

This cheeky whale shark was spotted off the coast of Indonesia taking a bite out of a fisherman's net that was bulging with a fresh catch of fish. Whale sharks in the area regularly follow fishing boats as they work, tearing through nets and swallowing vast quantities of fish in their gaping mouths, which can open up to 5 ft (1.5 m) wide.

Tall Cow

Blosom, a 13-year-old Holstein Friesian cow living on a farm in Orangeville, Illinois, stands an incredible 6 ft 4 in (1.93 m) tall, making her taller than Chicago Bulls basketball star Derrick Rose! Owned by Patty Hanson, Blosom weighs 2,000 lb (908 kg) and has her own Facebook page.

BLOOD SUCKER Before laying eggs, a female tick, in one feed, will drink up to 600 times her own bodyweight in blood.

HIDING PLACE Oliver, a cat owned by the Waterfield family from Devon, England, hid undetected in the engine of the family's camper van for four days while the vehicle was at a garage for maintenance. The mechanics had thoroughly examined the engine and changed the oil, but had not seen the cat.

FATAL CATCH A Brazilian angler was fishing off Icapui when he caught a small sole. He then bet his friends that he would be able to hold the slippery fish between his teeth for a minute, but the fish wriggled free, swam down his throat and became lodged in his windpipe, fatally choking him.

LOUD SQUEAKS If the high-pitched echolocation squeaks of the fishing bat were in human hearing range, they would be as loud as gunshots.

MILITARY MONKEYS The Chinese military has trained macaque monkeys to keep its air force safe by stopping birds from nesting near a major air base. As birds pose a hazard to planes, monkeys are taught to remove nests from treetops. They then leave a scent on the branches that discourages the birds from returning.

PIGEON SUSPECT A pigeon was blamed for starting a 2014 fire in an apartment in London, England. Firefighters believe the bird dropped a smoking cigarete butt into its nest in the roof of the apartment, causing a blaze that required the attention of four fire trucks and forced nine residents to flee the building.

MUTANT OCTOPUS After catching a six-legged octopus off the coast of Greece, Labros Hydras cooked it for supper—but later discovered from a biologist that it was only the second hexapus recorded anywhere in the world. The first was discovered in 2008 at an aquarium in Blackpool, U.K.

DOGGIE BOOTS Bluey, an eight-year-old Weimaraner dog, wears a special pair of $80 Canadian-made boots to cope with his grass allergy. Before he got his boots, the dog's paws used to become red and inflamed after just a few minutes playing outside his home in Pembrokeshire, Wales. He would lick and bite them for hours and his owner, Julie Farr, even tried tying plastic bags around his feet to ease the problem.

TWO-HEADED DOLPHIN The corpse of a two-headed dolphin was washed up on a beach in Izmir, Turkey, in August 2014. The conjoined dolphin, which had a single tail, was about one year old, 3 ft 3 in (1 m) long, and one pair of its eyes was not fully formed.

CHIMP CHEF Kanzi, a 34-year-old male bonobo chimpanzee who lives at the Great Ape Trust in Des Moines, Iowa, can break twigs to build a fire, light them with matches and then toast marshmallows over the fire on a stick.

GOOSE IMPACT Shannon Jergenson escaped serious injury when a goose smashed through her car windshield and wrapped itself around the steering wheel while she was driving at 50 mph (80 km/h) along Highway 76 near Denver, Colorado. Although Shannon later discovered her hair was full of shattered glass, she suffered only a small scratch on her face.

FARM DOG

Lemon, a Giant Schnauzer, stands on his hind legs to plow potato fields on the farm of his owner, Aleksandr Matytsin, in Omsk, Russia. As well as learning how to push the plow, Lemon has been trained to plant potatoes, collect the harvested crops, carry buckets of water and pump water from a tap.

PURR-FECT PAIR

Abdullah Sholeh's friendship with this 10-ft (3 m) long Bengal tiger is truly an astonishing demonstration of love and trust.

Abdullah, 33, grew close to Mulan Jamilah—a full-grown, six-year-old female tiger—when he became her full-time caregiver at an Islamic school in Malang, Indonesia. He has cared for the 382-lb (149-kg) tiger since she was a three month old cub, and even sleeps beside her with only metal bars separating them. Unafraid to show his love, Abdullah is often seen taking her in his arms, and even allows Mulan to "kiss" him!

FALLEN HERO Just after winning a prize for obedience at Crufts Dog Show in Birmingham, England, Eddie, a five-year-old Akita, sank his teeth into a dog trainer's knee and hand. Eddie was posing for a celebratory photograph when he took a dislike to another nearby Akita and lunged forward twice, clamping his jaws into the flesh of Louise Nelson as he did so.

WARM WELCOME When threatened, the turkey vulture vomits the foul-smelling, semi-digested contents of its stomach at predators. The high level of acid in the vulture's stomach, which allows it to eat rotten meat safely, means that the vomit will burn any enemy that gets too close.

SWALLOWED BALL Trixie, a border terrier owned by Melanie Pounder of Sunderland, England, lived for two years with a ball in her stomach. She was playing in the garden in 2012 when the ball slipped down her throat, but seeing as veterinarians could find no trace of it, they assumed it had passed through her system. It was only when the ten-year-old dog began getting sick two years later that she went for an X-ray. The image of her insides showed the ball, which was then removed.

TRUNK CALLS Elephants use over 70 kinds of vocal sounds and can identify more than 100 other elephants from their calls at a distance of several miles.

PUBLIC TOILET The Spanish town of El Vendrell has installed a public toilet for dogs. Designed by dog-lover Enric Girona, the roadside stainless-steel contraption consists of a canine potty and urinal that a dog's owner can flush when the dog has finished doing its business. It also features a water fountain to ensure the town's canines never go thirsty.

COVER BLOWN

Less than 0.39 in (10 mm) long, this tiny, pink pygmy seahorse (*Hippocampus bargibanti*) looks startled to have been spotted by British wildlife photographer Alex Mustard while it thought it was camouflaged against its coral home off the coast of Indonesia.

ROOF RIDE A cat was unhurt despite traveling for 22 mi (35 km) clinging on to the roof rack of a van that hit speeds of 70 mph (112 km/h) through Leicestershire, England. It is thought the cat climbed aboard when the van stopped at a gas station and then had to hang on for dear life once the van drove away. The cat, owned by five-year-old Connor Russell of Melton Mowbray, is appropriately named after Kick Buttowski, the daredevil U.S. cartoon character.

MIGHTY MITE The tiny moss mite *Archegozetes longisetosus* can resist 1,180 times its own weight—that's like a human holding back an airliner.

LONG MEMORIES Bottlenose dolphins can remember their former friends by their unique whistles even after being separated for as long as 20 years.

SAFETY DEVICE Sawfish give birth to live babies that have sheaths on their saws to protect their mother. Shortly after birth, the fibrous sheath wears away.

ELEPHANT DUET British musician Paul Barton plays the piano to entertain elephants at Elephantstay, a sanctuary in Ayutthaya, Thailand. For three years he played solo until one elephant, Peter, suddenly decided to join him in a duet, rhythmically bopping his head up and down as he hit the keys with his trunk.

DEADLY DIET Every day the desert woodrat, native to the Mojave Desert, eats enough poison to kill a mouse. The woodrat feeds on the creosote bush, a shrub whose leaves are covered in a toxic resin, but microbes in the woodrat's stomach neutralize the poison it consumes.

STRONG SENSE African elephants have 2,000 genes related to smell, the most found in any animal—more than twice that of dogs and five times more than in humans.

Fake Ants

Believe it or not, these are not ants on the wings of this fly, but the fly's own extravagant wing markings. *Goniurellia tridens*, a species of fruit fly found in the Middle East and Asia, bears what looks like an ant image on each wing, complete with six legs, two antennae, a head, thorax and abdomen. It is thought that the insect markings serve to confuse the fly's chief predator, a jumping spider.

DOMESTICATED REPTILE Retired prison officer Chris Weller has spent £23,000 ($35,000) converting his bungalow in Kent, England, to accommodate Caesar, his 6-ft-long (1.8-m) spectacled caiman. Chris moved into the loft to allow Caesar to roam around, but the pair still spend a lot of time together, watching TV or listening to classical music on the radio.

J-LO MITE A team of scientists from the University of Montenegro named a new species of water mite after Jennifer Lopez. After discovering the *Litarachna lopezae* mite on a coral reef off Puerto Rico, Vladimir Pesic and his colleagues decided to name it after J-Lo because they listened to her music while doing their research and also because her parents were born in Puerto Rico.

INFUSION CONFUSION In the late 17th century, some human patients were given transfusions of sheep's blood in an attempt to restore their virility, but most suffered fatal allergic reactions.

→ ON APRIL 14, 2012, A MAN IN DES PLAINES, ILLINOIS, DROWNED WHEN A SWAN ATTACKED HIM IN HIS KAYAK AND STOPPED HIM SWIMMING ASHORE.

CROC SHOCK When Kalpesh Patel went to take a shower in the bathroom of his home in Sojitra, India, he found a 5-ft-long (1.5-m) crocodile inside. Mr. Patel fled in shock, slammed the door behind him and told his wife and children not to go near the bathroom until forestry officials had arrived to remove the reptile. He had no idea how the croc got into the house or why it hid in the shower.

DOUBLE PUNISHMENT After having his hand bitten off by a 9-ft-long (2.7-m) alligator, Florida airboat captain Wallace Weatherholt was charged with unlawfully feeding the reptile. His hand was found following the attack, but surgeons were not able to reattach it.

ANIMAL ARTWORKS In February 2012, University College London's Grant Museum of Zoology staged the world's first art exhibition featuring paintings by a range of different animal species. The museum displayed abstract works created by chimpanzees, gorillas, orangutans and elephants.

SWALLOWED RING Rachelle Atkinson of Albuquerque, New Mexico, lost her $4,500 diamond wedding ring and discovered that her Basset hound, named Coraline, had eaten it—the apparently tasty morsel appeared in a veterinarian's X-ray of the dog's stomach. The vet inserted a tube down Coraline's throat and eventually managed to fish out the ring.

SPECIAL TALENT According to Ripley fan Dan Paulun, a rescue dog named Maddie—who is owned by U.S. photographer Theron Humphrey—can keep her balance on top almost anything, from a horse to a tree branch. The amazing canine talent has earned Maddie more than 782,000 followers on the social media site Instagram.

SALAD CORPSE After taking three mouthfuls of a "washed and ready to eat" supermarket baby leaf and rocket salad, James and Jasmine Watson from Gloucestershire, England, found what looked like a soggy fishcake—only to discover that it had a beak and was actually the corpse of a small bird.

EGG-STRAORDINARY

This is not a trick photo—this jellyfish really does look like a fried egg.

Cotylorhiza tuberculata (or the Fried Egg Jellyfish) lives in the Mediterranean Sea and gets its common name from its smooth, raised dome surrounded by a gutter-like ring. It can reach 14 in (35 cm) in diameter, but despite this large size its sting is harmless to humans.

04

TATTOO REDO

Tattoo fan *Keith Gordon from Essex, England, had tattoos on his arms removed so that he could get a white-collar job as an administrator, but he missed them so much that he had them re-inked—along with new tattoos that now cover the rest of his body and his entire head, including his lips, nose, ears and even his eyelids.*

Keith, who has spent more than $25,000 on redoing his body art, described getting his whole head tattooed as "a very extreme, intense experience." He confesses that his family and most of his work colleagues don't approve of his body art, which is at odds with his conservative lifestyle. His wife Lisa admits she would not have married him if he had looked that way when she met him. However, he remains unrepentant, saying: "I love the attention. I love being different and I love showing people that it is okay to be different."

Keith and Lisa Gordon on their wedding day in 2001.

Keith has reinvented himself as "the coolest looking guy in Essex," but his family isn't as sure. Son Ricky thinks his dad looks "kind of evil."

Keith with his wife and two of his four children before he had tattoos inked from top to toe, all over his body.

GIRL LIVES WITH LEECH IN NOSE

A 3-in-long (7.5-cm), blood-sucking leech lived in the nose of 24-year-old Daniela Liverani, from Edinburgh, Scotland, for more than a month. She had started suffering frequent nosebleeds while traveling around southeast Asia, so when she got home and saw something dark poking out of her nose she dismissed it as congealed blood. However, when she realized it was alive—sometimes protruding as far as her bottom lip—she rushed to the doctor who removed the leech with tweezers. The leech had been nesting in her nostril, feeding on her blood, and if it had not been removed it would probably have worked its way into her brain.

Yuck! 3-in (7.5-cm) leech

CHUTE FALL An eight-year-old boy survived a six-story fall down a trash chute in Honolulu, Hawaii. The boy had been taking out the trash when he slipped and plunged 60 ft (18 m) down the chute. He was rescued by a neighbor who lowered him a fire hose.

FAT REMEDY European executioners in the Middle Ages sold human fat from the corpses of those they had just killed as a health remedy for many ailments from toothaches to arthritis, and was available at pharmacies as late as the 17th century.

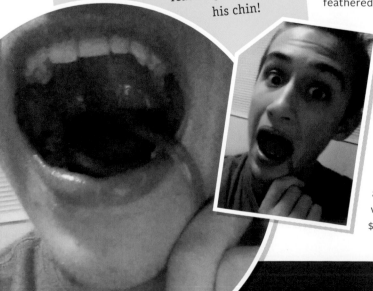

HUGE HAIRBALL Ayperi Alekseeva, an 18-year-old girl from Kyrgyzstan, had a huge 9-lb (4-kg) hairball removed from her stomach. She had been eating her own hair for years—a disorder known as trichophagia—but had come close to death because she had been unable to eat or drink.

DREAM WALK Four-year-old Thea Leinan Robertsen went sleepwalking for 3 mi (4.8 km) from her aunt's house to the town of Honningsvag, Norway, wearing just her underwear and a pair of old boots. Thea, who was out for several hours in the middle of the night, remembered dreaming that the house was on fire before putting on her boots and unlocking the front door.

SAMURAI BARBER Nguyen Hoang Hung, a barber in Da Nang City, Vietnam, cuts customers' hair with a razor-sharp Samurai sword traditionally used by Japanese warriors to behead an enemy. After practicing with the sword on wigs for four years, he can now cut beautiful hairstyles in minutes. He says the sword is especially good for creating a light, feathered look.

PERSONALITY CHANGE After suffering a stroke in 1989, chiropractor Jon Sarkin of Gloucester, Massachusetts, woke up to find that he had suddenly acquired a talent for painting. He previously had no flair for art at all but has gone on to become a prolific painter whose works sell for more than $10,000 each.

NO BLOOD Maisy Vignes from County Waterford, Ireland, miraculously made a full recovery despite being born without any blood. When she was born six weeks premature in 2009, instead of blood she had just a thin, plasma substance in her veins because her mother Emma had absorbed all the blood during pregnancy. Maisy was not expected to survive but, against all the odds, four years later she was able to start school.

MILITARY MUSTACHES Mustaches were compulsory for British Army soldiers until 1916—and shaving the upper lip could result in a court martial.

EYEBALL LICKER Hava Cebic, a 77-year-old grandmother from Crnjevo, Bosnia, claims to be able to cure people's eye ailments by licking their eyeballs. She says her tongue has healing properties and can cure allergies, dry and tired eyes, conjunctivitis and ocular hypertension. She always douses her tongue in alcohol before a lick in order to prevent infection.

HELPING HAND Sixteen-year-old Mason Wilde of Louisburg, Kansas, used a public library's 3-D printer to craft a prosthetic hand for a family friend, nine-year-old Matthew Shields, who was born without fingers on his right hand. Mason spent eight hours printing 20 pieces on the printer, putting them together using screws, nylon string, a drill and pliers. Matthew's new mechanical hand opens and closes, enabling him to pick up a pen and play catch, and to high-five his brothers.

EAR, EAR! Kala Kaiwi, a tattoo artist from Hilo, Hawaii, has stretched his ear lobes so much that he can fit his fist through them. He has created 4.3-in-wide (10.9-cm) flesh tunnels in his ear lobes to match the smaller ones in his nostrils and lower lip. The extreme body-modification enthusiast also has silicon horns implanted in his head, bolt holes inserted into his forehead with metal spikes screwed in, tattooed eyebrows, a tattooed eyeball and a split snake-like tongue, which he created himself using dental floss. Many of his body tattoos were achieved by scarification, where the designs are cut into the skin with a scalpel.

MELODIC MANIA Suffering from the medical condition tinnitus, Susan Root of Essex, England, endured an earworm of Patti Page's rendition of the song "How Much Is That Doggie In the Window?" non-stop for four years—when, just as mysteriously, she switched to hearing Judy Garland's "Somewhere Over the Rainbow."

BRAIN WAVES Aiste Noreikaite, a Lithuanian artist now based in London, England, has invented a hi-tech helmet that allows the wearer to hear his or her own thoughts. The Experience Helmet uses electroencephalography (EEG) technology to translate brain activity into electronic sound signals and play them back. The sounds are higher when wearers have clear minds but become faster and more rhythmic when they focus on particular subjects.

POOP REWARD A laboratory in Medford, Massachusetts, offered people $40 a day for their poop! The stools were used for fecal transplants to fight the superbug *C. difficile*, which kills 14,000 Americans every year.

HIDDEN SPIDER Georgian-born singer Katie Melua lived with a small spider inside her ear for a week. She felt a rustling sensation in her ear until a doctor using a micro-vacuum removed the live creepy crawly. She believes the spider had been living in a pair of earbud headphones that she had worn on a flight.

SEVERED SALE After Leo Bonten of the Netherlands lost his leg in an accident he had the amputated limb turned into a lamp. When he tried to sell the lamp in 2014 for over 100,000 euros ($131,000), eBay pulled the auction—it has a rule against selling body parts!

EXTRA COLORS Artist Concetta Antico, from San Diego, California, has a condition called tetrachromacy, which enables her to see 100 times more colors than an average person. Most people have three cones that absorb wavelengths of light and transmit them to the brain, but Concetta has four. She can see up to 99 million colors instead of one million.

HAIRY LANDSCAPES

The Egyptian pyramids and Sphinx.

British hair stylist Daniel Johnson cuts images of famous landscapes—including Sydney Harbour, the Egyptian pyramids, the New York City skyline and Stonehenge—into chest hair!

He calls the art form "manscaping" and he achieves it by clipping the men's chest hair to different lengths. Each design takes over 2 ½ hours and requires more than 170 individual cuts.

SPOT THE DIFFERENCE Born just one minute apart, identical twins Anna and Lucy DeCinque from Perth, Western Australia, share everything—a house, a job, a car, a Facebook account and even a boyfriend. Even though they are medically identical, they have spent $200,000 on cosmetic surgery to look even more like each other.

EAR PLANT Doctors in Beijing, China, removed a dandelion that had sprouted inside the ear of a 16-month-old girl. She had been suffering from an ear infection for four months and when she started scratching it regularly, her family took her to hospital where doctors discovered the flower, which had grown to 0.8 in (2 cm) in the humid conditions of the ear canal.

WINKING SPASM Blepharospasm is a rare eye condition that can cause people to wink thousands of times per day—and in extreme cases, sufferers may be unable to prevent their eyes from clamping shut, leaving them temporarily blind.

HEAVY SLEEPER Morag Fisher of Lincolnshire, England, broke eight bones, including her neck, spine, nose and jaw, when she fell down a flight of stairs while sleepwalking—but still did not wake up. She was found fast asleep lying in a pool of blood with life-threatening injuries. She regained consciousness only when paramedics woke her in the ambulance on the way to the hospital.

SELF-SURGERY Attacked by a shark, which clamped its jaws around his leg while he was standing in water fishing near Invercargill, New Zealand, doctor James Grant fought off the fish, sewed up the wounds with a first-aid kit and then went to the pub for a beer.

FROZEN TATTOOS Peter van der Helm has opened a tattoo shop in Amsterdam, the Netherlands, which removes tattoos from the bodies of dead people and freezes them in order to preserve them as works of art.

STONE TEARS When 12-year-old Yemeni girl Saadiya Saleh cries, she sheds tears of stone. In a condition that has baffled doctors, small, hard stones form under her eyelids, get pushed to the front of her eyes, then emerge as tears. In a few hours, she can produce enough stones to fill a small box.

KEN LOOKALIKE Rodrigo Alves, a Brazilian air steward living in the U.K., has spent $150,000 in the past ten years on cosmetic surgery to transform himself into a real-life Ken doll. He has had over 20 procedures, including nose jobs, abdominal and pectoral implants, calf shaping and laser comb hair treatment.

↑
TATTOOED EYEBALLS

Brazilian tattoo artist Rattoo has tattoos all over his face and has even inked his eyeballs blue. Eyeball, or scleral, tattooing can have freaky side effects—another Brazilian man who had his eye inked, Rodrigo Fernando dos Santos, wept black tears for the next two days.

PARASITIC WORM Discovering a parasitic worm crawling around in his face, biologist Jonathan D. Allen from The College of William and Mary in Williamsburg, Virginia, removed it himself by pulling it from his cheek with a pair of tweezers. He first became aware of the 1-in-long (2.5-cm) worm, which is usually found on cattle, during a lecture. However, for the first few months it was inaccessible at the back of his throat and it was not until it moved to his lips and cheek that he was finally able to extract it.

DEADLY BEAUTY Ladies of Renaissance Europe used eye drops made from the juice of the belladonna berry—poisonous deadly nightshade—to make their pupils appear larger and more attractive.

PARASITIC TWIN A two-year-old boy, Xiao Feng of Huaxi, China, "gave birth" to his own parasitic twin brother after he was found to be carrying an undeveloped fetus inside his stomach. The unborn fetus, which Xiao had absorbed in his mother's womb and which took up two-thirds of his stomach, measured 8 in (20 cm) in width and had formed a spine, limbs, fingers and toes. Doctors said the parasitic twin would have killed Xiao if it had been left untreated.

LUCKY ESCAPE While building a deck for his neighbor, Minnesota carpenter Eugene Rakow accidentally shot himself in the heart with a nail gun—and lived to tell the tale. A heart surgeon at Abbott Northwestern Hospital in Minneapolis said that if the nail had penetrated just a fraction further, it would have hit the coronary artery and Eugene would have been killed instantly.

NO FINGERS Even though she was born without any fingers, Annette Gabbedey from Somerset, England, has become an expert goldsmith, creating items of jewelry that sell for $40,000. Making the most of the sensitivity and movement that she retains in her hands, she ties a leather strap around her wrist to hold a file and uses a vice to keep the pieces of gold in place while she works.

SPIDER PHOBIA To overcome his phobia of spiders, Eric Ortiz of Deltona, Florida, had an image of a deadly black widow spider tattooed on his face.

MILEY FAN Carl McCoid, 40, from Bridlington, Yorkshire, England, has more than 20 body tattoos relating to actress and singer Miley Cyrus, including inked portraits as well as lyrics from her songs.

PIP and FLIP
TWINS from YUCATAN

Pip and Flip, real names Elvira and Jenny Lee Snow, were sisters and sideshow performers in the 1920s and 30s.

They suffered from microcephaly, a condition characterized by a small skull, relatively large face, short stature and limited mental capabilities. Sufferers were often referred to as "pinheads" on the sideshow circuit and Elvira and Jenny performed as "twins" Pip and Flip, Pipo and Zipo, or Zippo and Flippo in various circuses. It was often claimed they were found in Mexico's Yucatan peninsula, or were wild children from Australia, making them seem even more exotic. In reality, they were born in Georgia—Elvira in 1900, and Jenny Lee 12 years later. In the 1930s, they became the biggest draw at Sam Wagner's World Circus Sideshow at Coney Island, New York. They were paid $75 a week, three times the average American wage at the time, and returned home to Georgia in the off-season. In 1932, Pip and Flip were immortalized in the movie *Freaks*, featuring other famous sideshow characters such as Johnny Eck, the half-man, and the Earle family of midgets.

WORLD CIRCUS SIDE SHOW
CONEY ISLAND

CRAZY HAIRCUTS

Customers can get more than just a haircut when they go to see Rob "The Original" Ferrel, a hair artist based in San Antonio, Texas—they can have a lifelike portrait of their favorite actor, singer or sports hero etched onto the back of their head. Using the hair and scalp as his canvas, Rob says he can replicate any design or image in a client's hair—just with standard barber clippers and razors plus colored eyeliner for the finishing touches.

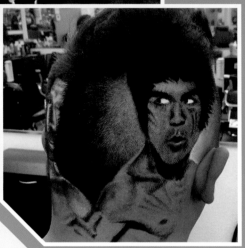

SWEATING BLOOD Delfina Cedeno, a young woman from Veron in the Dominican Republic, cries and sweats blood. Sometimes blood also seeps out of her fingernails, belly button and nostrils. She once bled for 15 days, becoming so ill that she needed a blood transfusion, and when she suffers an anxiety attack, her blood pressure rises to the point where she sweats blood.

CHAINSAW HORROR Following a freak accident 15 ft (4.6 m) up a Scots Pine, tree trimmer James Valentine was rushed to a hospital in Pittsburgh, Pennsylvania, with the blade of a chainsaw embedded in his neck. The razor-sharp blade sliced into his neck and shoulder, but luckily missed his spine and all major arteries. He still needed emergency surgery to seal the wounds with 25 stitches and ten staples.

ANTIQUE HAIR A lock of hair belonging to Emperor Franz Joseph I, who ruled Austria-Hungary from 1848 to 1916, sold at an auction in Vienna in 2013 for $18,000—more than 20 times its estimated value.

SURPRISE ADDITION Expecting triplets, Kimberly Fugate instead gave birth to identical quadruplets in Jackson, Mississippi, beating odds of 13 million to one. The fourth girl had gone undetected by ultrasound imaging throughout the pregnancy.

ROACH REMOVAL Woken by a sharp pain in his right ear, Australian warehouse worker Hendrik Helmer was left doubled up in agony as a 0.8-in-long (2-cm) cockroach burrowed deep into his ear canal. He tried to suck it out with a vacuum cleaner, but eventually went to a hospital in Darwin where doctors drowned the insect by pouring olive oil into the ear canal and then removed it with forceps.

BRAIN WORM A British man lived with a 4-in (10-cm)-long parasitic tapeworm inside his brain for a period of more than four years. The 50-year-old first visited medics in London in 2008 complaining of headaches, seizures, memory loss and a changed sense of smell, but despite exhaustive tests, no one could find anything wrong—until 2012, when they found the ribbon-shaped larval worm among his brain tissue. The man was given drugs to kill the worm and made a complete recovery.

HAIR COAT Xiang Renxian, a retired teacher from Chongqing, China, spent 11 years knitting her husband a coat and hat out of her own hair. When her long hair started to fall out naturally as she got older, she began using the hair that she was shedding, weaving it into clothing. She used 116,058 hairs to make the lightweight coat, which weighs just 13.47 oz (382 g).

LEECH TREATMENT After badly damaging his left hand in a roller press at work, machine operator Sam Leon of DeKalb, Illinois, applied 1,482 blood-sucking leeches to the injured limb to keep it from being amputated. Leeches secrete a powerful blood thinner that allows a wound to continue draining until the patient's veins have reformed.

SLEEPING SICKNESS Since April 2010, dozens of villagers in Kalachi, Kazakhstan, have been periodically hit by a mysterious illness that causes them to fall asleep suddenly, sometimes for up to six days. Those affected often fall asleep while standing up—and sometimes several people doze off simultaneously. One woman, Lyubov Belkova, has been hit by the sleeping bug seven times.

BODY SENSORS Software developer Chris Dancy from Brentwood, Tennessee, has 700 sensors, devices, services and apps that monitor his every mood and move. He spent four years connecting all the gadgets he wears on his body to smart technology. He carries two smartphones and wears a smartwatch (which provides him with updates from his phones), a heart monitor, a posture sensor and a device to track his sleep patterns. He even has a pet GPS system to track what his two dogs are doing and sometimes wears a Google Glass headset that records everything he sees.

WAYWARD NAIL A 3.2-in-long (8-cm) steel nail ripped into the skull of 55-year-old Mr. Yang of Nanjing, China, while he was using a cutting machine—but he did not even know about it until he started to feel sick. It had penetrated his eye socket and yet miraculously surgeons were later able to remove the nail without damaging his vision.

STEREO BLIND Five percent of the world's population, including actor Johnny Depp, are stereo blind, meaning they are unable to see movies in 3-D.

IMAGE CONSCIOUS Alan, a 20-year-old from Tokyo, Japan, spent $150,000 on plastic surgery so that he looked more like Michelangelo's Renaissance statue *David*. He is so obsessed with his appearance that he constantly monitors his face by taking at least 1,500 selfies a month and has 4,000 pictures of himself on his smartphone.

BALDNESS CURE The Greek philosopher Aristotle (384–322 BC) rubbed goat urine on his head to try to cure his baldness.

STEP MASSAGE As a form of body massage, without having to involve anyone else, 51-year-old Li Chia slowly rolls down and up 20 concrete steps every morning at a park in Xi'an, China. As soon as he reaches the bottom of the steps, he rolls back up again, and in the three years he has been doing it, he says he has never suffered even a bruise.

DIFFERENT LANGUAGE Ben McMahon, 22, from Melbourne, Australia, woke from a week-long coma following a car crash to find that he could speak only Mandarin Chinese. Although he had studied the language while he was at school, he had never been able to speak it fluently. It took him another three days to remember how to speak English.

Lip Service

Nail technician Kristina Rei of St. Petersburg, Russia, has had 100 silicone injections to give herself huge lips because she wants to look like animated-movie heroine Jessica Rabbit.

Although she has already spent $6,200 on the enhancements, the 25-year-old says she would like to make her lips even bigger and also wants pointed ears like an elf. "It's good to be different," she says.

When she was only four, she already thought her lips were thinner than everyone else's and decided that one day she would get them plumped up. She says she was bullied at school because of how she used to look, but since having her first lip injection at 17, she has become more confident. That initial injection was extremely painful, but she liked the result so much she started having injections regularly. Now she is pleased when people film her on their cell phones.

"I loved Jessica Rabbit's huge lips," she says. "She was my idea of the perfect woman. I want to look like a cartoon character. I am addicted to it. I love it."

AFTER: Her large lips may look awkward, but Kristina says she can eat, speak and kiss the same as before.

BEFORE: At 15, Kristina looked beautiful to most people, but she herself thought her lips were too small.

Body modification enthusiast Joel Miggler from Küssaberg, Germany, has created giant cheek holes in his face which give an alarming side view of his teeth.

He has 1.4-in wide (3.6-cm) flesh tunnels in both cheeks through which he can blow out cigarette smoke, but he has to plug them while eating soup or drinking. He also has to take smaller bites of food than before the tunnels were put in. Joel's first modification was at the age of 13, when he had his earlobes stretched. Now 23, he has 27 piercings, as well as several tattoos and implants, and has even had his buttock branded.

BEDBUG TATTOO Matt Camper, an entomologist at Colorado State University, created a temporary tattoo from 1,000 bedbugs feeding simultaneously on his flesh. His tattoo kit consists of the bugs and a jar with a wire mesh rabbit pattern on the top. When the jar is inverted onto his skin, the bugs crawl through the mesh and feed on him. Two hours later, the bites swell up and turn red in the pattern of the rabbit.

EAR MAGGOT A 48-year-old Taiwanese woman found she had a maggot living inside her left ear. After suffering an earache for 24 hours, she went to a hospital in Taipei where doctors removed a fruit fly larva that was moving around inside her ear. She had worn a hearing aid for many years, and that made her ear warm and an ideal home for larvae.

DEAD BODIES The Monroe Moosnick Medical and Science Museum in Lexington, Kentucky, has a dissectible life-sized wax figure of a woman that was created by casting organs and tissues from 200 human corpses.

BODY HEAT Tibetan Buddhist monks can raise their body temperature by the power of thought alone, producing enough heat in around an hour to dry cold, wet sheets draped over their shoulders in a frigid room.

IN DENIAL Blind people with Anton-Babinski syndrome refuse to believe that they cannot see. The condition is believed to be caused by a rare form of brain damage and most often occurs following a stroke or head injury.

POT (HOLE) LUCK Ray Lee of Wiltshire, England, was being rushed to a hospital with crippling chest pains and a potentially fatal heart rhythm of 186 beats per minute when the ambulance hit a large pothole in the road—and the resultant jolt caused his heart rate to plummet immediately to a safe 60 beats per minute.

TOWERING NOSES Students in China have been paying up to $10,000 to have their noses reconstructed to resemble the shape of the Eiffel Tower. The iconic Paris landmark's elegant curves are viewed as the ideal profile for ambitious young Chinese people.

MUSICAL FINGER
Body modification enthusiast Rich Lee of St. George, Utah, has had a pair of small magnet headphones implanted in his ears. When he wears a coil device around his neck, he channels magnetic fields, allowing the magnets to function as speakers. The undetectable implants are in the tragus, the hard bit of flesh in front of the ear canal. When he connects his music player to the coil, he can listen to music without blocking out other sounds. He also has a magnet implanted in one of his fingers so that when he puts his finger in his ear, he can hear music coming from his finger! As he has very poor vision in one eye, he also plans to hook up the implants to an ultrasonic range-finder so that he can use echolocation like a bat.

BATTERY BRAIN Known as "Cyber AJ," New Zealander Andrew Johnson has been fitted with a battery-operated brain to combat Parkinson's disease. In a procedure called deep brain stimulation, doctors planted electrodes in his head to counter the neurons responsible for causing shakes and tics, and now if his hands start to shake or he feels wobbly, he simply hits a switch to make the symptoms disappear.

FINGER PRINTS Paul McCarthy of Marblehead, Massachusetts, borrowed his friend's 3-D printer to build his 12-year-old son Leon a functional prosthetic hand after watching an online instruction video. The hand cost him just $5 to make, compared to a conventional prosthesis that would have cost over $30,000. Leon was born without fingers on one hand, but thanks to his new hand he can now pick up objects and even ride a bicycle.

PANIC ATTACK In June 2014, 26 students at a girls' high school in Yanagawa, Japan, fell ill in an apparent panic attack, forcing the school to close for the day. Shortly afterward, a student suddenly shrieked and collapsed in the middle of a class, as did two others in the same class and then students from other classes who had gone to check on the incident. Psychiatrists say adolescenct children can experience excessive tension and anxiety, which are highly contagious behaviors and can lead to group panic attacks.

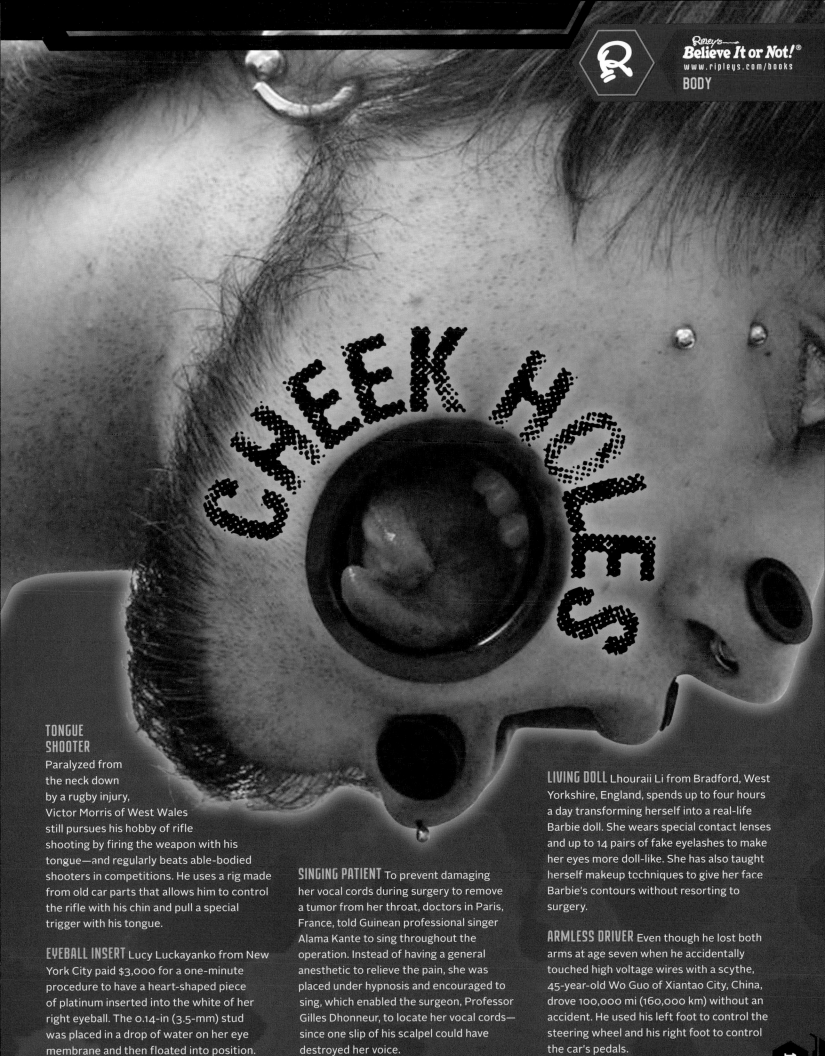

SEEK HOLES

TONGUE SHOOTER

Paralyzed from the neck down by a rugby injury, Victor Morris of West Wales still pursues his hobby of rifle shooting by firing the weapon with his tongue—and regularly beats able-bodied shooters in competitions. He uses a rig made from old car parts that allows him to control the rifle with his chin and pull a special trigger with his tongue.

EYEBALL INSERT Lucy Luckayanko from New York City paid $3,000 for a one-minute procedure to have a heart-shaped piece of platinum inserted into the white of her right eyeball. The 0.14-in (3.5-mm) stud was placed in a drop of water on her eye membrane and then floated into position.

SINGING PATIENT To prevent damaging her vocal cords during surgery to remove a tumor from her throat, doctors in Paris, France, told Guinean professional singer Alama Kante to sing throughout the operation. Instead of having a general anesthetic to relieve the pain, she was placed under hypnosis and encouraged to sing, which enabled the surgeon, Professor Gilles Dhonneur, to locate her vocal cords—since one slip of his scalpel could have destroyed her voice.

LIVING DOLL Lhouraii Li from Bradford, West Yorkshire, England, spends up to four hours a day transforming herself into a real-life Barbie doll. She wears special contact lenses and up to 14 pairs of fake eyelashes to make her eyes more doll-like. She has also taught herself makeup techniques to give her face Barbie's contours without resorting to surgery.

ARMLESS DRIVER Even though he lost both arms at age seven when he accidentally touched high voltage wires with a scythe, 45-year-old Wo Guo of Xiantao City, China, drove 100,000 mi (160,000 km) without an accident. He used his left foot to control the steering wheel and his right foot to control the car's pedals.

The sacred
HAIRY FAMILY OF BURMA

Moung-Phoset (left), his mother Mah-Phoon and his sister Mah-Me.

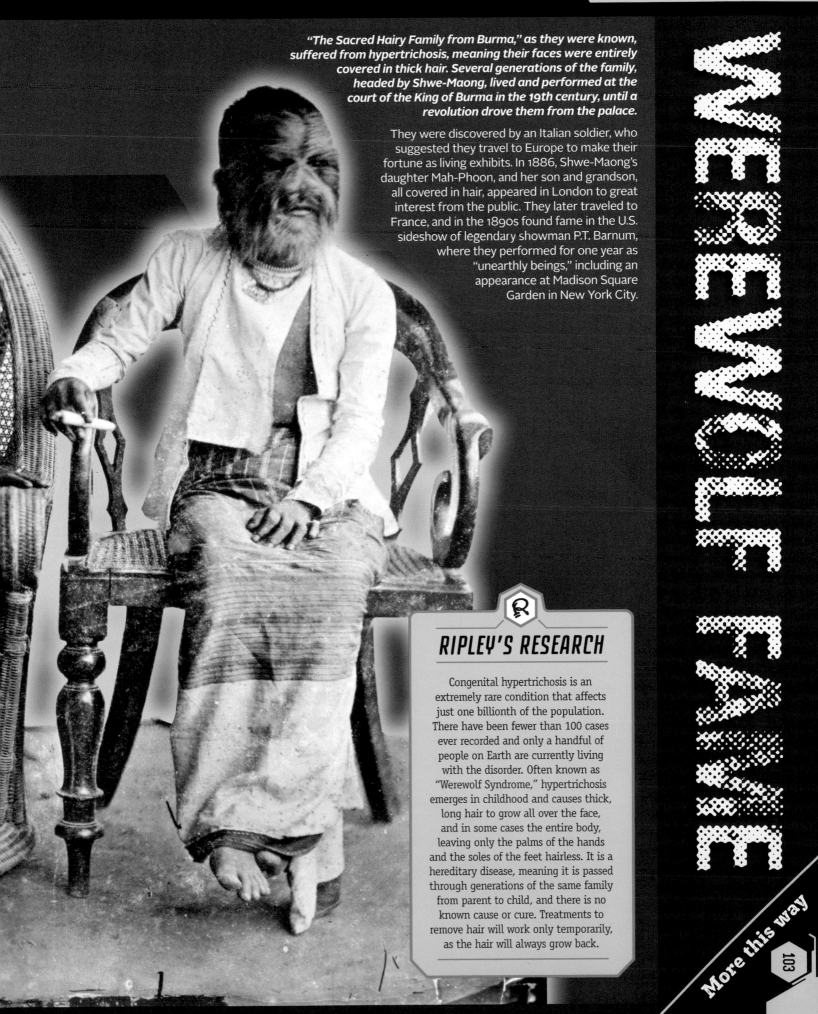

"The Sacred Hairy Family from Burma," as they were known, suffered from hypertrichosis, meaning their faces were entirely covered in thick hair. Several generations of the family, headed by Shwe-Maong, lived and performed at the court of the King of Burma in the 19th century, until a revolution drove them from the palace.

They were discovered by an Italian soldier, who suggested they travel to Europe to make their fortune as living exhibits. In 1886, Shwe-Maong's daughter Mah-Phoon, and her son and grandson, all covered in hair, appeared in London to great interest from the public. They later traveled to France, and in the 1890s found fame in the U.S. sideshow of legendary showman P.T. Barnum, where they performed for one year as "unearthly beings," including an appearance at Madison Square Garden in New York City.

WEREWOLF FAME

RIPLEY'S RESEARCH

Congenital hypertrichosis is an extremely rare condition that affects just one billionth of the population. There have been fewer than 100 cases ever recorded and only a handful of people on Earth are currently living with the disorder. Often known as "Werewolf Syndrome," hypertrichosis emerges in childhood and causes thick, long hair to grow all over the face, and in some cases the entire body, leaving only the palms of the hands and the soles of the feet hairless. It is a hereditary disease, meaning it is passed through generations of the same family from parent to child, and there is no known cause or cure. Treatments to remove hair will work only temporarily, as the hair will always grow back.

More this way

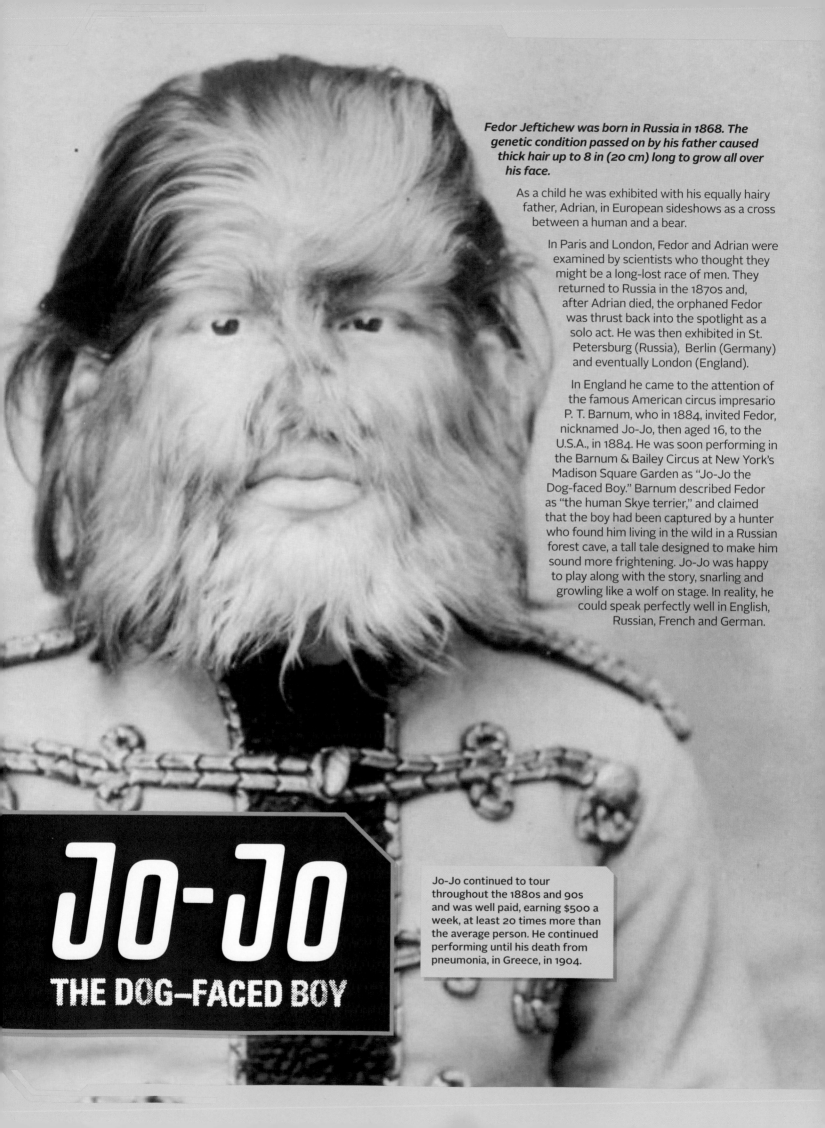

Fedor Jeftichew was born in Russia in 1868. The genetic condition passed on by his father caused thick hair up to 8 in (20 cm) long to grow all over his face.

As a child he was exhibited with his equally hairy father, Adrian, in European sideshows as a cross between a human and a bear.

In Paris and London, Fedor and Adrian were examined by scientists who thought they might be a long-lost race of men. They returned to Russia in the 1870s and, after Adrian died, the orphaned Fedor was thrust back into the spotlight as a solo act. He was then exhibited in St. Petersburg (Russia), Berlin (Germany) and eventually London (England).

In England he came to the attention of the famous American circus impresario P. T. Barnum, who in 1884, invited Fedor, nicknamed Jo-Jo, then aged 16, to the U.S.A., in 1884. He was soon performing in the Barnum & Bailey Circus at New York's Madison Square Garden as "Jo-Jo the Dog-faced Boy." Barnum described Fedor as "the human Skye terrier," and claimed that the boy had been captured by a hunter who found him living in the wild in a Russian forest cave, a tall tale designed to make him sound more frightening. Jo-Jo was happy to play along with the story, snarling and growling like a wolf on stage. In reality, he could speak perfectly well in English, Russian, French and German.

JO-JO
THE DOG—FACED BOY

Jo-Jo continued to tour throughout the 1880s and 90s and was well paid, earning $500 a week, at least 20 times more than the average person. He continued performing until his death from pneumonia, in Greece, in 1904.

Ripley's Believe It or Not!®
www.ripleys.com/books
BODY

WHO'S WHO?!
THE P.T. BARNUM PERFORMERS
(FROM LEFT TO RIGHT)

LALOO
Eight-limbed Man

YOUNG HERMAN
Expanding-chest Man

J.K. COFFEY
Skeleton Man

JAMES MORRIS
Stretchy-skin Man

JO-JO
The Dog-faced Boy

This advertisement for P.T. Barnum's circus featured a cartoon of Jo-Jo before the Russian Czar, with one of Barnum's agents at the door. In order to boost audiences, Jo-Jo's promoters pretended that he was the property of the Czar of Russia, and claimed that he was soon required to return to him.

BEARDED LADY

Harnaam Kaur from Slough, England, has polycystic ovary syndrome, which caused dark hair to appear on her face when she was 11 before spreading to her arms and chest. During her early teens, she waxed twice a week in an attempt to remove her beard and also tried bleaching and shaving. However, she decided to stop cutting her facial hair at 16 after being baptized as a Sikh—a religion that forbids the cutting of body hair. Now 23, she feels proud of her bushy beard, which she says makes her feel more empowered and feminine, and she has received many kind messages of support.

ULTIMATE SACRIFICE Dr. Jesse Lazear of Baltimore, Maryland, died at the age of 34 in 1900 after allowing himself to be bitten by mosquitoes that were infected with yellow fever. His sacrifice helped confirm to science that the insects were instrumental in spreading disease.

SECRET SKELETON Doctors in Nagpur, India, removed the skeleton of an unborn baby that had been left inside its mother for 36 years. Kantabai Thakre became pregnant at the age of 24 in 1978, but doctors warned her that there was little chance of her baby surviving after it was found growing outside her womb. Terrified of an operation, she fled back to Paipariya, her village, without having the fetus removed. However, when she started experiencing severe stomach pain nearly four decades later, a scan revealed the presence of the baby's skeleton encased in a calcified sac.

PAPER PHOBIA For more than 25 years, Diane Freelove of Rochester, Kent, England, has suffered from a fear of newspapers. She hates the look, smell and touch of newspapers and says that if anybody holding one approaches her, she freaks out. She thinks her phobia may stem from a childhood incident when her mother playfully hit her father over the head with a newspaper.

UNDERWATER VISION The Moken people of southeast Asia, who have deep-dived for food for centuries, have underwater vision that is twice as sharp as the average person. They constrict their pupils to the smallest point possible—20 percent smaller than the average pupils—and this helps them to spot tiny shellfish underwater without the aid of goggles.

FALL GUY Tom Stilwell, a 20-year-old Englishman, fell from the 15th floor of an apartment block in Auckland, New Zealand and, despite breaking several bones, survived to tell the tale. He plummeted 13 floors before landing on the roof of an adjacent building, which probably saved his life.

YOUNG HERO When Coy Jumper suffered a stroke and fell into deep water near Swansea, South Carolina, his ten-year-old granddaughter Cara leaped in and saved him from drowning. She then dragged her 230-lb (104-kg) grandfather ¼ mi (0.4 km) through the woods, got into his car and drove him 3 mi (4.8 km) back home to safety.

232 Teeth

A normal adult mouth contains 32 teeth—but 17-year-old Ashik Gavai from a village in Mumbai, India, underwent a seven-hour operation to remove an unbelievable 232 teeth from his mouth. He had been complaining about a painful swelling and when doctors operated they found a complex composite odontoma—a benign tumor deep in his lower jaw that contained hundreds of small pearl-like white teeth. After chiseling out the tumor and the tiny teeth, they still left him with 28 ordinary teeth.

ANCIENT ANATOMY

AXE HORROR Sheldon Mpofu from West Yorkshire, England, cheated death by millimeters after the sharp head of a pickaxe entered his skull. He was working in his garden when he swung the pickaxe, but on the way down it hit a washing line and the pointed end of the axe flew into his forehead. Luckily the axe head narrowly missed his brain and lodged in a sinus—an empty space in the skull.

SONIC GENE There is a gene in the human body called sonic hedgehog. It plays a vital role in ensuring that all our limbs and organs are in the correct place.

BAD BLOOD Thousands of people in India are choosing to shun modern medicines in favor of the ancient tradition of bloodletting, which they believe can cure arthritis and heart disease. At open-air clinics, patients bound with ropes stand in the heat for half an hour to make the blood flow more readily while a practitioner makes tiny nicks in the skin of the affected body area with a razor blade so that the "bad blood" can be removed.

3-D HEART When 14-month-old Roland Lian Cung Bawi of Owensboro, Kentucky, needed urgent heart surgery, his life was saved thanks to a super-sized 3-D printout of his heart. Engineers at the University of Louisville teamed up with Kosair Children's Hospital to create a three-piece reproduction of the boy's heart 1 ½ times its actual size, which enabled surgeons to develop a detailed plan and complete the repair in a single operation.

BRAIN PATTERN *Cutis verticis gyrata* is a rare skin condition that makes the scalp look like the brain. The skin of the scalp thickens to form convoluted folds and furrows, which resemble the pattern of the brain. Although the creases are soft and spongy, they cannot be corrected with pressure and the only known medical treatment is cosmetic surgery.

TALL TEEN Rumeysa Gelgi of Safranbolu, Turkey, at age 17 stands over 7 ft (2.1 m) tall. She also has 10-in (24.5-cm) hands and 12-in (30-cm) feet, meaning that she has to get her shoes custom-made in the U.S.A. She must use a walker to get around because she is so tall she finds it difficult to keep her balance. She suffers from a rare genetic disorder called Weaver Syndrome, which causes rapid growth, but she is now not expected to get any taller.

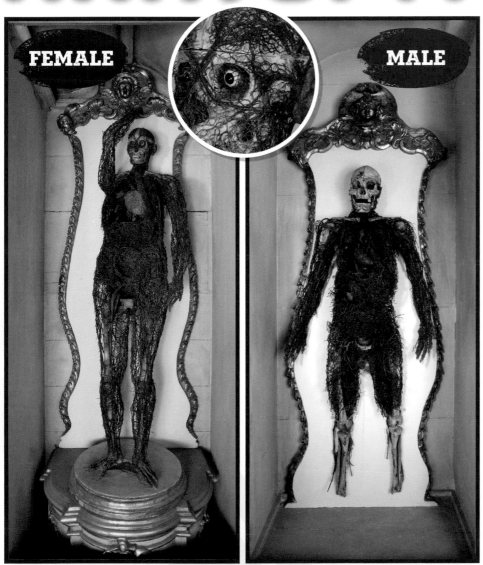

FEMALE

MALE

Housed in two glass cases in the crypt of the Museo Cappella Sansevero in Naples, Italy, are the real skeletons of a man and a pregnant woman showing their artery and vein systems in perfect detail.

These "Anatomical Machines" were made in 1763–64 by Palermo doctor Giuseppe Salerno, whose process of applying materials such as beeswax, iron wire and silk to the bodies preserved their circulatory systems for 250 years. The skeletons were built on the orders of the Prince of Sansevero, who may have had two of his servants killed to provide the bodies for the models.

WALTER HUDSON

Ripley's has immortalized Walter Hudson in a life-sized wax figure on display in several Ripley's Odditoriums.

Walter Hudson of Hempstead, New York, was one of the largest men ever to have lived. In 1987, at the age of 42, his weight was at least 1,200 lb (544 kg), heavier than an average horse, and he was easily the biggest man on Earth at the time.

Walter's insatiable appetite led to his ballooning to 125 lb (57 kg) by the age of six. At age 15 he weighed as much as two grown men and rarely left his house. By the 1980s, his waist was 103 in (261 cm) in circumference and, at 55 in (140 cm), his legs were wider than most people's waists.

He spent almost all of his life in bed and could not stand without help, which made calculating his exact weight difficult. In 1987, an attempt was made to weigh him on an industrial scale, with a group of local weightlifters enlisted as support. The scales read their maximum—1,000 lb (454 kg)—and then broke. Walter's size meant that he wore only a bed sheet, as he didn't have clothes to fit him.

Walter's Daily Diet

Walter generally consumed up to 20,000 calories a day—that's more than the suggested WEEKLY intake for a normal person. This would typically consist of:

Two boxes of sausages	12 eggs	Eight hamburgers
Eight baked potatoes	18 cupcakes	Eight portions of fries
	One loaf of bread	Two chickens
1 lb (454 g) of bacon	Three ham steaks	6 quarts (6 l) of soda

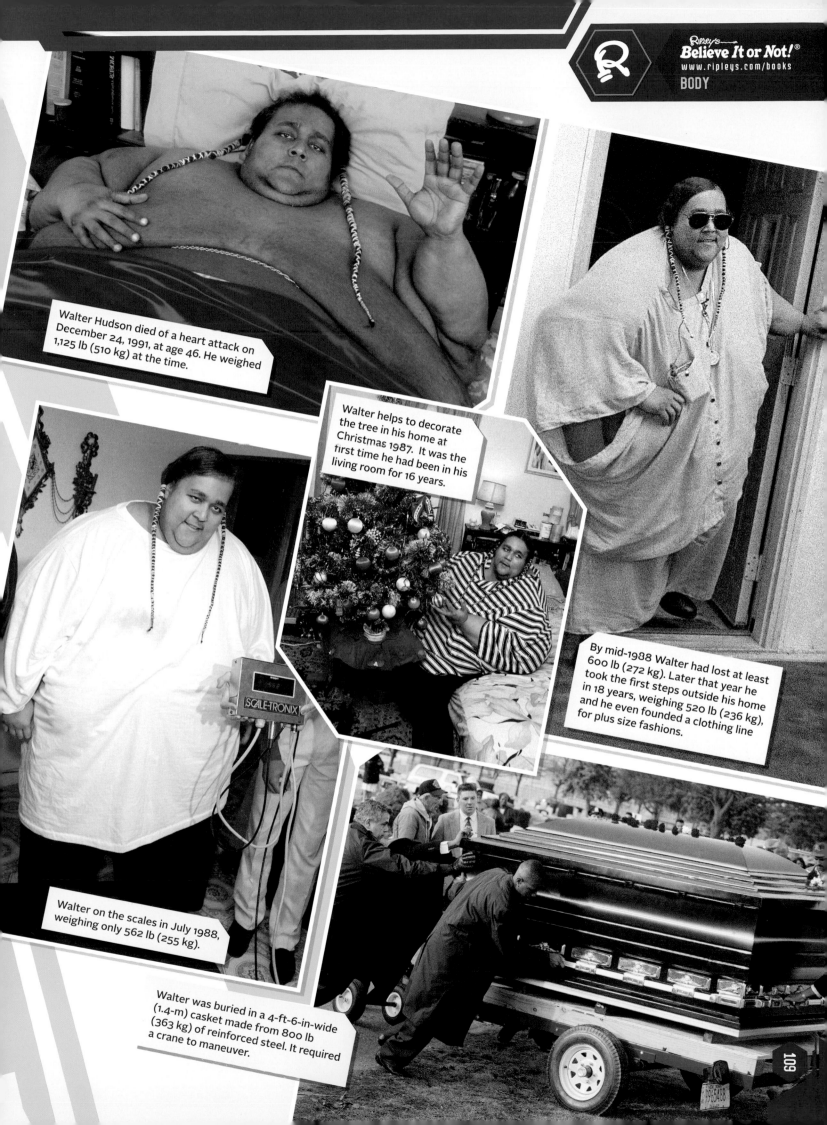

Walter Hudson died of a heart attack on December 24, 1991, at age 46. He weighed 1,125 lb (510 kg) at the time.

Walter helps to decorate the tree in his home at Christmas 1987. It was the first time he had been in his living room for 16 years.

By mid-1988 Walter had lost at least 600 lb (272 kg). Later that year he took the first steps outside his home in 18 years, weighing 520 lb (236 kg), and he even founded a clothing line for plus size fashions.

Walter on the scales in July 1988, weighing only 562 lb (255 kg).

Walter was buried in a 4-ft-6-in-wide (1.4-m) casket made from 800 lb (363 kg) of reinforced steel. It required a crane to maneuver.

SECOND SKELETON Student Seanie Nammock from Birmingham, England, suffers from a rare condition that causes a second skeleton to grow on top of the original one. *Fibrodysplasia ossificans progressiva*, or "stone man syndrome," turns muscles, ligaments and tendons into solid bone. It affects just 600 people worldwide, but Seanie has had it for more than six years and, with her back and neck frozen solid, she is unable to lift her hands above her waist.

HAIR TRADE The Lord Venkateshwara temple in Tirumala, southern India, makes more than $32 million a year by selling human hair. The temple employs 600 barbers to shave the heads of as many as 20,000 pilgrims a day. It collects 500 tons of hair a year, which it then sells to extension makers.

SKELETON REPLACEMENT The average 70-year-old human has grown and replaced seven whole skeletons during their lifetime.

BAD JOKES Witzelsucht is a brain disorder that compels the sufferer to tell inappropriately silly jokes and stories.

DISTINCTIVE SMELL No two people's body odor smells exactly the same—apart from identical twins whose smell is too similar to differentiate.

FLYING TOOTH
Meredith Cahill from Cherry Hill, New Jersey, sent Ripley's this picture of a tooth that flew out of her nose when she blew it! Her dentist had noticed the canine tooth in her upper gum five years earlier and it must have worked its way from the gum into her nasal passage.

HUGE TUMOR Nine doctors in Beijing, China, carried out a 16-hour operation to remove a 242-lb (110-kg) tumor from the lower back of 37-year-old Yang Jianbin. He had been born with a dark birthmark that had ballooned until he was unable to stand up. During the operation he received over 10½ pt (5 l) of blood, which is similar to what an adult's entire body holds.

THIN SKIN Count Orloff "The Transparent Man," a popular American sideshow performer in the late 19th century, had such thin skin that spectators could actually see the blood flowing through his veins—and a light shone on one side of his body could be seen from the other side. Born Ivannow Wladislaus von Dziarksi-Orloff in Hungary in 1864, he began experiencing muscular wasting as a teenager, which left him too weak to stand and led to him also being known as "The Human Window Pane."

WALKING BILLBOARD Edson Aparecido Borim of Sao Paulo, Brazil, makes his living by selling space on his body for tattooed advertisements. He started in 2006 and now has around 50 ads inked on his chest, back and arms. Walking around shirtless, he charges up to $148 a month for a tattoo, depending on its size and body location, and if companies do not pay or if they cancel an ad, he simply crosses out the tattoo.

BACK FROM DEAD Two hours after being declared dead by doctors in Salvador, Brazil, 54-year-old Valdelucio Goncalves was found alive and wriggling inside a zipped-up body bag. He was discovered by grieving relatives who had gone to the morgue to dress his body in readiness for his funeral later that day. They had already paid for a death notice in a newspaper and bought the coffin.

Little Star

One of Australia's greatest contortionists, Little Verlie first performed onstage in 1911 at the age of six and went on to amaze audiences by twisting her body into a series of complex poses. Her speciality was a one-legged skipping rope dance, which she performed while the other leg was twisted around her neck. She was adopted by Brisbane vaudeville trainer Lilian Ross, who later also adopted a young boy, Wee Darrell, to form a child contortionist double act. Verlie eventually tired of the arrangement and ran away in 1922, never to perform again. She never lost her flexibility and could still walk on her hands when she was in her fifties.

WILD

Since giving up his job as a heavy equipment mechanic in the late 1990s, former Marine Mick Dodge has lived like a wild man in the Hoh Rain Forest near Forks, Washington, bartering for essentials and sleeping in tree stumps.

He climbs the region's mountains barefoot, and to illustrate his love of the environment he has images of tree roots tattooed on his feet. He eats whatever he finds on his travels, including maggots, an elk killed by a cougar, and a sea lion he found washed up on a beach.

NOODLE BATH At the Hakone Kowakien Yunessun health spa in Japan, bathers combat aging by soaking their bodies in pools of wine, chocolate, or even ramen noodle soup. As well as noodles, the ramen broth contains pepper collagen, which is designed to rejuvenate the body and cleanse the skin.

NO SMILING Fifty-year-old Tess Christian, from London, England, has deliberately not smiled or laughed for 40 years so that she can avoid getting wrinkles. She has trained herself to control her facial muscles if she finds something funny, and although she was overjoyed when her daughter was born she still managed to resist smiling.

HAND CHIP Workers at the hi-tech Epicenter office block in Stockholm, Sweden, gain access to the building by using microchips implanted under their skin. Instead of swiping ID cards as security recognition, they move their hands across scanners to detect the injected chip, which is about the size of a grain of rice.

EYEBALL TATTOO Fifty years after suffering a serious eye injury as a child, which left his iris looking permanently white and cloudy, New Yorker William Watson had the damage repaired with an eyeball tattoo. The hour-long procedure, which involved injecting colored ink into his left eye, was performed by a doctor—and a tattoo artist who practiced beforehand on a grape.

DARING HANDSTANDS Acrobat Conor Kenny, from London, England, has performed thousands of handstands in daring locations, including on the edges of train platforms and highway overpasses, on the railing of London Bridge, England, and even on the sea floor while scuba diving in Greece.

PLANE CRASH Motorcyclist Loon Singh was hit by a MiG-27 fighter plane as it crashed into a field in Rajasthan, India, in January 2015—yet both he and the pilot survived. Singh, who suffered minor burns and a fractured hand, had been delivering invitations to his wedding when the plane landed on him.

IMAGINARY STARDOM People suffering from the medical condition *Truman Show* delusion—named after the 1998 Jim Carrey movie—believe that they are the stars of an imaginary TV show and are being filmed at all times. There have been more than 40 recorded cases in the world.

EXPLODING EYEBALLS Liz Hodgkinson, from Mold, North Wales, suffers from a rare degenerative disorder that causes her eyeballs to explode. The condition, *keratoconus*, causes the front of the eyeball to thin and bend out of shape so that the cornea (the usually dome-shaped window that covers the iris and the pupil) changes shape, thins out and then on very rare occasions splits. Liz's eyeballs have exploded on three separate occasions—the first time during a driving lesson on a divided highway, when her instructor had to grab the wheel. She has now had cornea transplants and even though her vision has been affected, it has not stopped her working as an artist.

EARLY BIRTH While being driven to a hospital in Plymouth, Devon, England, by her husband, Vicki McAteer gave birth to baby daughter Niamh in the leg of her jogging pants.

SKIN LARVAE After being bitten three times by mosquitoes on a trip to Belize, Harvard entomologist Piotr Naskrecki found that the bites contained botfly larvae. He removed one of the larvae with a suction device, but then deliberately allowed the other two maggots to grow under his skin for two months and then filmed the moment they finally crawled out of his body.

HUMAN BUOY Libby Tucker, a 67-year-old swimming teacher from Kent, England, can float upright and unaided in water without sinking. She does not need to tread water and can even cross her arms and legs without going under the surface. The gravity-defying grandmother has been able to perform the trick for as long as she can remember and once floated for 9 ½ hours for charity.

ARM DOODLES Keith Anderson from Peterborough, Ontario, Canada, has covered his arms in tattoos of his son Kai's doodles and drawings. He started inking the images onto his skin in 2008 when Kai was just four years old, and has added a new image every year since. To make sure there's enough room on his body to keep going, Keith has asked his son to draw smaller pictures!

LINCOLN HAIR A lock of hair that was removed from Abraham Lincoln's head by Surgeon General Joseph K. Barnes shortly after the President was fatally shot on April 14, 1865, sold at auction for $25,000 in Dallas, Texas, in 2015.

NIMBLE FEET Unable to use her hands properly after contracting polio as a child, Bai Aixiang, from Heyuan, China, cooks, washes, embroiders and even shaves her husband's head with her feet.

DRANK URINE After falling 65 ft (20 m) from a construction site in Hunan Province, China, and breaking his arms, legs and cell phone, 28-year-old Yang Hsieh survived by drinking his own urine for six days until he was rescued. Unable to move, he tried calling for help, but nobody came until eventually a passerby heard his feeble plea.

DANCING PLAGUE In July 1518, more than 400 people in Strasbourg, France, mysteriously began dancing for days without rest until many died from heart attacks, strokes or exhaustion. No explanation has ever been given for "The Dancing Plague." After about a month, it stopped as suddenly as it had started.

Julia Pastrana was a famous 19th-century performer, billed as the "ugliest woman in the world." Born in 1834 in Sinaloa, Mexico, Julia was covered from head to toe in thick black hair, a rare case of the genetic condition hypertrichosis. She also had protruding lips and gums, a result of gingival hyperplasia.

In 1854, at the age of 20, the American M. Rates persuaded Julia that she could make money from her curious appearance, and brought her to New York City to be exhibited. There, Julia was described as resembling a bear or an orangutan, and nicknamed the "semi-human," or "ape woman." She would sing and dance for paying audiences and for scientists who were eager to examine her. One doctor in Cleveland declared her to be an entirely new species! However, Julia was far from the wild creature she was portrayed to be—she was a graceful dancer and spoke three languages.

In New York, Julia met the showman Theodore Lent, who became both her new manager and her husband. Lent took Julia on a European tour, performing shows from London to Moscow, promoting her as a mysterious "nondescript."

In 1859, Julia became pregnant and, while in Moscow, gave birth to a boy, Theodore, who was also covered in hair. Tragically, he did not survive, and Julia passed away soon afterward. This should have put an end to Julia's remarkable journey, but after Lent had sold her body to St. Petersburg University to be mummified, along with young Theodore, he decided that the show must go on, and took the preserved corpses back on the road.

Mother and son spent the next few decades being exhibited at sideshows around Europe, finding their way to Norway in the 1920s, where they were displayed until the 1970s, before being looted by fairground vandals. Sadly, Theodore was lost, but Julia was rescued by the Oslo University Hospital, where she was placed in storage until 2013, when her story took one more incredible twist. Following a longstanding campaign from a Mexican artist, Julia's body was repatriated to her hometown in Sinaloa, where she was finally laid to rest in a Catholic funeral, more than 150 years after her death.

BILLED AS: THE UGLIEST WOMAN IN THE WORLD

STATIC HAIR Born after her mother Kendra Villanueva was struck by lightning, Kimberly Gordon of Albuquerque, New Mexico, still had static hair that stood perfectly straight a year later. It was a miracle that Kimberly survived the electrical jolt, which knocked out her heavily pregnant mother instantly as she took shelter under a tree during a violent storm. Kimberly had to be delivered by emergency C-section.

DREAM ON! Most people over the age of ten have between four and six dreams every night, working out at over 1,000 a year, but remember only five percent of them. As people reach their sixties, 80 percent of their dreams tend to be in black and white rather than color. By contrast, 80 percent of people under the age of 30 dream in color.

MATH GENIUS After being punched in the head in a bar near his home in Tacoma, Washington State, 31-year-old furniture salesman Jason Padgett came round to find that he had become a math and physics genius. He had shown little academic interest before, but the brain injury he had suffered in the attack unlocked part of his brain that makes everything in his world appear to have a mathematical structure. He has been diagnosed with acquired savant syndrome, where once-ordinary people become skilled in math, art or music following a brain injury.

BRAIN WORM Doctors in Chengdu, China, removed a 6-in (15-cm) parasitic worm from the brain of a 60-year-old man suffering from headaches. They blamed the man's condition on eating uncooked frogs and eels, which contain parasites that can enter the human body.

BROKEN BONES Darryle See, 22, survived with just a few broken bones after being hit full-on by a Chicago-bound Amtrak train travelling at 110 mph (177 km/h). The impact, near Michigan City, Indiana, was so powerful it hurled him 20 ft (6 m) from the tracks.

TEAM SWAP Paul Warburton a Manchester City Football Club fan, received a life-saving stem cell transplant from his brother Martin in 2003—only after he agreed to sign a contract promising to change his allegiance to arch rivals Manchester United.

THIRD SET Kristian Vollick of Arizona tells Ripley's that his great-grandmother Edith West grew her third set of teeth at the age of 102. Whereas most people only get two sets of teeth in a lifetime, Edith, who was born in 1911, started losing her second set when she was 98, only to grow more teeth four years later.

SIX FINGERS

Spanning four generations, all 14 members of the Silva family from Brasilia, Brazil, were born with six fingers on each hand as a result of a genetic condition known as polydactyly.

Far from being downhearted, they have learned to use their condition to their advantage. For example, 14-year-old Joao de Assis da Silva has become a talented guitarist with the help of his extra fingers.

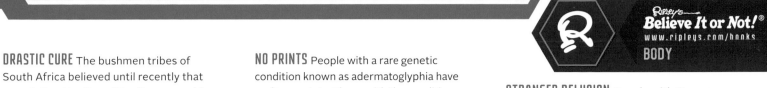
Ripley's Believe It or Not!®
www.ripleys.com/books
BODY

DRASTIC CURE The bushmen tribes of South Africa believed until recently that amputating the tips of the fingers could cure sickness.

SOLDIERS' TEETH In the 19th century, dentures were known as "Waterloo teeth" because many of them were made from teeth taken from dead soldiers after battles such as Waterloo, where the British defeated the French in 1815.

NO PRINTS People with a rare genetic condition known as adermatoglyphia have no fingerprints. Those with the condition can spend hours trying to get through border control, giving it the common name "immigration-delay disease." Only four families in the world are known to have it.

HAPPY ENDING In 1936, 30-year-old Samuel Ledward from North Wales, was pronounced dead by doctors following a motorcycle accident, but on the way to the mortuary his hand twitched and he went on to make a full recovery. In 2014, he celebrated his 108th birthday.

STRANGER DELUSION People with Capgras syndrome are convinced that all friends and family are imposters, but anyone with Fregoli syndrome believes just the opposite—that all strangers are really friends and family members in disguise. A woman in Pittsburgh, Pennsylvania, who had Fregoli syndrome following head trauma from a car accident told hospital staff that a fellow patient was her boyfriend, that a visiting social worker was her sister and that her mother was posing as one of the nurses.

STABBING PAIN A 42-year-old man from Trenton, New Jersey, awoke with a strange pain—and was told that he had been sound asleep with a knife in his back for ten hours.

PUSH-UPS Georgian Corporal Temur Dadiani lost both his legs in an explosion in Afghanistan in 2011, but, by balancing on his arms only, the double amputee can perform 36 push-ups in just 38 seconds.

A-Z OF BEARDS New York graphic designer Mike Allen created a new typeface—Alphabeard—out of his own facial hair. Over a period of two years, he sculpted his beard into the shapes of every letter from A to Z. He photographed each letter, shaved and had to wait two weeks before sculpting the next.

WORLD MAP Retired lawyer Bill Passman of Pineville, Louisiana, has a tattoo showing a map of the world on his back and every time he visits a new country, he has it colored by a tattoo artist. He only began traveling in 2006, but he has already been to all seven continents, including Antarctica, and has more than 70 countries inked in.

Jorge Iván Latorre Robles has some very unusual talents—he can stretch his skin, pop out his eyes and dislocate his joints.

The 24-year-old from Puerto Rico, known by his friends as "Chicle" (meaning "chewing gum" in Spanish), didn't discover his talents until he was 18, when he was breakdancing and found that his flexibility meant that he could perform tricks unlike the other dancers.

Jorge was diagnosed with Ehlers-Danlos Syndrome, a condition that affects his body's production of collagen (which provides strength and structure to the skin), causing the skin to loosen.

He mostly uses his talents to entertain people, performing at theaters, working as a street performer and volunteering at the hospital entertaining sick children, who often think he is a superhero with stretchy skin powers.

Jorge has been a fan of Ripley's since he was young, when he was into "weird" stuff, and felt he finally became a part of the Ripley family when he discovered his skills. He loves Ripley's so much he said he could happily live in a Ripley's Believe It or Not! Odditorium!

STRETCHY SKIN!

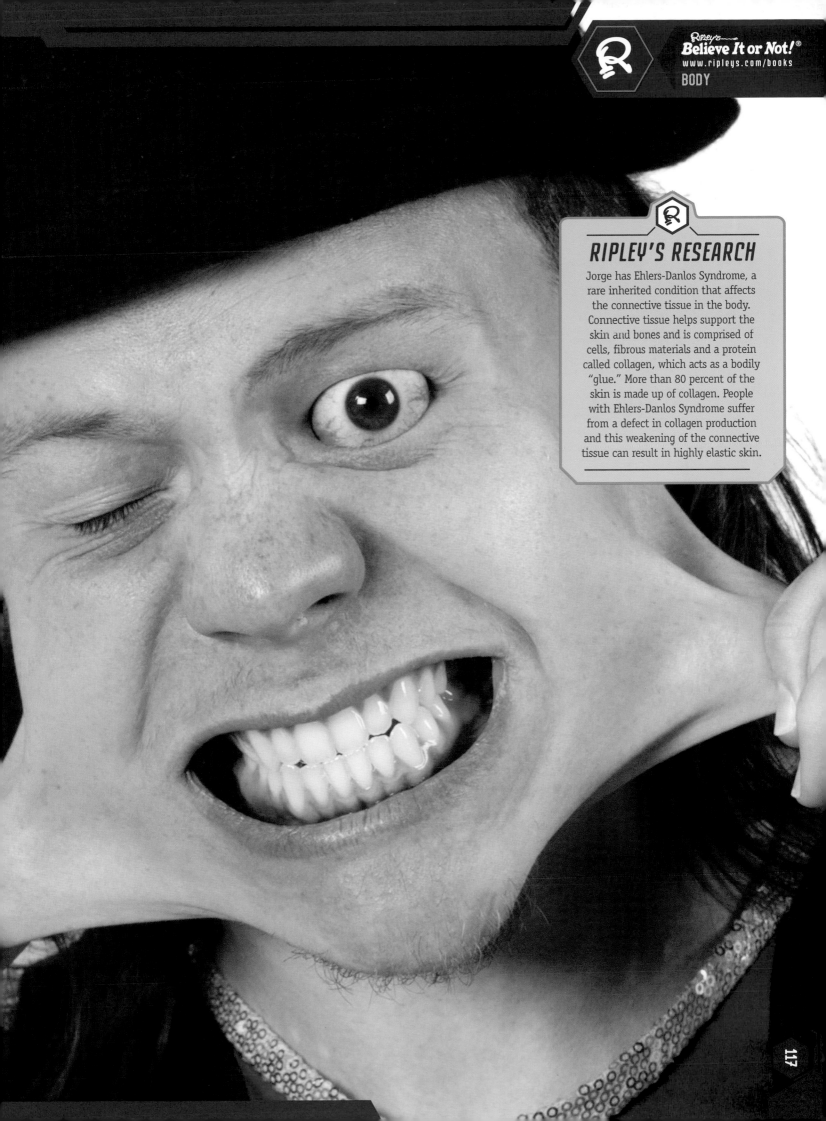

RIPLEY'S RESEARCH

Jorge has Ehlers-Danlos Syndrome, a rare inherited condition that affects the connective tissue in the body. Connective tissue helps support the skin and bones and is comprised of cells, fibrous materials and a protein called collagen, which acts as a bodily "glue." More than 80 percent of the skin is made up of collagen. People with Ehlers-Danlos Syndrome suffer from a defect in collagen production and this weakening of the connective tissue can result in highly elastic skin.

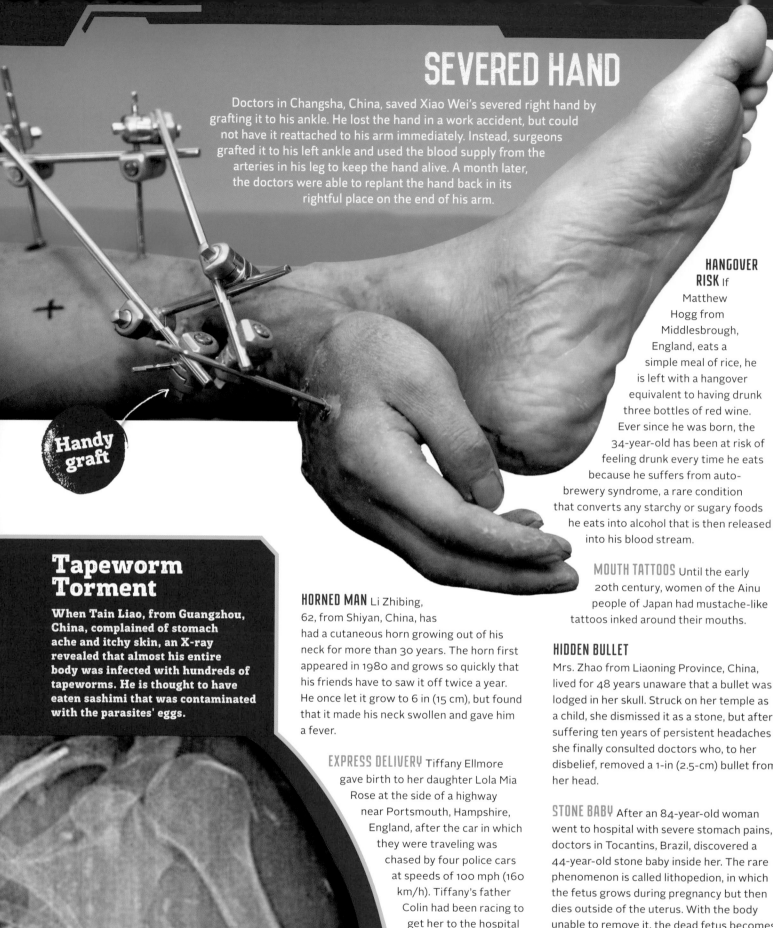

SEVERED HAND

Doctors in Changsha, China, saved Xiao Wei's severed right hand by grafting it to his ankle. He lost the hand in a work accident, but could not have it reattached to his arm immediately. Instead, surgeons grafted it to his left ankle and used the blood supply from the arteries in his leg to keep the hand alive. A month later, the doctors were able to replant the hand back in its rightful place on the end of his arm.

Handy graft

Tapeworm Torment

When Tain Liao, from Guangzhou, China, complained of stomach ache and itchy skin, an X-ray revealed that almost his entire body was infected with hundreds of tapeworms. He is thought to have eaten sashimi that was contaminated with the parasites' eggs.

HORNED MAN Li Zhibing, 62, from Shiyan, China, has had a cutaneous horn growing out of his neck for more than 30 years. The horn first appeared in 1980 and grows so quickly that his friends have to saw it off twice a year. He once let it grow to 6 in (15 cm), but found that it made his neck swollen and gave him a fever.

EXPRESS DELIVERY Tiffany Ellmore gave birth to her daughter Lola Mia Rose at the side of a highway near Portsmouth, Hampshire, England, after the car in which they were traveling was chased by four police cars at speeds of 100 mph (160 km/h). Tiffany's father Colin had been racing to get her to the hospital in time, but Lola wouldn't wait and arrived just as their car was surrounded by police officers who thought the speeding vehicle was stolen.

HANGOVER RISK If Matthew Hogg from Middlesbrough, England, eats a simple meal of rice, he is left with a hangover equivalent to having drunk three bottles of red wine. Ever since he was born, the 34-year-old has been at risk of feeling drunk every time he eats because he suffers from auto-brewery syndrome, a rare condition that converts any starchy or sugary foods he eats into alcohol that is then released into his blood stream.

MOUTH TATTOOS Until the early 20th century, women of the Ainu people of Japan had mustache-like tattoos inked around their mouths.

HIDDEN BULLET Mrs. Zhao from Liaoning Province, China, lived for 48 years unaware that a bullet was lodged in her skull. Struck on her temple as a child, she dismissed it as a stone, but after suffering ten years of persistent headaches she finally consulted doctors who, to her disbelief, removed a 1-in (2.5-cm) bullet from her head.

STONE BABY After an 84-year-old woman went to hospital with severe stomach pains, doctors in Tocantins, Brazil, discovered a 44-year-old stone baby inside her. The rare phenomenon is called lithopedion, in which the fetus grows during pregnancy but then dies outside of the uterus. With the body unable to remove it, the dead fetus becomes covered in calcium as a form of protection, resulting in a stone baby.

FOREST FOOD Lost for 18 days in California's Mendocino National Forest, 72-year-old hiker Gene Penaflor of San Francisco, survived by eating squirrels, snakes and lizards.

NEW LOOK Rene Koiter, a 29-year-old graphic designer from Lake Forest, California, spent 10 months transforming himself into the terrifying Khal Drogo from the TV series *Game of Thrones*. He underwent vigorous workouts—pumping iron to build up his body muscles—grew his hair, and learned to mimic his character's speech and mannerisms. Rene was already fluent in five languages before he added Khal Drogo's fictional tribal dialect.

CLOWN FACE

NASAL TICK Tony Goldberg, a biology professor at the University of Wisconsin-Madison, discovered a new insect species—up his nose! He felt a pain in his nose three days after returning from a research trip to Uganda and used a pair of forceps to remove a previously unknown species of African tick, which had allegedly buried itself more than an inch (2.5 cm) deep in his nostril.

HANDLESS JUGGLER Jamie Andrew of Glasgow, Scotland, had all of his hands and feet amputated following a French mountaineering accident in 1999. However, despite his loss, he has continued climbing 19,000-ft-high (5,800-m) mountains and has taught himself to juggle.

Richie the Barber from West Hollywood, California, has the face of a clown tattooed over his own face.

Tattoos of big red eyebrows arch above the real ones he shaves daily, and he has a clown's red-nose tattoo, plus oversized red lips that protrude beneath his own mustache. The rest of his face is inked blue, including his ears and eyelids. On the sides of his head he is growing Bozo the Clown hair, which he has dyed bright red, and he has a tattoo of Bozo on the back of his head. He also has a third eye tattooed on his face, and the words "Good" and "Luck" inked on his eyelids.

05

CARDBOARD BOX OFFICE

A couple in Australia have recreated dozens of their favorite movie scenes using cardboard boxes and everyday junk.

When Leon Mackie, Lilly Lang and their baby son Orson moved from New Zealand to Sydney, they were left with a lot of boxes. So the movie buffs started Cardboard Box Office, where each week they would build a film set from old household materials and a few toys, and re-enact iconic scenes, usually with Orson taking center stage. When they posted the results online, the response was overwhelming.

Raiding their own wardrobes for costumes and building cheap props and sets, they tackled everything from *The Lion King* to *Pulp Fiction*. They built a cardboard rocket to represent *Apollo 13* and a Great White Shark for *Jaws*; the creature in *Alien* is a sock puppet with plastic teeth and the blood is made from red yarn.

As Orson is the star of the show, all of their works have baby-related titles, like *Kid Kong*, *Parents of the Caribbean*, *Fleece Willy*, *The Lord of the Teething Rings* and *The Good, The Bad and The Dribbly.*

Kid Kong

The Little Lebowski

The Dark Knighty-Knight

Bubbalien

Wah Wars

How do you choose the scenes you want to show? We just think of movies and, if they fit the requirements, we make them. Generally, the films need to be well known. They also need to have an iconic set, creature or vehicle.

Where do you create the scenes? In our house, but house lighting is terrible for photos because it nearly always comes from above and doesn't spread very far. We use lamps to highlight faces and shadowed parts of the sets. We now have a lot of lamps.

Is baby Orson easy to work with? Yeah, he's great. He never really makes a fuss. **Star Wars** was probably the most challenging. We needed Orson to look serious, but he kept laughing.

How long does each scene take to set up? It ranges from one to five hours, depending on how many props need to be made and the complexity of the set. The one that's taken the longest to set up to date has probably been **The Dark Knight** as we had to make each of the buildings in "Gotham City" by hand. It took hours.

Which is your favorite scene? Probably **Lord of the Rings.** The set, costumes and props all came together really well. I also especially like the lighting in that scene.

Lord of the Teething Rings

"Houston, We have a poopy..."

E.TED

The Lion Kid

Walk, Forrest, Walk!

"You're Gonna Need a Bigger Baby..."

The Birdies

Castababy

Parents of the Caribbean

Goonies Never Say Cry!

Vader Burner

Star Wars fan Alex Dodson from Barnsley, England, turns scrap metal into movie-themed fireplaces. His first creation was Darth Vader, and after getting a positive reaction on the Internet, the technology teacher is now making the fireplaces to order, using 42-lb (19-kg) metal gas bottles. As well as re-creating Darth Vader's iconic mask, the self-taught welder turns scrap metal into the "minions" from *Despicable Me*, and *Star Wars* stormtroopers.

AUTOGRAPH HUNTER Paul Schmelzer of Minneapolis, Minnesota, collects autographs with a difference—because he asks famous people to sign his name rather than theirs. More than 70 people have responded favorably to his request, "Can I have my autograph?" including Yoko Ono, architect Frank Gehry, and Dan Castellaneta, the voice of Homer Simpson.

ROLE MODELS When Japanese video game maker SEGA launched *Sonic the Hedgehog* in 1991, they gave him red-and-white sneakers based on a pair of boots worn by Michael Jackson. They modeled his adventurous character on future U.S. President Bill Clinton.

NATIONAL PRIDE For over 20 years, Brazilian lawyer Nelson Paviotti has worn only yellow, green, blue and white clothing—the colors of the country's soccer team. He had promised to wear the colors if Brazil won the 1994 World Cup, which they did. To add to the patriotic flavor, his office has yellow walls and his car is painted blue, yellow and green.

JACKSON TRIBUTE The 225-piece Ohio State University Marching Band moonwalked across the football field during half-time at an OSU game against Iowa in October 2013 while playing a selection of Michael Jackson hits and forming a giant silhouette of him.

CELEBRITY HUNTER New York City bar worker Vanessa Sky Ellis spends up to 12 hours a day hunting for celebrities and has had selfies taken with more than 10,000 stars, including Brad Pitt, Al Pacino, Katy Perry, Johnny Depp and Lady Gaga.

FLYING PHOBIA U.S. singer-songwriter R. Kelly had a 1996 hit with "I Believe I Can Fly," but he used to have a terrible fear of flying and would travel everywhere by boat.

WHEEL SCREENS For motorcyclists who want to personalize their rides, Thai company World Moto uses the latest technology to turn bike wheels into full-color, eye-catching LED TV screens. Each Wheelie has 424 LED lights mounted on an eight-spoke wheel, turning the wheel into a spinning screen, although amazingly the image appears static as the wheel turns. A computer tracks the wheel's speed and the position of each spoke, and also controls the lighting of the LEDs.

CHURCH REGULAR Martha Godwin became the pianist at Macedonia United Methodist Church in Southmont, North Carolina, in 1940 at age 13 and has held the position for more than 74 years.

FUTURISTIC DRESS Dutch designer Daan Roosegaarde has created a futuristic dress that becomes transparent if the wearer encounters someone they find attractive. The dress has leather strips that are embedded with electronic foils. Beneath the garment, tiny, hidden sensors are placed to detect changes in the wearer's body temperature and heart rate, and when those readings increase, the foils change the color of the dress.

CALIFORNIA DREAMIN' Rap duo Silibil N' Brains—Billy Boyd and Gavin Bain from Dundee, Scotland—posed as Californians for 4 ½ years, fooling record companies, partying with Madonna and touring with Eminem before their hoax was finally exposed.

LIVING COLOR

The drag queen and performer Detox made people look twice when he arrived at a celebrity event in Hollywood in May 2013, with ingenious make up creating the illusion that an old black-and-white movie star had arrived on the red carpet. He achieved the look using head-to-toe white paint and a silver wig to expertly re-create the gray effect of a genuine black-and-white photo.

Amazing paint job!

Ripley's Believe It or Not!®
www.ripleys.com/books
POP CULTURE

STREET JAM In 2013, a street musician from Berlin, Germany, was performing Bronski Beat's 1984 hit song "Smalltown Boy" and couldn't believe his eyes when Scotsman Jimmy Somerville, the former Bronski Beat frontman, wandered over and joined in. Somerville, 52, happened to be walking his dog in the area.

EARLY JOB Actor Tom Hanks once worked as a bellboy at the Hilton Hotel in his hometown of Oakland, California, and carried the luggage of stars such as Cher, Bill Withers and Sidney Poitier.

GAME PROPOSAL Robert Fink from Oregon City, Oregon, created a video game to propose to his girlfriend. He and two friends devised *Knight Man, A Quest For Love*, in which a knight collects a gold ring that he uses to propose to his princess. Robert proposed by asking his partner Angel White to test the game.

1,290 SHIRTS Between July 2011 and January 2015, Isac Walter from Los Angeles, California, wore a different rock band T-shirt for 1,290 consecutive days—without repeating a single band.

Famous Fingers

Mel Brooks

SEPT. 8 2014

Comedian Mel Brooks left his mark at the TCL Chinese theater in Hollywood in September 2014, where the hand and footprints of legendary celebrities are immortalized in concrete on the sidewalk.

The director of *Blazing Saddles* made sure his own prints would stand out by arriving with a fake sixth finger attached to his left hand, a trick that went unnoticed until he left a six-fingered imprint in the wet concrete.

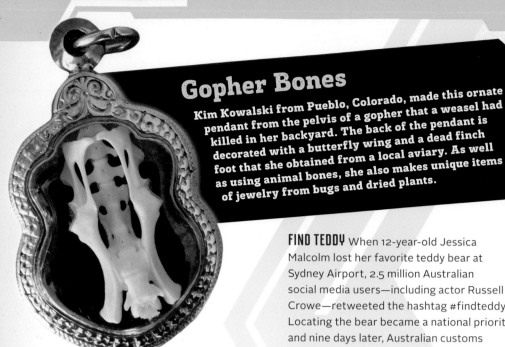

Gopher Bones

Kim Kowalski from Pueblo, Colorado, made this ornate pendant from the pelvis of a gopher that a weasel had killed in her backyard. The back of the pendant is decorated with a butterfly wing and a dead finch foot that she obtained from a local aviary. As well as using animal bones, she also makes unique items of jewelry from bugs and dried plants.

FACEBOOK MILESTONE Colombian singer-songwriter Shakira became the first person in the world to acquire 100 million fans on Facebook. If all of those fans were to join hands, they would wrap around the world four times. Seventeen percent of her fans are named Maria and 4 percent are José.

CONGRESS LIBRARY The U.S.A.'s Library of Congress has approximately 838 mi (1,348.63 km) of shelf space holding more than 151 million items.

FIND TEDDY When 12-year-old Jessica Malcolm lost her favorite teddy bear at Sydney Airport, 2.5 million Australian social media users—including actor Russell Crowe—retweeted the hashtag #findteddy. Locating the bear became a national priority and nine days later, Australian customs officials finally found Teddy and returned him to Jessica.

ROBOT NEWSREADER Japanese robotics professor Hiroshi Ishiguro has created the world's first newsreading android. His youthful-looking female robot, Kodomoroid, delivered a pitch-perfect report of an earthquake and an FBI raid to journalists at Tokyo's National Museum of Emerging Science and Innovation.

NONAGENARIAN ACTOR In December 2013, Romanian actor Radu Beligan starred in a French play, *The Egoist*, at the Metropolis Theater, Bucharest—at age 95. He made his stage debut in 1937 and has since appeared in almost 100 productions.

AUTO WRECKERS More than 500 cars were destroyed in the making of the 2011 movie *Transformers: Dark of the Moon*. All the cars were previously flood-damaged and therefore of no value.

TROLL DOLLS Ray Dyson of Edmonton, Alberta, has a collection of more than 1,750 troll dolls—including Viking trolls, biker trolls and elephant trolls.

ROYAL TREKKIE While still a prince, King Abdullah bin al-Hussein of Jordan appeared as an extra in a 1996 episode of *Star Trek: Voyager*. A huge fan of *Star Trek*, he asked his aides to arrange for him to make a cameo appearance as an unnamed, uncredited ensign briefly glimpsed in a corridor.

TOUGH WATCH The Kaventsmann Triggerfish bronze wristwatch, made in Germany, can withstand a blast from 10 lb (4.5 kg) of plastic explosives.

DEATH WISH Chuck Lamb from Galloway, Ohio, used to work as an IT engineer, but since 2005 he has been earning $1,500 a day playing corpses in movies and TV shows. He even has his own website, deadbodyguy.com. He says one of the reasons he makes a good corpse is because he is bald, meaning that any wig will fit him.

WORLD DANCE Three men from Dublin spent a year Irish dancing their way around the world, visiting 23 countries. Chris McGrath, Kevin Cobbe and Iain McNamara set off at the start of 2013 and danced in such iconic locations as the Amazon rain forest, the Machu Picchu Inca site in Peru, and Australia's Sydney Opera House.

BATTLE SURVIVORS English fantasy authors and friends C.S. Lewis and J.R.R. Tolkien, who wrote *The Chronicles of Narnia* and *The Lord of the Rings* respectively, both survived the bloody Battle of the Somme in World War I.

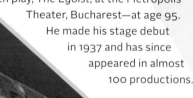

SIMPSONS TATTOO

Michael Baxter, a prison officer from Melbourne, Australia, has more than 200 characters from *The Simpsons* inked on his back. The 52-year-old grandfather spent $10,000 and 130 hours under the needle over the course of a year to get his giant tattoo, which also depicts locations from Springfield, including Moe's Tavern, the nuclear plant and the Simpson family's famous sofa.

SMELL PHONE Dr. David Edwards, a biomedical engineer at Harvard, has invented the oPhone, a device that enables you to send smells instead of texts. An app allows the user to compose and send a smell message by text or email, based on a set menu of over 300 different aromas, including coffee, chocolate and pizza, built into the device.

ANTIQUE BOOK A copy of the *Bay Psalms Book,* the first book printed in America, in 1640, was sold for $14.2 million in November 2013. Sold at Sotheby's auction house, the book is one of only 11 surviving copies.

PENNY PINCHING British actor David Suchet perfected the quick, mincing walk of Agatha Christie's fictional Belgian TV detective Hercule Poirot by clenching a penny coin between the cheeks of his butt and walking so that it didn't drop.

TOO CLEVER Essen-based School of Economics and Management, in Germany, sued its student Marcel Pohl for graduating too quickly. The university claimed loss of income after Pohl completed his bachelor's and master's degree studies in about a quarter of the time it takes most of its students to finish.

PEACE, LOVE AND POTATO SALAD Ohio's Zack "Danger" Brown won the Internet when his Kickstarter campaign to fund his first foray into making potato salad exceeded his goal of earning just $10—to the tune of more than $55,000! Zack used the cash he'd earned not only to make his salad, but also to throw a huge public party—which was dubbed PotatoStock 2014—benefitting hunger and homelessness charities.

COMFORT ZONE

Cinemagoers in Moscow, Russia, were able to watch a movie while lying in bed.

For two weeks in December 2014, furniture retailer IKEA ripped out all the traditional seats in one of the theaters at the Kinostar De Lux Multiplex in the suburb of Khimki and replaced them with its own furniture, including 17 double beds. The bed sheets were changed by the staff after each screening.

ODD TOGETHER NOW

CONGRESS of FREAKS with RINGLING BR

POP PLATES

Los Angeles, California, artist Angela Rossi buys "orphaned and unloved" decorative, vintage plates and turns them into fun, contemporary pop artworks by applying portraits of cult TV and movie characters and icons.

Using a special heat technique, she seals onto the plates images of the likes of Yoda and R2-D2 from *Star Wars*, Mr T from *The A-Team*, and the Starship Enterprise.

Couples compete in a marathon event on a ship off the coast of California. The dance was halted by authorities concerned for the health of participants.

Competitors showing the strain during a dance marathon in Washington, D.C., in 1924.

Some dance contests, known as "walkathons," resembled modern marathon races, with dancers traveling several miles between locations on public roads. In 1927 hundreds of couples danced 20 mi (32 km) around Los Angeles in California, accompanied by an orchestra on wheels.

The Ringling Brothers and Barnum & Bailey Circus ran a successful sideshow in the 1920s and 30s featuring some of the most famous oddities and performers of the era.

Each year, the renowned New York photographer Edward J. Kelty, who specialized in capturing images of the circus, would gather together the sideshow acts, at what he called the "Congress of Freaks," for a photograph at Madison Square Garden, New York City. The 1927 ensemble included more than 35 bizarre characters, including circus legends such as Major Mite the dwarf, giant Jack Earle, and Lionel the dog-faced boy.

ERS AND BARNUM & BAILEY COMBINED CIRCUS.

SEASON — 1927

1. Lady Olga, Bearded Lady

Born Jane Barnell in North Carolina in 1871 with a hairy face, Lady Olga was sold to a showman by her mother and toured with sideshows from a very young age. She performed in at least 25 circuses, and appeared alongside other sideshow stars in the 1932 movie *Freaks*. Despite her unconventional appearance, she married four times.

2. Daisy Earles, the Dancing Doll Family

Harry, Gracie, Daisy and Tiny, were born Kurt, Frieda, Hilda and Elly Schneider in Germany in the early 20th century. Gracie and Harry were taken to California by Bert W. Earles, where they joined a Wild West Show in 1916, changing their names and taking Earles' name. Later joined by the rest of the family, they performed with the Ringling Brothers and Barnum & Bailey Circus for 30 years, riding horses and singing and dancing. All four appeared as Munchkins in the 1939 film *The Wizard of Oz*, and Harry and Gracie played significant parts in the 1932 horror movie *Freaks*. Tiny was the last member of the group to die, aged 90, in 2004.

3. Giant Jim Tarver

Jim Tarver, born 1885 in Texas, was described as being 8 ft 6 in (2.6 m) tall, but 7 ft 3 in (2.2 m) is more likely. He performed for several circuses, and was billed as the "tallest man in the world" until Jack Earle (see 17) visited the sideshow and discovered he was even taller!

4. Baron Paucci

Baron Paucci, who stood only 27 in (69 cm) tall, was born in Sicily, Italy, in 1894. He performed at Lilliputia—a town full of little people—in Coney Island, New York, for 15 years. He was infamous for his drinking and outrageous behavior, which eventually led to him leaving Lilliputia and joining the Ringling Circus sideshow. Baron Paucci married a woman of normal size, but unfortunately their marriage was short-lived.

5. & 15. Carlson Sisters

Flo and Dot Carlson were billed as the "Boxing Fat Girls" and would spar on stage.

6. "Twisto the Human Knot" Contortionist

7. Lillian Maloney, Fairy Airy

Lillian Maloney was a glamorous albino Irish woman, characterized by her bright hair and pale skin. At the time, albinism was not a well-known condition and was regarded as a curiosity.

8. Clico, "The Wild Dancing South African Bushman"

Clico was a South African tribesman whose real name was Franz Taibosh. His stage name was inspired by the clicks he used in his native language. Franz's talent for dancing was noticed by Irish settler, Paddy Hepston, who was working in South Africa, and he took Clico to England in 1915 to work as a dancer. He was a sensation and soon caught the attention of American impresarios. He joined Sam Gumpertz's Coney Island sideshow before touring with the Ringling Brothers for many years. He died aged 83 in 1940 in New York.

9. Tiny Earles, the Dancing Doll Family (see 2)

10. Miss Londy

Eleanor Wagner was over 7 ft (2.1 m) tall, although she was sometimes billed as being more than 8 ft (2.4 m) tall. She performed at Coney Island, New York, and was known as the "Viennese Giantess," the "German Giantess" and "Miss Londy."

11. Major Mite

Standing 26 in (0.7 m) tall and weighing only 20 lb (9 kg), Major Mite was one of the most famous midget performers of the era. The Ringling Brothers and Barnum & Bailey Circus signed him up in 1923, when he was just ten years old, and he starred in the sideshow for more than 25 years. As well as his successful circus career, Major Mite (whose real name was Clarence Chesterfield Howerton) was one of the smallest Munchkins in the movie *The Wizard of Oz* (1939), and had several other Hollywood roles. He died in 1975, aged 62 years old.

12. Koo-Koo

Koo-Koo the "Bird Girl," born Minnie Woolsey in Georgia in 1880, was part of the Ringling Brothers circus sideshow for many years.

Ripley's Believe It or Not!®
www.ripleys.com/books
POP CULTURE

13. Haig, the Elastic Skin Man

14. The Mighty Ajax, Sword Swallower
Joseph Milana was born in Washington D.C. in 1886, and enjoyed a long career. As a young man he toured with Buffalo Bill's Wild West Show and once performed for King George V of England. He spent years at the Dreamland Circus sideshow at Coney Island and was only with the Ringling Circus for the 1927 season.

15. Carlson Sister (see 5)

16. Harry Earles, the Dancing Doll Family (see 2)

17. Giant Jack Earle
Jack Earle, born in 1906, stood 7 ft 7 in (2.3 m) tall, and had a career in the movies until the tumor that caused his extreme height resulted in problems with his eyesight. He performed with the sideshow from the 1920s to 1940.

18. Gracie Earles, the Dancing Doll Family (see 2)

19. Miss Kitty, the Armless Wonder
Kitty Smith was born into poverty in Chicago in 1882, and both her arms were amputated at the age of nine after being badly burned. The young Kitty learned to draw, selling her autobiography and drawings to support herself, and eventually found work on the sideshow circuit, performing at Coney Island and the Ringling Circus sideshow.

20. Professor Henri, India-Rubber Man
Professor Henri's real name was Clarence H. Alexander. He spent more than 20 years in sideshows as a contortionist who could reportedly stretch his neck 7 in (18 cm) and his arms and legs out by 12 in (30 cm). Tragically, he killed himself on stage because of his unrequited love for the tattooed lady Miss Mae Vandermark (see 23).

21. Freddie Esele, the Armless Wonder
Born without arms in New York in 1888, Freddie was a fixture on the circus sideshow circuit for many years.

22. Jolly Irene
Irene was said to weigh almost 700 lb (318 kg) and also performed at Coney Island.

23. Miss Mae Vandermark, Tattooed Woman
Born in Pennsylvania, Mae Vandermark Patton trained as a stenographer, but moved to New York in search of adventure. She befriended the tattooed lady Miss Pictoria (see 33), who persuaded her to join the profession, and "Professor" Wagner of the Bowery, New York, completed her full body tattoos in less than a year. She got a job at Coney Island before landing the role with the Ringling Brothers, marrying a man in the circus business and spending more than 30 years on the road.

24. Unknown

25. & 26. Sadie and Rosie Anderson, "The Spotted Women"
African-Americans with vitiligo, which causes the skin to turn white in places, were often exhibited as "leopard" or "spotted" people. Sadie, Rosie and other members of the Anderson family were exhibited in sideshows from an early age, and both girls had long careers with touring circuses.

27. Lionel the Dog-Faced Boy
Lionel, the Lion-Faced Man, or Dog-Faced Boy, was born in Poland in 1891 as Stephan Bibrowski. His entire body was covered in long, thick hair, which he claimed was caused by his mother seeing his father killed by a lion while she was pregnant. It is far more likely that he suffered from hypertrichosis, sometimes known as "werewolf disease." Lionel was famous at Coney Island during the 1920s, where he performed a gymnastic act at the Dreamland Circus sideshow.

28. Tom Ton
Tom Ton, a stage name used for more than one sideshow performer, weighed 645 lb (293 kg) at the age of 21.

29. Ho-Jo, the Bear Boy

30. Madame Adrienne, Bearded Lady
Madame Adrienne's real name was Adele Kis, and she was born in Hungary in 1884. She was married to a circus lion tamer. Adele was touring America when a rival performer cut off her beard while she was sleeping. Adele successfully sued for thousands of dollars in damages.

31. & 32. Eko and Iko, the Albino Twins
Eko and Iko, black albino twins, were kidnapped in 1899 by sideshow bounty hunters for their unique appearance. They were variously known as the "Ecuadorian Cannibals," the "Sheep-Headed Men" and the "Ambassadors from Mars," and played saxophone and guitar on stage. They toured unpaid until 1927, the year of this photograph, when their mother tracked them down and demanded that they be freed from performing. They were freed, but soon returned to sideshows with a contract that ensured them a great deal of money, and they played venues such as Madison Square Garden to more than 10,000 people. They toured the world in the 1930s, performing for the Queen of England among others, and returned to the U.S.A. to perform right up until 1961.

33. Miss Pictoria
Billed as the "Human Art Gallery," Victoria James was a well-known tattooed lady in the 1920s and 30s. Her extensive tattoos, like those of Mae Vandermark, were drawn by "Professor" Charles Wagner in New York.

34. "Baby Bunny"
Helen "Baby Bunny" Smith left school to work on sideshows as a fat lady who claimed to weigh over 500 lb (227 kg). She married the "skeleton man" Peter Robinson (see 35) and the unlikely pair became minor celebrities.

35. "Skeleton Man"
Born in 1874, Peter Robinson was said to weigh only 50 lb (26.68 kg). He met his future wife, the "fat girl" Baby Bunny (see 34) in 1919, and they would dance together on stage. A 1924 newspaper described him as "one of the biggest moneymakers in the business," owing to the rarity of "human skeletons," and he spent more than a quarter of century in the circus.

36. King Roy, the Scottish Albino
King Roy, also billed as a contortionist, was the son of Rob Roy—a famous albino who performed for the Barnum and Bailey Circus in the 19th century—and Annie Roy, a sword swallower. He is said to have had six albino children.

HAPPY MEALS

Mike Fountaine has spent almost half a century collecting more than 75,000 items of McDonald's memorabilia, including cups, uniforms, Happy Meal toys and even a giant Ronald McDonald. He started his collection in 1969 with a pin badge when he was 16 and his paraphernalia now fills nine rooms and more than 2 mi (3 km) of shelving at his home in Allentown, Pennsylvania. The collection has become so big that he has had to build a separate 2,400-sq-ft (223 sq m) barn to house everything.

FASHION VICTIM Mahbub Ali Khan (1866–1911), ruler of Hyderabad, India, never wore the same clothes twice and owned a walk-in closet 120 ft (36.6 m) long.

LONG WAIT In August 2014, English singer Kate Bush played her first concert in 35 years. Although she recorded eight studio albums during that time, she had not performed live since her first and only tour ended in 1979.

SILENT GIGS U.K. death metal band Unfathomable Ruination played a series of 2014 London gigs inside an airtight, soundproof steel box—so that nobody could see or hear them—until the oxygen inside ran out, usually after about 15 minutes. The 6-ft (1.8-m) cube was an art installation by a Portuguese artist named Joäo Onofre.

DONKEY CHARGERS To stay connected to the Internet, village herdsmen in Izmir, Turkey, strap solar panels to the backs of their donkeys and use them as mobile charging points. The farmers stay online during their long overland journeys by plugging their laptop or phone charger into the panels, which can produce up to 7 kilowatts of energy—enough to charge more than 1,000 cell phones.

WHISTLESTOP TOUR U.S. country music star Hunter Hayes played ten shows in ten cities in just 24 hours. He began in New York at 8.17 a.m. on May 9, 2014, then moved on to Boston and Worcester, Massachusetts; Providence, Rhode Island; New London, New Haven and Stamford, Connecticut; South Orange and Asbury Park, New Jersey; and finally, at daybreak on May 10, he performed in Philadelphia, Pennsylvania.

HAIR STRINGS Lithuanian violinist Eimantas Belickas played a tune on a violin that had strings made of human hair. The long hair of Tadas Maksimovas was divided into strips, hardened with resin and stretched along the length of the violin while still attached to his head.

13,450 FT WEDDING GOWN

A bridal gown measuring a staggering 13,450 ft (4,100 m) in length winds back and forth for nearly 3 mi (4.82 km) across a flower field in Chengdu, China. The 5-ft-wide (1.5-m) gown took a month to make and was priced at almost $7,000.

JEDI RAZOR The handheld communicator that Liam Neeson's character, Jedi master Qui-Gon Jinn, uses in the 1999 movie *Star Wars: The Phantom Menace* is based on a Gillette Sensor Excel female razor.

TWIN SUIT Hot on the heels of the craze for wearing all-in-one suits known as "onesies," a company in Lancashire, England, marketed a "twinsie"—an outfit for two people. It has three legs, four arms and two hoods and is sold as being ideal for couples who want to keep warm together in winter.

SURPRISE ENDING A performance of the musical *Peter Pan: The Never Ending Story* in Glasgow, Scotland, in 2014 had a surprise ending when the actor playing Peter Pan proposed for real to the actress playing Wendy. Dutchman Sandor Sturbl popped the question on stage to Scottish actress Lilly-Jane Young. To a chorus of cheers from the audience, she accepted.

KFC NECKLACE Lexington, Kentucky, jewelry designer Meg C has created a range of gold necklaces from discarded KFC chicken bones. She cleans and dries the bones, coats them with varnish, covers them in copper and then has them electroplated in gold.

FLYING QUARTET German composer Karlheinz Stockhausen wrote a piece to be played by a string quartet in four hovering helicopters. The music was first performed in the skies above Amsterdam, the Netherlands, in 1995.

FLOWER POWER Experiments conducted by British horticultural students show that plants thrive when played heavy metal music—particularly by the band Black Sabbath—developing larger flowers and becoming more resistant to disease.

CHOCOLATE DISK Croatian rock star Gibonni released a version of his 2013 album *20th Century Man* made entirely of chocolate. Both the record and the label are edible—and the disk actually plays.

MUSIC FITS Zoe Fennessy, from Nottinghamshire, England, suffers epileptic seizures whenever she hears a song by American R&B star Ne-Yo. Surgery to remove a large chunk of her left temporal lobe has failed to cure the problem, so she has to wear earphones when she goes out in case one of his songs is played in a store.

ICE CASTLE Over a period of three weeks, 60 ice sculptors from 12 countries used shovels, hatchets, saws and 600 tons of water to create Disney icons—including Captain Hook, Peter Pan, Snow White and Alice in Wonderland, and Sleeping Beauty's entire castle—from ice at the 2014 Disney Dreams Ice Festival in Belgium.

ICEBERG GIG

British rock band The Defiled played the world's first-ever gig on a floating iceberg. They performed for 30 minutes on the berg in the middle of the Greenland Sea—while their audience watched from a flotilla of fishing boats. It took several days to find an iceberg that was sufficiently large and thick enough to hold the four-man band and all their equipment, which was plugged into an electricity generator.

BIRD WATCHING The population of the world has collectively spent more than 200,000 years playing *Angry Birds*—about the same length of time that modern humans have existed.

PAPER PRODUCER Finnish cell phone company Nokia, founded in 1865, was best known for making toilet paper up until the 1980s. It used to supply the U.K. with 30 percent of its toilet paper needs.

SHOE FUND U.S. actor Conrad Cantzen (1867–1945) bequeathed his estate to a fund that still helps "down-at-heel actors" buy new shoes for auditions. He left $226,608.34 to establish the Conrad Cantzen Shoe Fund, and in the first ten years alone it filled more than 7,000 requisitions for shoes.

MINI ME To attract the attention of potential employers, freelance photographer Jens Lennartsson from Malmo, Sweden, enhanced his resumé by mailing out 400 ten-in-high (25-cm) plastic models of himself.

SELFIE SPREE Mark E. Miller and Ethan Hethcote took 355 selfies in an hour at South Beach, Miami, Florida—with a different person in each picture.

Carved Crayons

California artist Hoang Tran hand carves beautifully detailed images of characters from *Star Wars*, *Game of Thrones*, *Doctor Who* and *Breaking Bad* into the tips of ordinary wax crayons. The former dentist uses his old dental tools to do the carving and sometimes adds melted wax from different colored crayons to make the sculptures more realistic.

DANCING BANANA When she was 15, future Hollywood star Megan Fox had a job where she used to dance in the street wearing a giant banana costume to attract customers to a smoothie bar in Florida.

ZOO JEANS A new line of distressed jeans has been "designed" by lions, tigers and bears. To raise funds for the Kamine Zoo in Hitachi, Japan, volunteers wrap the animals' favorite toys in a sheet of denim and let them rip it apart. Humans then collect what remains of the denim and cut and sew it into shape to form a pair of unique Zoo Jeans.

FAVORITE FILM *101 Dalmatians* fan Nelson Vergara of Santiago, Chile, loved the Disney movie so much he didn't just paint black spots on his white van, he also adopted more than 40 real Dalmatians!

FOOD FASCINATORS

Israeli designer Maor Zabar uses felt, plastic and wire to create amazingly realistic models of food dishes, which he then fixes to hats. His fashionable designs include a berry pie beret, a salad sombrero, a prawn salad fascinator and even a hat in the shape of an inverted, melting ice-cream cone.

PROFITABLE LUNCH During one lunch in 1994, Pixar creatives John Lasseter, Pete Docter and Joe Ranft came up with the ideas that would eventually become the hit movies *A Bug's Life*, *Finding Nemo*, *Monsters Inc.* and *WALL-E*.

MAGNETIC SHOES Inspired by comic book character Magneto, inventor Colin Furze from Lincolnshire, England, created a pair of magnetic shoes that enable him to walk upside-down along metal ceilings. He built the magnet in the shoes using a microwave transformer, with one of the coils removed, and hooked it up to a car battery. Then, he placed the transformer on a shoe-shaped plate and clamped his foot to it before attaching straps to the shoes with switches, which power the flow of electricity and allow him to walk. His only fear was that if there were a sudden power outage while he was walking on the ceiling, he would fall off.

DOG SHOW Every Thursday at 3 p.m., BBC London 94.9 presents *Barking at the Moon*, the world's only weekly radio show for dogs. It is hosted by dog lovers Jo Good and Anna Webb and their dogs Matilda (an English bulldog) and Molly (a miniature bull terrier). The show has over half a million listeners, from as far away as Hawaii and Australia.

DOUBLE LIFE For part of the year Sonia Gill is a Bollywood superstar in India having starred in five blockbuster movies and numerous TV ads, and having legions of fans—but for the rest of the year she works at Oxfordshire County Council in England, issuing parking permits.

HIGH HEELS High-heeled shoes known as *chopines*, some 18 in (45 cm) high, were worn in 16th-century Venice by women as a sign of status—and also to help keep their feet dry when the Venetian canals flooded.

SMURF LOVER Karen Bell from Ayrshire, Scotland, has been collecting *Smurf* figurines and stickers for over 30 years—and now has about 5,000 pieces of *Smurf* memorabilia.

KEEN COLLECTOR Bill McBride, from Washington, D.C., has spent more than $270,000 on building up a collection of over 60,000 items of Darth Vader memorabilia. The *Star Wars* fan has been collecting figurines, artwork and replica lightsabers since the 1980s and even rejected the offer of a real Porsche 911 sports car in exchange for a few of his most select pieces.

Ripley's Believe It or Not!®
www.ripleys.com/books
POP CULTURE

EVER PRESENT Canadian musician Bruce Rickerd played guitar in 10,000 consecutive performances of *Mystère* in Las Vegas, Nevada, between 1993 and 2014, never missing a single show in 21 years.

➜ AS ALL SNOWFLAKES ARE UNIQUE, THE TEAM WORKING ON DISNEY'S *FROZEN* BUILT SOFTWARE TO CREATE 2,000 DIFFERENT SNOWFLAKES FOR THE MOVIE.

TWO NOTES German vocalist Anna-Maria Hefele can sing two notes at once. The eerie technique is called "polyphonic-overtone singing" and allows her to sustain a constant low note while simultaneously singing a high-pitched scale.

BABY SELFIES A new crib mobile toy allows babies to take selfies and post the results on Facebook and Twitter. New Born Fame, created by Dutch designer Laura Cornet, features soft toys shaped as a Facebook logo and a Twitter bird, which automatically take a picture or video when the youngster reaches for them.

PEAK PLAYER William Cruz, from Provo, Utah, played the video game *Far Cry 4* for 79 minutes on the summit of the 18,569-ft-high (5,660-m) Himalayan mountain Kala Patthar in freezing temperatures of −17°F (−8°C).

Japanese shoe designer Masaya Kushino has created a range of high-heeled footwear inspired by a rooster.

With their metal claw heels, beak-like toes, and uppers made out of feathers and brocade, his "Bird-Witched" stiletto designs certainly look unusual, but he insists they are perfectly wearable.

FLYING CHOP To promote his book *Meatspace*, author Nikesh Shukla launched a lamb chop into space from a field in Gloucestershire, England. Attached to a fork hanging from a weather balloon, the chop soared 82,000 ft (25,000 m) high before the balloon burst, sending it plunging back to Earth.

BLIND CRITIC Since 2011, Tommy Edison, from Milford, Connecticut, has reviewed dozens of movies on YouTube even though he is unable to see any of them because he was born blind. Instead he judges each movie on what he hears, and his videos have proved so popular that they have racked up more than a million views combined.

BEACH BOX Brian Wilson, lead member rock band The Beach Boys, once had a giant sandbox built around the piano in his house so that he could feel sand beneath his feet, which he believed would provide inspiration for his song writing.

ROOSTER SHOES

FANTASY WEDDING

Kerry Ford and Darren Prew enjoyed a *Game of Thrones*–themed wedding at Eastnor Castle, Herefordshire, England, dressing up as characters from the TV series for a ceremony that was attended by wolves, wildings and white walkers. The bride arrived on a white horse and the couple sliced their five-tier wedding cake, which featured a chocolate crown, with a 4-ft-long (1.2-m) broadsword.

EXPENSIVE GUM A piece of KISS front man Gene Simmons' used chewing gum from his appearance on the U.K. TV sports show *Soccer AM* in September 2013 attracted 29 bids on eBay, eventually selling for £210 ($317) in aid of charity.

KEEN TREKKIE Line Rainville, a social worker from Notre-Dame-des-Prairies, Quebec, is such a massive *Star Trek* fan that she has spent $30,000 to create a replica of the *Enterprise* spaceship—complete with bridge, transporter room and observation deck—in her basement. It took her over a year sourcing the Internet for items.

FAMOUS LOGO Nike paid designer Carolyn Davidson, then a student at Portland State University, Oregon, $35 for their famous swoosh logo in 1971, with Nike cofounder Phil Knight saying of the design: "I don't love it, but maybe it will grow on me."

HOBBIT VILLAGE *Lord of the Rings* fan Svatoslav Hofman, a student from Orlickych Horach, Czech Republic, has created his own accurate, replica Hobbit-sized village, complete with a pub—and he did it all from memory.

LITERARY TUSK A narwhal whale tusk was engraved with the name Cornelius Fudge—the same name as the Minister for Magic in the *Harry Potter* books—over a century before author J.K. Rowling first wrote about the boy wizard. The tusk's owner, John Jeffries from Cornwall, England, assumed that Rowling must have somehow heard of sailor Cornelius Fudge, to whom it was originally presented in 1881, but she said she had made the name up and that it was just an amazing coincidence. The ivory with literary links sold at an auction for $60,000 in 2013.

Pringles Spider

The Kidney Garden Spider (*Araneus mitificus*) of Asia gets its name from the dark, kidney-shaped marking on its abdomen—but to many people its markings look just like the Pringles man! However, the arachnid prefers to eat flies and bugs rather than Pringles.

WALKING BACKWARD French TV screened a nine-hour-long program showing Parisian director Ludovic Zuili walking backward through the busy streets of Tokyo, Japan. However, the film, *Tokyo Reverse*, was shown backward so that it looked as if Zuili was the only person walking normally.

HIGH CULTURE On April 23, 2014, British actors Simon Cole, Gary Fannin and William Meredith, members of the Reduced Shakespeare Company, performed a selection of the Bard's plays at an altitude of 37,000 ft on board a flight from Gatwick, West Sussex, to Verona, Italy. Using the length of the airplane as their stage, they performed the "Shakes on a Plane" routine for almost an hour to mark the 450th anniversary of Shakespeare's birth.

CONFETTI PARADE When astronaut John Glenn returned from 1962's Mercury 6 mission, 3,474 tons of confetti were thrown during a New York City parade in his honor.

HOT HIT Sammy Cahn and Jule Styne wrote the song "Let It Snow! Let It Snow! Let It Snow!" in Los Angeles, California, on one of the hottest days of the summer of 1945.

POP PLATES

Los Angeles, California, artist Angela Rossi buys "orphaned and unloved" decorative, vintage plates and turns them into fun, contemporary pop artworks by applying portraits of cult TV and movie characters and icons.

Using a special heat technique, she seals onto the plates images of the likes of Yoda and R2-D2 from *Star Wars*, Mr T from *The A-Team*, and the Starship Enterprise.

Couples compete in a marathon event on a ship off the coast of California. The dance was halted by authorities concerned for the health of participants.

Competitors showing the strain during a dance marathon in Washington, D.C., in 1924.

Some dance contests, known as "walkathons," resembled modern marathon races, with dancers traveling several miles between locations on public roads. In 1927 hundreds of couples danced 20 mi (32 km) around Los Angeles in California, accompanied by an orchestra on wheels.

DANCE MARATHONS

On April 1, 1931, in a Chicago ballroom, exhausted dancers Mike Ritof and Edith Boudreaux struggled to stay on their feet after winning an epic dance contest.

Since the event began on August 29, 1930, they had danced nonstop for an unbelievable 5,154 hours 48 minutes—that's 214 days, or seven months. Couples were required to remain in motion for 45 minutes every hour. During the 15-minute rest period, men and women retired to separate sleeping quarters for a nap. Any dancer who failed to wake up in time was either slapped or dunked in a tub of ice water.

PHOTOS SOLD HERE MADE BY

'Rdm' Studio

OPEN DAY & NIGHT.

A dancer supports his sleeping dance partner at a 1930 Chicago dance marathon. If a competitor's knees touched the floor, they were disqualified. Contestants used a range of tricks to keep each other awake and upright, including pinpricks, pinching, smelling salts and ice packs. In extreme cases exhausted partners were fastened together with chains to prevent them drifting apart.

HEDGEHOG SUPERSTAR

The Japanese owner of Marutaro the hedgehog has created an Internet sensation with his website, hedgehogblog.com. He posts daily selfies of the animal to his 78,000 Twitter fans, adding homemade expression sticks so that followers can see his imagined emotions. Marutaro also has a Tumblr calendar, a YouTube channel and a Vine account where more than 115,000 followers watch videos of his eventful encounters with brushes and pinecones, which he appears to think are other hedgehogs.

BEARS' AUTOGRAPHS Superfan Glenn Timmerman has 126 autographs of Chicago Bears players past and present tattooed on his body. He started in 2005 when he met former Bear Otis Wilson and asked him to sign his body. Timmerman then drove straight to his favorite tattoo parlor and had Wilson's signature inked permanently into his skin.

KING PONG Frank Lee, a professor at Drexel University, Philadelphia, Pennsylvania, played a supersized version of the trailblazing 1972 video game Pong on the side of a city skyscraper. He re-created the classic Atari game on the 29-story Cira Centre, turning it into a 60,000-ft-sq (5,575-sq-m) screen as hundreds of embedded LED lights replicated the game's ball and paddles, which were controlled by a joystick about a mile away.

HISTORIC VIOLIN The violin that was played to calm passengers as the *Titanic* sank in the North Atlantic in 1912 sold for $1.45 million in just 10 minutes at a 2013 auction in Wiltshire, England. It was played by the doomed ship's bandleader, Wallace Hartley, who died along with 1,517 others. The violin survived in a leather case found strapped to Hartley's body and was eventually returned to his fiancée, Maria Robinson.

MISSING LETTER Los Angeles, California, rap artist Andrew Thomas Huang has recorded a song "Rap Without The Letter E"—which lasts 2 minutes 39 seconds and in which none of the lyrics contain the letter "e."

FONDUE FOOTWEAR Inspired by people dipping vegetables into melted cheese, Japanese designer Satsuki Ohata has created fondue footwear. By dipping his or her feet one at a time into colorful melted PVC, the wearer creates an exact foot mold. Once dry, the mold can be peeled off and on.

VIRTUAL GIRLFRIEND Matt Homann from St. Louis, Missouri, has launched an app to help single people convince friends and family that they really have a partner. The app, *Invisible Girlfriend*, provides virtual phone calls, voicemails, random gifts and even a Facebook relationship.

TRACTOR ORCHESTRA A contemporary music festival in Valencia, Spain, opened with a 30-minute piece played by 12 farm tractors. Swedish conductor Sven-Ake Johansson led the four-wheeled orchestra through a range of diesel-engined whines, groans and roars.

FRIENDS REUNITED When young Phoebe Simpson from Yorkshire, England, accidentally left her favorite teddy bear, Roar, on a train in London, she feared she would never see him again—but passenger Lauren Bishop Vranch found the bear and launched a campaign on Twitter and Facebook, which soon reunited Roar with his owner.

SEWER CONCERT The sewerage system of Cologne, Germany, hosts jazz and classical music concerts. Built by the Romans in the 1st century A.D., the system's Kronleuchtersaal space was later fitted with chandeliers and can accommodate audiences of up to 50 people.

Text Lane

To reduce the number of collisions among pedestrians while they are texting on cell phones, the Chinese city of Chongqing has opened a street lane designated solely for people who walk while texting. The sidewalk has been divided into two lanes —one for phone users, the other for nonusers.

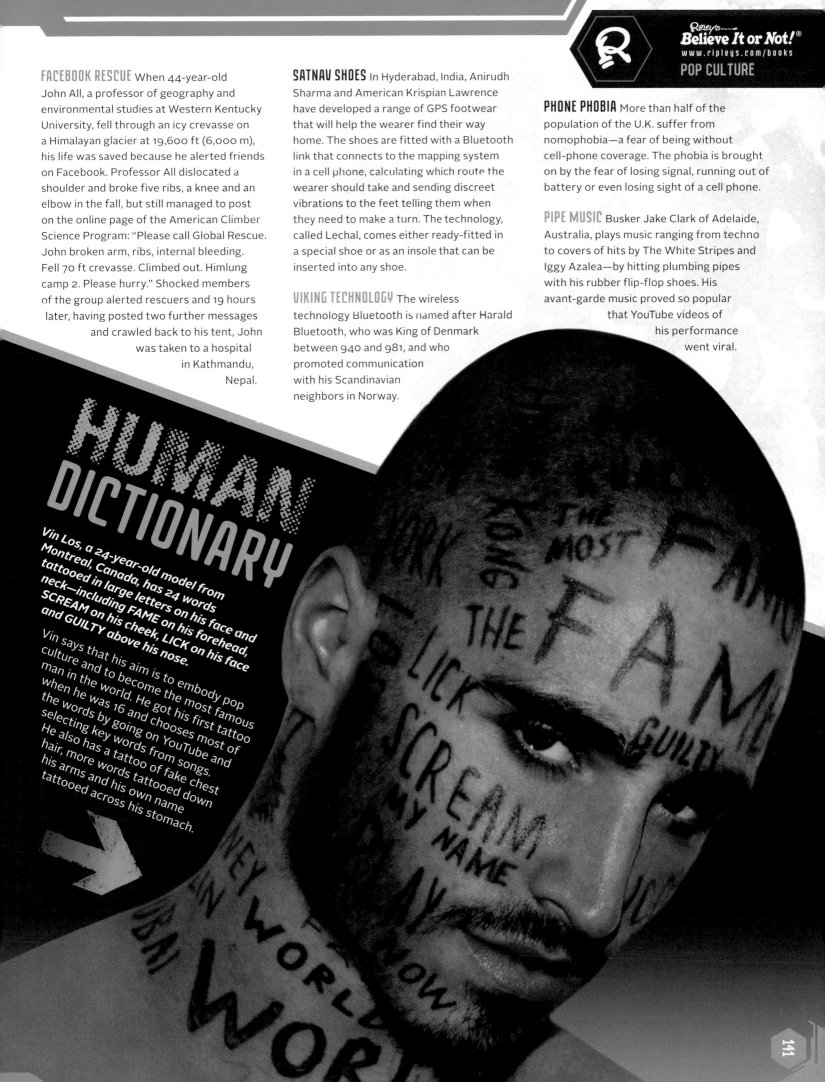

FACEBOOK RESCUE When 44-year-old John All, a professor of geography and environmental studies at Western Kentucky University, fell through an icy crevasse on a Himalayan glacier at 19,600 ft (6,000 m), his life was saved because he alerted friends on Facebook. Professor All dislocated a shoulder and broke five ribs, a knee and an elbow in the fall, but still managed to post on the online page of the American Climber Science Program: "Please call Global Rescue. John broken arm, ribs, internal bleeding. Fell 70 ft crevasse. Climbed out. Himlung camp 2. Please hurry." Shocked members of the group alerted rescuers and 19 hours later, having posted two further messages and crawled back to his tent, John was taken to a hospital in Kathmandu, Nepal.

SATNAV SHOES In Hyderabad, India, Anirudh Sharma and American Krispian Lawrence have developed a range of GPS footwear that will help the wearer find their way home. The shoes are fitted with a Bluetooth link that connects to the mapping system in a cell phone, calculating which route the wearer should take and sending discreet vibrations to the feet telling them when they need to make a turn. The technology, called Lechal, comes either ready-fitted in a special shoe or as an insole that can be inserted into any shoe.

VIKING TECHNOLOGY The wireless technology Bluetooth is named after Harald Bluetooth, who was King of Denmark between 940 and 981, and who promoted communication with his Scandinavian neighbors in Norway.

PHONE PHOBIA More than half of the population of the U.K. suffer from nomophobia—a fear of being without cell-phone coverage. The phobia is brought on by the fear of losing signal, running out of battery or even losing sight of a cell phone.

PIPE MUSIC Busker Jake Clark of Adelaide, Australia, plays music ranging from techno to covers of hits by The White Stripes and Iggy Azalea—by hitting plumbing pipes with his rubber flip-flop shoes. His avant-garde music proved so popular that YouTube videos of his performance went viral.

HUMAN DICTIONARY

Vin Los, a 24-year-old model from Montreal, Canada, has 24 words tattooed in large letters on his face and neck—including FAME on his forehead, SCREAM on his cheek, LICK on his face and GUILTY above his nose.

Vin says that his aim is to embody pop culture and to become the most famous man in the world. He got his first tattoo when he was 16 and chooses most of the words by going on YouTube and selecting key words from songs. He also has a tattoo of fake chest hair, more words tattooed down his arms and his own name tattooed across his stomach.

06

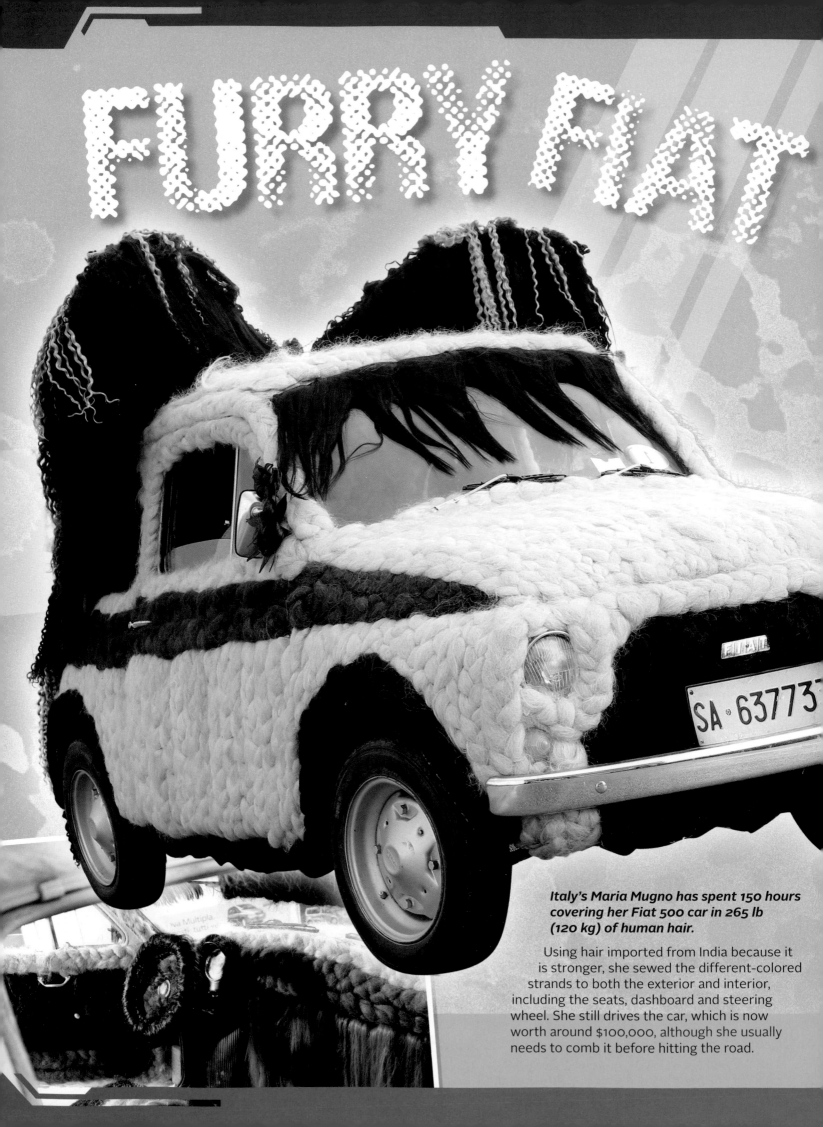

FURRY FIAT

Italy's Maria Mugno has spent 150 hours covering her Fiat 500 car in 265 lb (120 kg) of human hair.

Using hair imported from India because it is stronger, she sewed the different-colored strands to both the exterior and interior, including the seats, dashboard and steering wheel. She still drives the car, which is now worth around $100,000, although she usually needs to comb it before hitting the road.

SA · 637737

POOP BUS ➜

A bus powered by human poop has gone into service between the English cities of Bath and Bristol. The 40-seater, environmentally friendly Bio-Bus runs on gas generated through the treatment of sewage and food waste. The annual waste produced by one busload of passengers would provide enough power for it to travel the length of Britain and back—a distance of 1,760 mi (2,832 km).

This GENeco Bio-Bus is powered by your waste for a sustainable future GENeco

PUMPKIN VOYAGE Artist Dmitri Galitzine from London, England, sailed 4 mi (6.4 km) across the Solent seaway from Hampshire to the Isle of Wight in a boat made from an 800-lb (363-kg) pumpkin. The voyage took him nearly two hours in the hollowed-out pumpkin, which was fitted with a small outboard motor.

PLANE HIKER Since July 2012, New York travel writer Amber Nolan has been hitching rides on private aircraft across the U.S.A. She has visited nearly every one of the 50 states and more than 250 towns and cities.

MOOSE BEWARE One in five road accidents in Sweden involves a moose. The accidents occur mostly at dawn or sunset and are caused because the heavy animals are capable of running at over 30 mph (48 km/h).

BURIED FERRARI In 1978, cops working on a tip dug in the mud outside a house in Los Angeles' West Athens district and uncovered a dark green Ferrari Dino 246 GTS completely buried in the soil. Investigators revealed that the car, which was in surprisingly good condition and would be worth over $300,000 today, had been stolen in 1974 as part of an elaborate insurance scam.

INSECT DEBRIS Cars competing in France's annual Le Mans 24-hour endurance race are on average 11 lb (5 kg) heavier at the finish than when they started owing to dirt and squashed insects that they have collected.

BICYCLE LIFT A bicycle lift called the CycloCable helps cyclists ride up a steep 426.5-ft (130-m) hill in Trondheim, Norway, without having to pedal. The device, which is integrated into the road, works like a ski lift with the cyclist being carried uphill at a leisurely 6½ ft (2 m) per second.

EMERGENCY STOP A pilot landed a light airplane on a highway in Sichuan Province, China, and then taxied to a nearby gas station to refuel. He climbed onto the wing of the plane to reach the fuel cap and, with the help of staff, managed to extend the gas pump nozzle far enough to fill up.

PIZZA-COPTER Dirk Reich from Hamburg, Germany, created a radio-controlled "pizza-copter" by attaching four engines and a flight controller to a regular pizza box. In a trial run at his home, his flying pizza box lifted off the ground and glided through a doorway before landing on a table. He hopes to improve the prototype by making the box lid open automatically as it lands.

BACKWARD TAXI Indian taxi driver Harpreet Dev, aged 30, of Bhatinda, Punjab, is renowned for his amazing reverse driving skills—after 11 years of successful rear-first steering, he even has a special government license that allows him to drive backward in any state in the northern part of India.

THREE GENERATIONS A Morris Minor car, owned by John Anthony from Neath, Wales, has been in his family for three generations spanning more than half a century. The car, which still runs was bought new by his grandfather, Idris Evans, in 1956.

JET SURF A cross between a surfboard and a jet-ski, the $12,000 Jet Surf has a 2.5 l (0.66 gal) fuel tank and a 100 cc engine attached to the back, enabling users to surf at nearly 35 mph (57 km/h) for an hour and a half.

DAY TRIP England's Matthew Winstone rented a 50-lb (22.7-kg) bicycle for the day, transported it in a van to the French Alps—a distance of more than 700 mi (1,125 km)—rode it to Mont Ventoux's 6,273-ft-high (1,912-m) summit, and, with the help of friends Ian Laurie and Robert Holden, returned it to the London rental station with 22 seconds to spare before the 24-hour rental agreement expired.

ROMANTIC CROSSING Harry Martin-Dreyer of London, England, rowed 3,000 mi (4,800 km) across the Atlantic Ocean to Barbados in a charity race so he could propose to his girlfriend, Lucy Plant. The voyage took him and crew mate Alex Brand more than 50 days, battling 50-ft-high (15-m) waves in places. At one point Harry, who carried the diamond engagement ring in a waterproof bag, was hit in the face by a flying fish. Luckily it was all worth it as Lucy said yes.

Road Blanket

To prevent a stretch of road in Jinan, China, from cracking in the cold winter weather during its construction, it was covered with thousands of cotton quilts. The quilt blankets were placed over an area 650 ft (200 m) long and 52 ft (16 m) wide.

145

MIND THE GAP

Commuters on a train in Perth, Australia, came to the rescue of a man who fell and got stuck fast between a train and the station platform on a rush-hour morning in August 2014. The passengers exited the carriage and in a superhuman effort tilted the 80,000-lb (40-ton) train far enough to free the man, who was trapped by one leg. Unbelievably, he was not badly hurt and caught the next train!

GARDEN RUNWAY
Commercial airline pilot Mike Clark built a working replica of a German Fokker Eindecker World-War-I fighter plane—and then constructed a runway in the back garden of his home in West Sussex, England, so he could fly it.

MASS PRODUCTION
China produces more than 18 million cars per year—and a new car rolls off the country's production lines once every 1.7 seconds.

EXPENSIVE PARKING
An underground parking space near the Royal Albert Hall in Kensington, London, England, sold for £400,000 ($680,000) in 2014—2 ½ times the cost of an average U.K. home and 15 times the average annual U.K. salary. For the same amount of money, a motorist could park their vehicle just ½ mi (0.8 km) away at another parking lot for 31 years.

AXE ATTACK A driver and passenger traveling at 65 mph (105 km/h) along a busy highway north of Boston, Massachusetts, had a lucky escape when an axe flew off the back of a truck in front of their car and crashed through the windshield, but missed them and became lodged in the dashboard.

CLOSE SHAVE After falling onto the New York subway tracks at the 49th Street station, 22-year-old Mary Downey was run over by three trains—but survived with only a broken shoulder.

HOMEMADE TANKS Li Guojun from Liaoning Province, China, built his own working tanks. The two 20-ft (6-m) -long vehicles have a top speed of 12 mph (19 km/h) and can tackle any terrain.

➡ **DRIVERS IN WASHINGTON D.C. SPEND AN AVERAGE OF 67 HOURS IN TRAFFIC EVERY YEAR!**

CATTLE ALERT A Korea Air Boeing 747 jumbo jet was forced to make an emergency landing at London's Heathrow Airport after 390 cows on board overheated the cabin and set off fire alarms over the Irish Sea. As well as emitting large amounts of methane, cows have higher body temperatures than humans.

SHOCK FIND Nursery worker Charlie Wise from Berkshire, England, was cleaning out the Volkswagen Golf she had just bought online for £200 ($340) when she looked in the trunk and found a 3-ft-long (0.9-m) boa constrictor curled up in a corner. She thought it was a cuddly toy until the snake flicked out its tongue.

HOME RAILROAD Todd Miller has built mini working steam locomotives, 11,000 ft (3,353 m) of track and a 400-ft-long (122-m) tunnel on the grounds of his home outside Portland, Oregon. It took him eight years to build some of the locomotives for the railroad, which is so big that up to 40 passengers can ride on it at a time.

Porsche Prayer

Buddhist monks are used to blessing people, births, weddings and homes, but in August 2014 monks at Xinqian temple in Xiaogan, China, took the unusual step of blessing a brand new Porsche. The car's businessman owner requested the ceremony for good luck and to ensure that he would be kept safe on journeys.

TERRIBLE TRAFFIC

In August 2010, drivers in Beijing, China, were stuck in a traffic jam that stretched for more than 70 mi (112 km) and lasted for an incredible 12 days.

Cars caught in the back-up took up to five days to make the trip along China National Highway 110 in the growing smog, sleeping under their vehicles to escape the summer heat and buying supplies from locals who set up stalls selling water and noodles. The epic jam was caused by holiday traffic, construction work, and an unusually high number of heavy coal trucks.

ROBOT COPS To tackle road congestion on the streets of Kinshasa, capital of the Democratic Republic of Congo, city authorities replaced traffic lights with robot traffic officers. The 8-ft-tall (2.4-m), solar-powered humanoids, which are made of aluminum and stainless steel, wear trademark police sunglasses, have rotating chests, and have cameras installed inside their bodies to help them record traffic flow.

JET TRUCK Neal Darnell of Springfield, Missouri, has built a jet-powered truck that can reach speeds of nearly 380 mph (612 km/h), making it faster than a Japanese bullet train. Named Shockwave, the 4-ton truck has three jets taken from U.S. Navy trainer aircraft and which generate 36,000 horsepower. It can cover a ¼ mi (0.4 km) in just 6.5 seconds and has to be stopped by using two military parachutes.

TOP BANANA Steve Braithwaite of Kalamazoo, Michigan, spent two years and $25,000 making a bright yellow car in the shape of a banana. Powered by a Ford V8 engine, the banana has a top speed of 85 mph (137 km/h).

OLYMPIC ODYSSEY Farmer Chen Guanming said he rode a three-wheeled rickshaw for more than two years all the way from his remote Chinese village to London, England, in time for the 2012 Olympics. His 37,500-mi (60,000-km) journey took him through 16 countries, floods, war zones, mountain passes and temperatures of −22°F (−30°C).

RECUMBENT RIDE Riding a recumbent bike, 48-year-old Bruce Gordon from Halfmoon Bay, British Columbia, cycled 18,100 mi (29,000 km) around the world in 153 days.

FIVE MORE GIGANTIC JAMS

● **New York, U.S.A., August 1969**—Revelers traveling to the Woodstock music festival caused a 20-mi (32 km) jam on the nearby New York Thruway, and drivers abandoned their cars to enjoy the event.

● **Tokyo, Japan, August 1990**—Holiday traffic and a typhoon caused an 84 mi (135 km) jam between Hyogo and Shiga, trapping 15,000 cars.

● **Germany, April 1990**—18 million cars lined up at the border between East and West Germany during the first Easter holiday after the fall of the Berlin Wall.

● **France, February 1980**—The Lyon–Paris road was brought to a standstill by a 109-mi-long (175-km) jam caused by skiing vacationers returning to Paris in bad weather.

● **England, April 1985**—Good Friday 1985 saw a giant traffic jam on the M6 motorway in Lancashire, involving 50,000 vehicles.

MAN DRIVES CAR WITH NO STEERING WHEEL

A 38-year-old man stopped by police in Adelaide, Australia, was found to be driving without a steering wheel. The car was controlled instead with just a set of vise grips, which had been attached to the steering column.

TURKEY PATROL A police officer called Butterball One—dressed as a giant turkey—patrols crosswalks in Las Vegas, Nevada, at Thanksgiving and squawks at drivers who fail to yield to pedestrians. Officers wait on the roadside to impose $200 fines on those who fail to stop.

SHORT RUNWAY The only runway at the airport on Saba Island in the Caribbean is located on the edge of a cliff and is only 1,300 ft (400 m) long—less than one tenth the length of the longest runway at New York City's John F. Kennedy International Airport.

CHEAP TRAVEL Students in Nantes, France, have invented the Microjoule, a superlight car that could be driven around the world on just $26 of fuel. Made of carbon fiber, the vehicle accommodates only the driver—lying horizontally—but can travel more than 2,000 mi (3,200 km) on ¼ gal (1 l) of fuel. It has an internal combustion engine and achieves its fuel efficiency by its aerodynamic shape and low resistance—when you spin its wheels, they revolve for several minutes without stopping.

DRIVEABLE SUITCASE He Liangcai from Changsha, China, has invented a driveable suitcase. The electric suitcase has a small motor that allows it to be ridden and can transport two adults at 12 mph (20 km/h) for up to 37 mi (60 km).

EIGHT WHEELS The Overland Octo-Auto, invented by U.S. automobile pioneer Milton Reeves in 1911, had eight wheels and was 20 ft (6 m) long. When it failed to sell, he replaced it the following year with a six-wheel version, the Sexto-Auto, which proved equally unsuccessful.

WATER BIKE Judah Schiller rode a bike 4 mi (6.4 km) across San Francisco Bay on September 27, 2013 on two pedal-powered inflatable pontoons. The following week he took his contraption to New York City and rode across the Hudson River in just 15 minutes.

MONSTER MACHINE Fabio Reggiani of Reggio Emilia, Italy, built a 16-ft-high (5-m), 33-ft-long (10-m) functional motorbike powered by a 5.7-liter V8 engine. The diameter of the tires is just under 6½ ft (2 m) and the machine is so big it needs stabilizers to prevent it toppling over when ridden.

PROUD MARY Launched in 2013, the Danish-registered *Mary Maersk* cargo ship holds 18,000 containers and would be 250 ft (76 m) taller than the Eiffel Tower if stood on end.

WRONG CAR A shopper in Stansbury, South Australia, accidentally drove home in the wrong car. The man got into a gray Hyundai hatchback instead of the near-identical Toyota that was parked in the next lot and only realized his mistake when stopped by police officers. Both vehicles had been left unlocked in the parking lot with the keys in the ignition.

BOARD GAME New drivers in Sierra Leone are required to play a board game to get their license. The game is called "The Drivers' Way" and players must give correct answers to traffic-related questions to progress around the board.

BIKE CRAZY Twenty-seven percent of all journeys taken in the Netherlands are on bicycles—compared with under 2 percent in the U.K. and North America.

FAKE LANDING

In 1929, Alfred E. Smith, former governor of New York City, announced that the planned Empire State Building was to have its height increased from 1,050 ft (320 m) to 1,250 ft (380 m) so that huge, 800-ft-long (244-m) zeppelin airships could use its mooring mast for docking. Passengers would descend a gangplank, he said, and seven minutes later they would be on the street. Sadly, however, the 40 mph (64 km/h) average winds at the top of the tower made the idea impractical and six years after the Empire State Building opened, the 1937 Hindenburg disaster, in which 36 people were killed when an airship exploded, effectively ended passenger travel in these vessels. This clever faked picture of the airship *Los Angeles* docking at the top of the Empire State Building in the 1930s shows what might have been.

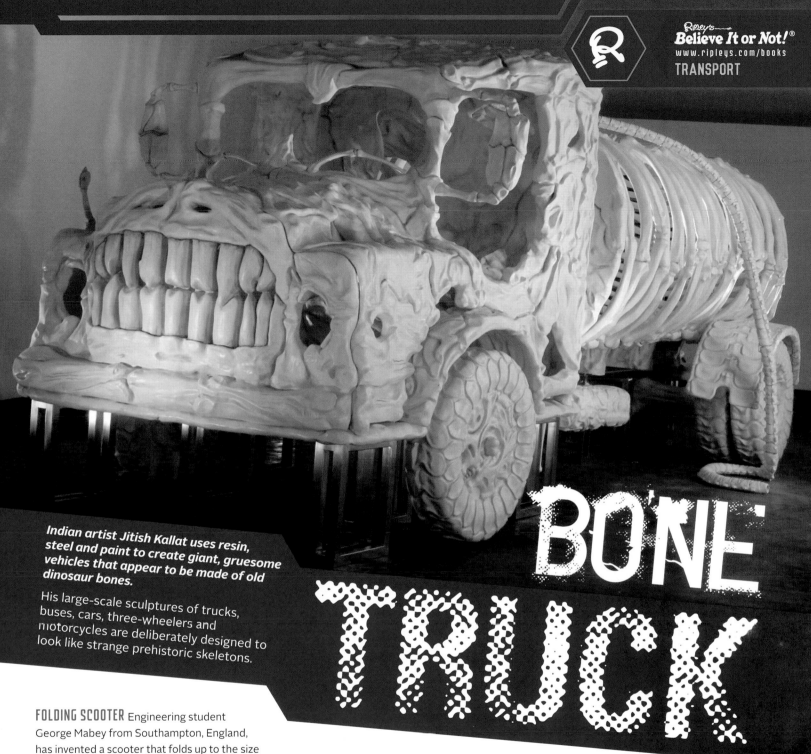

BONE TRUCK

Indian artist Jitish Kallat uses resin, steel and paint to create giant, gruesome vehicles that appear to be made of old dinosaur bones.

His large-scale sculptures of trucks, buses, cars, three-wheelers and motorcycles are deliberately designed to look like strange prehistoric skeletons.

FOLDING SCOOTER Engineering student George Mabey from Southampton, England, has invented a scooter that folds up to the size of a standard piece of paper—small enough to fit in a woman's handbag. The lightweight scooter works by linking aluminum parts with a cable, which, when tightened, pulls them together to support the weight of an adult.

FISH IMPACT Pilot Nick Toth had to abort takeoff from the MacDill Air Force Base in Florida after his Gulfstream IV jet crashed into a fish. The jet was halfway down the runway when he and his aircrew spotted a large osprey flying in front of them with something in its claws. As the bird disappeared underneath the plane, they heard a bang and taxied back to check—but found that the impact was with a 9-in-long (23-cm) sheepshead fish, which the osprey had probably dropped.

MAIL ROUTE The Australian mail route from Cairns, Queensland, to Cape York covers 900 miles (1,440 km) in a single day. The mailman flies by plane for nine hours, making 10 stops along the way.

→ **TEN CABS IN YOKOHAMA, JAPAN, ARE DESIGNATED AS TURTLE TAXIS, WHICH DELIBERATELY OFFER PASSENGERS AS SMOOTH A RIDE AS POSSIBLE.**

PEDAL PORSCHE Johannes Langeder of Linz, Austria, built a full-size, gold foiled Porsche sports car with a top speed of just 5 mph (8 km/h). The car took six months and $20,000 to build and is operated by pedal power.

DESTINATION ERROR Edward Gamson and Lowell Canaday of Washington, D.C., thought they had booked vacation tickets to Granada in Spain, but instead British Airways took them to the Caribbean island of Grenada. The couple realized the error only when their connecting flight from London began heading west rather than south.

MIGHTY CARGO A Chinese-owned, South Korean-built container ship, CSCL *Globe*, weighs 203,000 US short tons. At 1,312-ft-long (400-m), it could carry 156 million pairs of shoes, 300 million tablet computers or 900 million cans of beans.

Tight Fit

Driver Chen Zhongliang somehow managed to squeeze his 4x4 into a tiny parking space outside his home in Quanzhou, China, that was just a few inches bigger than his vehicle. More impressive still, he reversed into the gap in a single maneuver.

MISSING PLANE A Boeing 727 airplane was stolen from an airport in Luanda, Angola, on May 25, 2003, and it has never been found.

SUBMARINE HOTEL British company Oliver's Travels rents out a submarine that has been converted into a luxury hotel 650 ft (200 m) under water. "Lovers Deep" is staffed by a crew of three—captain, chef and butler—and can be harbored anywhere in the world from a starting price of $268,000 per night.

MECHANICAL SHEPHERD Instead of a dog, Marty Todd uses a remote-control miniature helicopter to herd the sheep on his farm in Nelson, New Zealand. The sheep react to the movement and sound of the whirring blades as the helicopter flies back and forth.

FARM FORDS Auto mechanic Spyros Droulias from Elis, Greece, converts abandoned family cars into farm machinery. More than a million cars have been discarded by their owners in cash-strapped Greece because they can no longer afford to run them and are unable to sell them. The enterprising auto-shop owner has set up a lucrative sideline that uses his mechanical skills to modify unwanted Fords and Toyotas into useful milking machines and ploughs.

MISSED TARGET A pilot who was supposed to drop 3,000 ping-pong balls that were redeemable for prizes onto a crowd who had gathered for the stunt at Blackfoot, Idaho, missed his target completely and instead scattered the balls over a nearby interstate where they bounced into high-speed traffic.

DENTAL CAR Rex Rosenberg from Great Bend, Kansas, covered a Subaru with more than 140 lb (64 kg) of dentures and dental impressions to create his art car ChewBaru. He found the dentures online, soaked them in bleach and glued them to the car along with toothpaste tubes and dental tools. He also found a discarded mannequin, cut it into pieces, inserted LED lights into the eyes and stuck the head to the roof of the car.

FUN RIDE After a trip to a theme park, Will Pemble built his children Lyle and Ellie a 180-ft-long (55-m) roller coaster in the back garden of the family home in San Francisco, California. It cost him more than $3,000 and took 300 hours to construct.

TOO HEAVY Four new submarines costing $3.2 billion commissioned by the Spanish Navy were found to be too heavy and, if launched, would have sunk like stones.

SHEEPDOG CAR

Farmer Dave Isaac from Sussex, England, covered his Peugeot estate car in fur so that it looked just like his favorite sheepdog Floss. He built a timber frame around the chassis and re-created Floss to the last detail, giving her a top speed of 40 mph (64 km/h). The replica was so accurate that when he drove it around his farm to round up the sheep they did not appear to notice any difference.

TRAM ON STILTS

It actually drove through the sea!

In 1896, engineer Magnus Volk opened an electric tramline that actually ran through the sea for 2.8 mi (4.5 km) between Brighton and Rottingdean in Sussex, England.

Advertised as "a sea voyage on rails," it consisted of a single tramcar raised on four 23-ft-high (7-m) tubular legs, which contained wheels plus a set of scrapers to sweep seaweed, crabs and shingle from the track. The rails were supported by concrete blocks embedded at 2.5-ft (0.8-m) intervals along the shore. Able to carry 160 passengers, the *Pioneer* (or "Daddy Long-Legs" as it was known) was equipped with a lifeboat and life preservers, but although it operated successfully in shallow water, it came to a near standstill at high tide. A violent storm badly damaged the tramway just a week after opening, but it trundled on for another few years before finally closing in 1901.

Harley Hearse

At his funeral in Mechanicsburg, Ohio, in 2014, 82-year-old motorcycle enthusiast Bill Standley was lowered into the ground in a see-through casket while sitting astride his beloved 1967 Harley-Davidson Electra Glide cruiser. He had bought three burial plots to accommodate the casket, which was built by his two sons. Five embalmers had then prepared his body—dressed in black leathers, a white crash helmet and gloves—with a metal back brace and straps to ensure he remained in the seat.

TOY TRAVEL Japanese company Unagi Travel offers people who are often unable to go on vacation the chance to send their cuddly toys instead. It charges between $20 and $55 for the service, depending on the destination and the size of the toy.

WOOD BEETLE Husband and wife Momir and Nada Bojic from Celinac, Bosnia–Herzegovina, made a driveable Volkswagen Beetle from 50,000 individually hand-carved pieces of oak, designed to replicate the tiled roofs of their homeland. Most of the car is carved from wood, including the bodywork, pedals, steering wheel, wipers, wheel caps, bumpers, tail lights, gearstick, dashboard, clock and even the radio antenna—and when Momir drives it, he wears a matching wooden cap! It took them nearly two years to transform the 1975 Beetle, because each wooden tile required no fewer than 23 separate procedures.

PIZZA TREAT When a delayed Frontier Airlines flight from Washington, D.C., to Denver, Colorado, was diverted to Cheyenne, Wyoming, because of bad weather, pilot Gerhard Bradner bought 35 Domino's takeout pizzas to feed the 160 stranded passengers.

ICONIC CAR Gordon Grant of England, spent 12 years building an exact replica of Chitty Chitty Bang Bang, the iconic car driven by Dick Van Dyke in the 1968 movie of that name.

DETECTOR SEAT Researchers at Nottingham Trent University, England, have developed a car seat that detects when drivers are falling asleep at the wheel. An electrocardiogram sensor system embedded into the fabric of the seat interprets heart signals, which indicate when a driver is becoming less alert. The system then issues a warning, and if that is ignored, active cruise control technology is deployed to slow down the vehicle.

STATIONARY WARSHIP In 1803, the British Navy registered a 575-ft-high (175-m) rock off Martinique as a British warship—*H.M.S. Diamond Rock*—and hoisted guns on top.

HUBCAP CREATURES

Artist Ptolemy Elrington from Brighton, England, creates incredible wildlife sculptures from car hubcaps. He has collected thousands of lost hubcaps from U.K. roadsides and turned them into imaginative sculptures of owls, dogs, wolves, lizards, sea creatures and chickens. A 33-ft-long (10-m) dragon that he built from 200 hubcaps sold for around $5,000. He cuts the hubcaps to shape with a craft knife and a hacksaw and joins them together with salvaged wire.

TOLL ROAD When highway construction near Bath, England, left drivers facing an hour-long detour, local businessman Mike Watts spent £150,000 ($250,000) of his own money to build a toll road across a field—the first private toll road to open in the U.K. for more than 100 years. The 1,197-ft (365-m) -long road took just ten days to build, and he charged motorists £2 ($3.40) to use it. On its first five days, it carried 4,000 cars.

HIGH-SPEED CHASE Malazum Hussain was jailed after leading police officers on a 5-mi (8-km), 85-mph (135-km/h), late-night car chase through Sheffield, England—even though he is legally blind and can see only a few feet in front of him.

OLD HOUSE While piloting a light aircraft over Northglenn, Colorado, Brian Veatch accidentally crashed into a house he had once owned. Brian, who was unhurt in the crash, sold the house in 2003 and now lives about a mile away.

DUAL POWER The Varibike, designed by Martin Kraiss from Ülm, Germany, can be propelled by both arms and legs. The bicycle has foot pedals and arm cranks connected to the wheels, thereby increasing the machine's power and speed by more than 30 percent.

→ **$500,000 IN LOOSE CHANGE WAS LEFT BEHIND AT AIRPORT SECURITY DESKS IN THE U.S.A. OVER THE COURSE OF 2013.**

BOTTLE BOAT To celebrate their graduation, four science and technology students from Chongqing, China, spent two months building a working rowboat from 1,528 used plastic bottles. The 16-ft-long (5-m) vessel can hold the weight of five adults. Armed with oars, the four students took the boat out onto the river to show that it was fully functional and would not sink.

ABSENT MINDED After police issued a Facebook appeal to trace the owner of a $108,000 boat that had been moored in Stromstad Harbour, Sweden, for two years, a wealthy Norwegian man came forward and said it was his, explaining that he had somehow forgotten all about the luxury vessel.

CANOE CROSSING Hungarian architect Gabor Rakonczay became the first person to paddle solo across the Atlantic Ocean in a canoe. Setting off from Portugal in December 2011, he made the 3,500-mi (5,600-km) crossing to Antigua in the Caribbean in 76 days in his 24½-ft-long (7.5-m) canoe, capsizing twice in rough waters and, because of a fault with his communcations equipment, going missing for six weeks amid fears that he had drowned at sea.

ART TRUCKS

Japanese truckers love to customize their vehicles with steel, chrome and gold, topped with brightly colored neon and ultraviolet lighting for a dazzling display at night.

Many *Dekotora* ("decorated trucks") also have landscapes, pictures of celebrities or images of characters from popular Japanese animation and comic books painted on the sides.

Vanishing Trick

Artist Laurent La Gamba from Paris, France, makes human models disappear by blending them in with high-performance sports cars. Using BMWs and Porsches as his backdrop, he spends up to two hours painting his models with acrylics before photographing them so that they are perfectly camouflaged against the bodywork of the car and the surrounding landscape.

WOODEN BIKE Russian carpenter Yuri Hvtisishvili made a life-sized replica of a classic IZH-49 Soviet motorbike—entirely from wood. It took him four months of carving to create the detailed model on which even the tires look real.

TINY BIKES Adults in Portland, Oregon, speed downhill at 35 mph (56 km/h) on tiny bicycles with 12-in (30-cm) wheels that are designed for use by three-year-old children. The craze is called "zoobombing," because the starting point is near the Oregon Zoo.

1930S TRAIN REACHES 140 MPH!

In the 1930s, Germany tested a high-speed railcar that looked like a zeppelin airship and was powered by an aircraft engine and a rear propeller. Designed by aircraft engineer Franz Kruckenberg, the lightweight, streamlined *Schienenzeppelin* could carry 40 passengers and reach a speed of 143 mph (230.2 km/h), making it the world's fastest gas-powered rail vehicle. However, only one was ever built and it was not considered safe enough for public service. It was dismantled in 1939 because the German army needed its construction materials at the start of World War II.

HIT BY TRAIN Kristopher Wenberg, a 25-year-old U.S. Army soldier, miraculously got up and walked away after being hit by a freight train. He was walking along railroad tracks in Topeka, Kansas, wearing headphones and therefore failed to hear an approaching train. Although the train slowed, it still hit Kristopher who survived with minor injuries to his leg and shoulder.

CONTINENTAL TREK Stopping only to collect roadkill to make stew, British couple Katharine and David Lowrie trekked the length of South America pulling a 220-lb (100-kg) trolley. It took them more than a year to travel the 6,400 mi (10,300 km) from the southern tip to the Caribbean, a journey that took them across rain forests, mountains and windswept pampas.

LOW MILEAGE A 1961 Triumph Herald car that was put up for sale in Norfolk, England, in 2013 had been driven just 20 mi (32 km) in 52 years—and not at all since the day it had been delivered brand new. It was listed in the auction catalogue as "a classic car with one careful lady owner."

TOY STORY A six-year-old boy was rescued by motorists after driving a miniature battery-powered ATV on to a busy six-lane highway in New York City. Three motorists slowed their vehicles and formed a shield around the toy car to protect it from traffic traveling at 50 mph (80 km/h) on the Bronx River Parkway.

DRIVEABLE DECK CHAIR British artist Solomon Rogers has created a four-wheeled buggy with two motor-powered deck chairs, a sound system, a fridge, a slushy drink maker and a parasol that can be driven around the beach to help vacationers find the best spot. The parasol is fitted with a GPS system that can tell where the sun is at any given time, providing the perfect level of shade for users.

TUBE CHALLENGE In August 2013, Geoff Marshall and Anthony Smith, both from the U.K., visited all 270 London Underground stations in 16 hours 20 minutes and 27 seconds. They were helped by a team of friends who warned them of possible obstacles along their route.

PASSENGER HERO Even though 77-year-old passenger John Wildey from South Yorkshire, England, had never flown an airplane before, he still managed to land a Cessna Skyhawk light aircraft safely after his pilot friend collapsed and died suddenly in midair. Guided by air traffic controllers, John flew the plane for 90 minutes, bringing it down from an altitude of 1,500 ft (450 m) to land in darkness at Humberside Airport on his fourth attempt.

MOBILE JACUZZI Phillip Weicker and Duncan Forster, engineering graduates from McMaster University, Ontario, spent six years transforming a 1969 Cadillac Coupe DeVIlle from a convertible car into a mobile jacuzzi. They removed the rear section of the vehicle and replaced it with a hot tub that can hold over 600 gal (2,271.25 l) of water. The "Carpool DeVille" has a 7.7-liter V8 engine that is used to power the car and heat the water in the tub to around 100°F (38°C).

STILL GOING Irv Gordon of New York has put more than 3 million mi (4.8 million km) on his Volvo P1800 since buying the car in 1966.

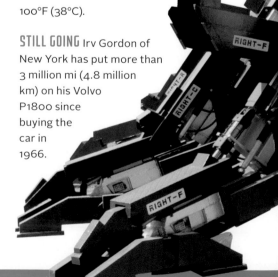

LONG PLATFORM Gorakhpur station, an important railway junction in Northern India, has a platform that measures 0.8 mi (1.35 km) long—more than the length of 12 American football fields.

WEDDING TRAIN To mark the tenth anniversary of the subway system in Wuhan, China, 14 grooms proposed to their loved ones on board a train before getting married in a mass wedding ceremony on a station platform.

TRAIN CROSSING The runway at New Zealand's Gisborne Airport, which handles more than 17,000 flights and 130,000 passengers a year, has a railway track running straight across it.

COSTLY SWERVE Driving home from work in Lower Saxony, Germany, Joerg Daecher caused $45,000 worth of damage to his luxury Ferrari Testarossa sports car when he swerved to avoid a hedgehog. The hedgehog escaped unhurt.

FLYING CAR Steve Saint of Dunnellon, Florida, has built a car capable of powered flight, using a deployable parachute as a wing. The 15-ft-long (4.5-m) Maverick Sport flying car, which comes complete with a 6-ft (1.8-m) rear-mounted aircraft propeller, is both street and air legal. It flies at 40 mph (64 km/h) and can reach speeds of 100 mph (161 km/h) on the road.

BEETLE ROBOT

Japanese engineer Hitoshi Takahashi spent 11 years building a functional, remote-controlled robot in the shape of a giant rhinoceros beetle.

The KABUTOM RX-03 is 36 ft (11 m) long and weighs 18 tons. It walks with the aid of its six diesel-powered legs and can blow smoke from its nose.

SUPERMAN

Is it a bird? Is it a plane?

To promote the 2014 Bethpage Air Show on Long Island, New York, five members of the Red Bull Air Force donned wingsuits to fly Superman-style over the Manhattan skyline, jumping from a plane 7,500 ft (2,286 m) above the Hudson River and falling at speeds of up to 120 mph (193 km/h) before landing on a barge.

Starting from the Financial District, the team of Jon Devore, Jeff Provenzano, Amy Chmelecki, Sean MacCormac and Andy Farrington soared for 2 mi (3.2 km) over the city skyscrapers and although their landing pad was narrow, they used their parachutes to reduce speed and touch down safely without ending up in the river. Their hi-tech suits add surface area to the body with extra fabric between the legs and arms, allowing them to descend like flying squirrels.

The incredible aerial views they obtained particularly impressed Jeff Provenzano, a native New Yorker. He said: "I've been dreaming about this since I was a kid. It's been years of looking up at the big buildings and wondering if there is a day that I can fly over them. That day was today."

SWOOPS
No, it's a wingsuit Flyer!

FAST FIZZ Frank Esposito, a restaurant manager in Long Island, New York, can use a saber to open 48 bottles of champagne in one minute.

SEVEN MARATHONS San Francisco, California, athlete Tim Durbin ran seven marathons in seven days on seven continents in January 2015. He completed marathons in Antarctica, Chile, Miami, Spain, Morocco, Dubai and Australia in an average time of around 5 hours 30 minutes. In 2013, Durbin began logging his miles for running, walking, cross-country skiing and swimming with the aim of completing a distance equivalent to traveling around the equator—24,901 mi (40,075 km)—by the year 2022.

DON'T LOOK DOWN Without using safety ropes, Scott Young from Hampshire, England, performed a daring handstand on the edge of the roof of a 40-story-high building in Shanghai, China. Usually when people do handstands they have to focus on the ground to keep their balance, but in Scott's case the ground is so far down that he has to block it out of his mind. He films his adventures, which have taken him to skyscrapers all over the world, on a camera built into his shoe and has also performed handstands on the back of moving motorcycles.

QUICK ARROWS Master archer Lars Andersen, from Denmark, is so fast and accurate he can throw a ring pull from a can into the air and hit it with an arrow before it falls to the ground. He can even hit other arrows as they are fired at him, splitting them in midair.

SKATER GIRL Nine-year-old Sabre Morris from Newcastle, Australia, can land an awesome 540-degree skateboard spin—but she still can't ride a bike! She learned to skate when she was six because her parents would not allow her to have a bicycle as their house has no garage.

BOWLING BACKWARDS Andrew Cowen of Rockford, Illinois, scored 280 points in a game bowling backwards. Facing away from the pins, he bowled ten straight strikes and except for a second-frame spare, he would have bowled a backwards perfect 300 game.

TOUGH TEETH Second-generation New York City strongman Mike Greenstein (known as Mighty Atom, Jr.) can pull a car across the street with his teeth—at age 93! The grandfather of three, and great-grandfather of two, stands just 5 ft 4 in tall (1.6 m) tall and weighs 140 lb (63 kg). His legendary father Joe could allegedly prevent an airplane taking off as it taxied down a runway at 150 mph (240 km/h) by using chains attached to his hair.

BOOK CHAIN To promote reading, a chain of 4,845 second-hand books was tumbled in domino fashion along a 2,014-ft-long (614-m) pathway at Belgium's 2013 Antwerp Book Fair. It had taken a team of 40 volunteers two hours to set up the lines of books so that they would fall in sequence.

BIRD'S EYE VIEW Doing their best impersonations of Superman, a team of five Red Bull wingsuit flyers jumped from a plane at an altitude of 7,500 ft (2,286 m) and soared above the New York City skyline at speeds of 120 mph (193 km/h) (1) before landing on a narrow strip on a barge on the Hudson River. As they approached the pad (2), the fearless five—Jon Devore, Jeff Provenzano, Amy Chmelecki, Sean MacCormac and Andy Farrington—deployed parachutes to slow down so that they were able to land expertly without even getting wet (3).

PAINFUL SLEEP

China's Zhou Jie suffered for her art for 36 nights by sleeping almost naked on an unfinished bed and pillow made of harsh, skin-piercing iron wire as part of a painful performance piece.

Visitors to the Beijing, China, exhibition hall watched her work to complete her stark wrought-iron bedroom, which, in addition to the bed, featured toy animal sculptures made from rough metal wire.

WINNING STREAK Pakistani squash player Jahangir Khan won 555 consecutive matches over a period of five years and eight months between 1981 and 1986.

MONSTER CARP Using just a piece of bread as bait, England's Andy Harman caught the world's biggest carp—a 150-lb (68-kg) monster—in Krabi, Thailand, in 2014. It took an hour of struggle to land the fish in a rectangular cage as it was too big for a net.

MILK CARTON IGLOO On a visit to his girlfriend Kathleen Starrie's family in Edmonton, Canada, Dan Gray, an engineering student at the University of Canterbury, New Zealand, built a full-size igloo from 500 milk cartons. The cartons were filled with water and food coloring and then frozen to create ice bricks. Using snow and water to hold the bricks together, he built the igloo in five days.

JORDAN SHOES A pair of shoes worn by Michael Jordan during the famous 1997 "Flu Game," where he led the Chicago Bulls to a vital victory over the Utah Jazz at the NBA finals despite suffering from the flu, sold at an auction for $104,765 in 2013. After the game the star gave the size 13 shoes to Utah Jazz ball boy Preston Truman who kept them locked in a bank safe-deposit box for 16 years, once turning down an $11,000 offer for them.

SPEEDING WAKEBOARDER

Five-time British wakeboard champion Jorge Gill was pulled along a flooded field in Lincolnshire, England, by a $1.7-million Ferrari at speeds of up to 84 mph (135 km/h). The thrill-seeking 19-year-old attached himself by a cord to the supercar's spoiler, jumped into the water-filled ditch and, as the Ferrari accelerated along an adjacent country lane, he clung on as it dragged him at speeds more than four times faster than he usually travels on a wakeboard.

MAN WALKS BACKWARD FOR 25 YEARS

Mani Manithan from Tamil Nadu, India, has been walking backward for over 25 years—since June 14, 1989—to promote world peace. He once walked backward, naked, for 300 mi (480 km). He even climbs stairs backward and has been walking in reverse for so long he has forgotten how to walk normally.

CHILD GENIUS At just two years old, Adam Kirby from London, England, took an IQ test that ranked him smarter than U.S. president Barack Obama and U.K. prime minister David Cameron. He started reading at nine months and by age two could count up to 1,000 in English and up to 20 in Spanish and Japanese. His parents knew he was special when at 23 months he potty trained himself after reading a book on the subject!

DOVE HUNT Olney, Texas, is home to an annual one-arm dove hunt in which hand and arm amputees gather for competitions such as billiards, golf, cow-chip throwing and skeet shooting in addition to dove hunting. The hunt started out as a joke in 1972 by local residents Jack Northrup and Jack Bishop ("the one-armed Jacks"), both of whom had a limb amputated at the shoulder.

HEAD OVER HEELS U.S. Army soldier Jalyessa Walker performed 49 consecutive backflips in the football stadium at the University of Texas, El Paso, in November 2012.

TWIN PEAKS Twenty-nine-year-old Nepalese mountaineer Chhurim Sherpa climbed Mount Everest twice in a week in May 2012—the first woman to climb the world's highest mountain twice in a season. She made her first ascent on May 12, then returned to base camp for a couple of days' rest before scaling the peak again on May 19.

→ NARAYAN TIMALSINA FROM PALPA DISTRICT, NEPAL, IS ABLE TO HOLD 24 TENNIS BALLS, BALANCED IN A PYRAMID IN HIS RIGHT HAND, FOR 90 SECONDS.

DOMINO CASCADE In July 2013, a team from Sinners Domino Entertainment toppled more than 270,000 dominoes at once in a sports hall in Büdingen, Germany.

SURFBOARD BALANCE Doug McManaman of Nova Scotia, Canada, balanced a 9-ft-long (2.7-m), 20-lb (9-kg) surfboard on his chin for 51.47 seconds.

WINE BUFF Alain Laliberte from Toronto, Ontario, has a collection of about 160,000 wine labels from around the world, carefully stored in over 120 shoeboxes. His oldest label comes from Germany and dates back to 1859. His fascination with wine does not stop at the labels—he samples an average of 5,000 wines a year.

DISNEY DAYS Southern Californians Tonya Mickesh and Jeff Reitz visited Disneyland every day during 2012—a total of 366 trips. They each walked up to 4 mi (6.4 km) per visit, meaning that between them they racked up a total of nearly 3,000 mi (4,800 km) in the course of the year. They also posted more than 2,000 photos of their adventure on Instagram.

BALLOON CROSSING Matt Silver-Vallance became the first person to float from Robben Island to Cape Town, South Africa, using only helium balloons. Attached to 160 balloons, he took about one hour to make the 3.7-mi (5.9-km) crossing above the shark-infested waters of the Atlantic. He carried bags filled with water that could be jettisoned to increase his altitude and an air gun and makeshift spear to pop the balloons to hasten his descent.

BIKE CLIMB Without his feet ever touching the ground, Italian Vittorio Brumotti cycled up 3,700 steps to the top of the tallest building in the world—the 2,715-ft (828-m)—high Burj Khalifa in Dubai. He jumped his way up the 160 floors in 2 hours 20 minutes.

BUBBLE POP On January 28, 2013, 336 students at Hawthorne High School, New Jersey, popped more than 8,000 square feet of bubble wrap in two minutes. The event celebrated the 13th Annual Bubble Wrap Appreciation Day—bubble wrap was invented in Hawthorne in 1960 by Marc Chavannes and Al Fielding.

Needle in a Haystack

New York-based Italian artist Sven Sachsalber achieved the supposedly impossible by finding a needle in a haystack. He had given himself 24 hours to locate with his bare hands the single silver needle which had been pre-inserted into an enormous haystack by the president of a Paris museum—but he managed to find it with six hours to spare. His previous performances have included sawing the branches off a tree while still sitting in it and spending 24 hours in a room with a cow.

NOSE PULL

Zhang Yilong managed to pull a van with just his nose at a car show in Zhoukou, China.

He attached one end of a chain to the vehicle and strapped the other end to two metal hooks, which he then inserted into his nostrils. Defying the pain, he moved the van inch by inch along the road to the delight of the cheering crowd.

BRAINS AND BRAWN Michael Kotch of Upper Milford Township, Pennsylvania, solved a Rubik's Cube with one hand in 25 seconds while simultaneously doing push-ups with the other arm.

DARING DORIS Great-great-grandmother Doris Long from Hampshire, England, celebrated her 99th birthday in May 2013 by abseiling down the side of a 110-ft-high (34-m) building.

PRAM PUSHER Dougal Thorburn from Dunedin, New Zealand, ran 6 mi (9.6 km) in 32 minutes 26 seconds—while pushing a pram containing his 2 ½ year old daughter, Audrey. His time was only six minutes slower than the world record for the same distance for athletes not pushing a pram!

POGO FLIPS In Tokyo, Japan, on December 18, 2013, Fred Grzybowski from the United States performed 17 consecutive backflips on a pogo stick.

BURNING RUBBER At the wheel of a specially modified replica 1937 Ford Sedan hotrod with a 1,200cc motorcycle engine, U.K. stunt driver Terry Grant spun his car 360 degrees (a donut) a total of 39 times in 100 seconds at a show in Devon, England. He averaged a donut every 2.5 seconds.

ICE WHEELIE Using special studs on his tires, Ryan Suchanek performed a motorcycle wheelie on ice at an incredible speed of 108.5 mph (174.6 km/h). He rode on one wheel for over 660 ft (200 m) on frozen Lake Koshkonong, Wisconsin.

MOUTH JUGGLER In June 2013, entertainer Mark Angelo from Hudson, Ohio, juggled two ping-pong balls using nothing but his mouth for a total of 212 spits and catches in 2 minutes 8 seconds. Mark, who first discovered his unusual talent by tossing popcorn in the air and catching it in his mouth, can also balance a golf club on his chin with a golf ball on top if it and another club spinning on top of the ball!

KEY COLLECTION The late Harley Yates of South Lake Tahoe, California, had a collection of more than 350,000 keys—including keys for cars, boats, handcuffs, vending machines, clocks, safes, suitcases and even a Mexican jail. Weighing in excess of six tons, his collection was accumulated over a period of more than 80 years and was stored in hundreds of plastic canisters.

Night Golfers

Night Sports U.S.A. has invented the perfect gift for golfers who want to play in the dark—LED golf balls that light up when they are hit and stay lit for eight minutes so that players can find them easily. The balls, which have a 40-hour battery life and come in four colors, also float in water, making them retrievable from lakes and streams. The company also produces illuminated tees and flags.

DEFYING THE ODDS

In 2007, Geoff Holt, who is **paralyzed** from the chest down following a diving accident, **sailed solo** 1,400 mi (2,253 km) around the coast of Great Britain on a voyage that took 109 days.

In 2011, soldier Joe Townsend, who **lost both legs** in Afghanistan, completed the arduous **Ironman UK challenge.** It took him 13 hours to swim 2.4 mi (3.86 km), cycle a 112-mi (180-km) ride and run a marathon.

Matt Stutzman of Fairfield, Iowa, won the silver medal at the 2012 **Paralympic archery** competition despite being born **without any arms.** Using his left foot to load the arrow, he pushes the bow with his right foot and releases it with a special apparatus strapped to his body.

Dutch **wheelchair tennis player** Esther Vergeer did not lose a single match between 2003 and her retirement in 2013. She ended her career with an **unbroken winning streak of 470 matches.**

South African Natalie du Toit **lost her left leg** in a road accident when she was 17, but went on to win 13 Paralympic swimming gold medals and was so fast she became the **first amputee to qualify for the regular Olympics,** in 2008.

OLDEST CLIMBERS Esther Kafer, 84, and her husband Martin, 85, of Vancouver, British Columbia, became the oldest people to reach the summit of Tanzania's 19,340-ft-high (5,895-m) Mount Kilimanjaro on September 30, 2012. The couple have been climbers for more than 60 years.

DARING BACKFLIP After speeding down a sheer drop, New Zealand mountain biker Kelly McGarry performed a sensational backflip across a 72-ft-wide (22-m) canyon gap in Utah during the 2013 Red Bull Rampage.

ICY SWIM In October 2013, Stig Severinsen swam for 250 ft (76.2 m) under 3-ft-thick (0.9-m) ice in a frozen lake in Greenland—with no wetsuit. The Danish freediver can also hold his breath underwater for 22 minutes, helped by the fact that he has a lung capacity twice that of an average person.

ARMLESS STAR

Ibrahim Hamadtou of Egypt lost both his arms in a train accident when he was ten years old, but that has not stopped him becoming a world-class table-tennis player. He began playing three years after the accident and at first tried holding the bat under his arm, but now he holds the bat in his mouth and serves by flicking the ball up with his foot. His ingenious technique has proved so successful that he won the silver medal at the African Para Table Tennis Championships.

SHALLOW SWIM Kenny Khong Jia Hin of Penang, Malaysia, uses a stroke that he calls the reverse swim to swim in water that is just 12 in (30 cm) deep—without touching the bottom of the pool. He learned the technique by accident when he nearly drowned while swimming in the sea as a boy. He lies on his back in a floating position and pushes himself forward by extending both arms in a circular motion.

CARD SHARP Even though he is blind, Richard Turner from San Antonio, Texas, never loses at cards. Having practiced up to 20 hours a day, seven days a week for years, he has developed an incredible touch sensitivity that allows him to manipulate the outcome of any card game. He has 50,000 card decks at home and is so obsessed with cards that he named his son Ace of Spades, or Ace for short.

SPRING SENSATION Sixteen-year-old gymnast Mikayla Clark, a student at Westlake High School, Atlanta, Georgia, can perform 44 consecutive back handsprings, or backflips.

Ripley's **Believe It or Not!®**
www.ripleys.com/books
FEATS

TOUR DE FORCE Frenchman Robert Marchand cycled 16.7 mi (26.9 km) in one hour around an indoor track in Paris in 2014—at the age of 102! Marchand had dreamed of becoming a professional cyclist in his younger days, but was told he was too small, so he worked instead as a lumberjack in Canada and a truck driver in Venezuela before finally taking up cycling again when he was 67.

TUNNEL VISION James Wilson from Surrey, England, solved a Rubik's Cube in 3 minutes 16 seconds while freefalling in an artificial wind tunnel where he fought wind speeds of 125 mph (200 km/h).

SOFT LANDING On the 18th hole of the 2013 PGA Championship at Oak Hill Country Club, Rochester, New York, Swedish golfer Jonas Blixt's tee shot landed in the back pocket of a spectator's pants—yet he still went on to make a birdie!

BLIND FAITH Seventeen-year-old Aaron Golub from Newton, Massachusetts, signed for the Tulane University football team even though he is legally blind. His right eye does not function at all and he has very little vision in the left, but his coach describes him as the best high-school long snapper he has ever trained.

CENTENARIAN TEACHER Agnes Zhelesnik teaches home economics for 35 hours a week at the Sundance School in North Plainfield, New Jersey—even though she had her 100th birthday in 2014. Believed to be the oldest working teacher in the U.S.A., she began teaching when she was 81.

CANADIAN ODYSSEY Jamie McDonald, from Gloucester, England, ran 5,000 mi (8,000 km) coast-to-coast across Canada from east to west in 11 months—dressed as comic-book superhero Flash. He ran the equivalent of more than 200 marathons and wore through ten pairs of running shoes.

RIVER WALK French tightrope walker Denis Josselin defied gravity by balancing on a thin rope 82 ft (25 m) above the River Seine in Paris, France, and walking nearly 500 ft (150 m) to the other side—without a harness or safety net. The walk took him 30 minutes to complete and halfway across he put on a blindfold for a short distance to make the stunt even more dangerous.

URBAN GOLFER Detroit, Michigan, news reporter Charlie LeDuff turned the city into an 18-mi-long (29-km) golf course by playing from one end of town to the other through abandoned houses, grassy fields and crumbling landmarks. Carrying only four clubs and playing each shot where it lay, he took 2,525 strokes.

NAIL POLISH Samantha Henderson of Philadelphia, Pennsylvania, has collected more than 1,300 bottles of nail polish.

MIGHTY WAVE

Brazilian surfer Carlos Burle rode a colossal wave measuring 100 ft (30 m) tall off the coast of Praia do Norte, Portugal, in October 2013.

The wave, which had been whipped up by an Atlantic storm, was the height of a ten-story building. Unbelievably Carlos rode it shortly after he had rescued a friend from nearly drowning.

HUMAN
CANNONBALLS

For 70 years, three generations of the legendary Zacchini family risked life and limb by defying gravity as human cannonballs. Audiences gasped as the Zacchinis were blasted into the air from a cannon at speeds of 90 mph (144 km/h) toward a net that was more than 150 ft (46 m) away.

The Zacchinis were already long-established circus performers when Maltese-born inventor Ildebrando Zacchini suggested to the Italian government that his new human cannon would be a good way of propelling soldiers into enemy lines during World War I. After the proposal was rejected for being too risky, Ildebrando decided to use the cannon in a family act, involving seven brothers and two sisters.

Ildebrando's eldest son, Edmondo, was the first to try out the spring-loaded cannon. It hurled him just 20 ft (6 m) and put him in hospital with a broken leg. In the 1920s the Zacchinis replaced the crude contraption with a cannon which enabled them to fly greater distances.

Inside the cannon!

The female as well as the male Zacchinis earned a living as human cannonballs. Here, Egle Zacchini is seen in her suit, crash helmet and asbestos mask just before a launch in the 1940s.

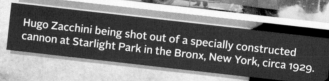

Hugo Zacchini being shot out of a specially constructed cannon at Starlight Park in the Bronx, New York, circa 1929.

During World War II, when her brothers Hugo and Mario were sent to fight, 18-year-old Victoria Zacchini took their places in the cannon. Here she is in Chicago in 1943 being blasted outward.

The famous Hugo Zacchini atop his cannon outside the Ringling Brothers and Barnum & Bailey Circus in Brooklyn, New York, in 1933.

HUGO ZACCHINI—HUMAN PROJECTILE
RINGLING BROTHERS AND BARNUM & BAILEY COMBINED CIRCUS

BROOKLYN, N.Y.
MAY 1ST 1933

REINDEER RACING

Being a reindeer racing jockey is not for the faint-hearted. Jockeys on skis harness themselves behind the de-antlered animals as they sprint around a frozen lake at speeds of nearly 40 mph (65 km/h) during the annual 2-mi (3-km) Kingship Cup race in Inari, Lapland, Finland. There are more than 500 registered racing reindeer and 100 professional reindeer jockeys in Finland, and around $22,000 is bet on the outcome of the race.

BED OF NAILS At Fremont, Indiana, Amy Bruney skipped rope 117 times on top of a 125-lb (57-kg) board that was fitted with 3,000 upturned nails, the points of which were painfully pressing onto the chest and stomach of her husband, Pastor Jon Bruney.

TOTAL FLIP At the 2012 Winter X Games at Aspen, Colorado, Heath Frisby of Middleton, Idaho, became the first person ever to front-flip a snowmobile, completing a 360-degree revolution in midair before landing safely.

GIANT SNOWMAN Greg Novak from Gilman, Minnesota, used farm equipment to build a 50-ft-high (15.2-m) snowman with a 45-ft-wide (13.7-m) base. It took him hundreds of hours to construct the snowman, who had plywood eyes, a barrel for a nose, garbage can covers for buttons, an 80-ft-long (24.3-m) scarf and carried a 35-ft-high (10.6-m) broom.

REVERSE SPEAKER Schoolboy Cameron Bissett from Bo'ness, Scotland, can speak fluent English backward. He started by imagining what words would sound like backward before progressing to full sentences. He can even pronounce the title of the *Mary Poppins* song "Supercalifragilisticexpialidocious" backward!

HUMAN TORCH Austrian stuntman Joe Tödtling managed to last for an incredible 5 minutes 41 seconds with his entire body on fire and without extra oxygen supplies before the heat finally became unbearable. For the stunt, Joe, who has appeared in movies such as *The Monuments Men* with George Clooney, wore a special suit and was set on fire by his wife Julia.

Toe Wrestling

One of England's craziest sports events is the World Toe Wrestling Championships, which takes place each year in Derbyshire, England. Competitors sit barefoot facing each other and lock their big toes together, the aim being to pin the opponent's big toe on the platform for three seconds. During the contest, hands must be kept flat on the floor and the non-fighting foot must stay in the air. The championships were devised in the 1970s by George Burgess, who wanted to give England the chance to be world champions in at least one sport!

Ripley's—Believe It or Not!®
www.ripleys.com/books
FEATS

STILETTO SPRINTER Eighteen-year-old Julia Plecher from Ruckersdorf, Germany, ran 100 meters in 14.53 seconds in 2013—while wearing high-heeled shoes. Her time was just 4.95 seconds slower than the world record achieved by Usain Bolt in more suitable footwear for running.

LONG STRIKE Joey Augustine, manager of Seaside Lanes Bowling Alley in Virginia Beach, Virginia, made a strike from a distance of 120 ft (36.5 m)—double the length of a bowling lane. Using a 14-lb (6.3-kg) ball, he stood at the entrance door of the alley, hurled the ball across the carpeted floor, past a sofa and down the lane, knocking down all ten pins.

FLYING SHOPPER Matt McKeown from Devon, England, broke the U.K. national road speed limit—while riding a shopping cart. He reached 70.4 mph (113.3 km/h) on the cart, which was powered by a Chinook helicopter starter engine and a 250cc Honda engine and was stabilized with go-kart wheels.

DARING DHERS Venezuelan BMX rider and five-times X Games gold medalist Daniel Dhers performed a series of amazing stunts, including 360s, tailwhips, no-handers and even a backflip, on ramps mounted on the backs of two trucks moving through traffic in Lima, Peru.

BEES' KNEES Sophia Hoffman, 11, and Kush Sharma, 13, proved such expert spellers that the 2014 Jackson County, Missouri, Spelling Bee went on for an incredible 66 rounds—before the organizers ran out of suitable words! It resumed two weeks later and, after a further 29 rounds, Kush finally won.

Australian aerial acrobat Simone Genziuk hangs upside down while lifting a 165-lb (75-kg) washing machine with her hair.

The washing machine, which hangs from a hook linked to a woven knot in her hair, weighs 33 lb (15 kg) more than she does! Simone used to be a trapeze artist, but then started lifting 4.4-lb (2-kg) weights with her thick, waist-length hair, even though it proved very painful. She has since conditioned her hair to lift bigger weights by putting olive oil on it and never brushing it.

LIVING DOLL Robyn Amato of Tampa, Florida, has been collecting Raggedy Ann dolls for more than 20 years and now has over 3,000. She has spent more than $20,000 on her hobby, and even dresses up as Raggedy Ann and takes some of her dolls out on day trips.

➡ **BRIAN JACKSON OF MUSKOGEE, OKLAHOMA, IS ABLE TO USE HIS MOUTH TO INFLATE AND BURST THREE HOT WATER BOTTLES IN JUST OVER A MINUTE.**

FINGER FORCE Malaysian kung fu master Ho Eng Hui can pierce coconut shells with just his index finger and with such force that the water inside the shell spurts out.

NARROW GAP Wearing aerodynamic wingsuits, French and Norwegian thrillseekers Ludovic Woerth and Jokke Sommer jumped from an airplane over Rio de Janeiro, Brazil, and flew through the narrow 26-ft-wide (8-m) gap between the city's 460-ft-high (140-m) Ventura Corporate Towers.

WATER GUNS Chris Reid of Renton, Washington, has a collection of more than 340 Super Soaker water guns. The pump-action toy was introduced in 1989 and Reid's first Super Soaker, a green and yellow 50, is autographed by its inventor, Lonnie Johnson.

SNOWMAN ARMY Volunteers in Ottawa, Ontario, Canada, built 1,299 snowmen in just one hour at the Winterlude event on February 1, 2015.

HAIR RAISING

BLIND SHOT Michael Quin of Springfield, Missouri, hit a three-pointer during a half-time challenge at the February 2014 basketball game between the College of the Ozarks and Bellevue to win himself free McDonald's meals for a year—and the 54-year-old nailed the shot despite being blind since 2010.

LATE GRADUATE Manuela Hernandez from Oaxaca, Mexico, graduated from elementary school at the age of 100 in June 2013. As a child, she had to leave school after just a year to work for her family, but resumed her studies when she was 99 on the advice of one of her grandchildren.

BACKWARD STUNT Sitting backward on the handlebars, Norwegian daredevil Eskil Ronningsbakken cycled in wet conditions at speeds of up to 50 mph (80 km/h) down a 2.8-mi (4.5-km) winding mountain road that runs from the 2,788-ft-high (850-m) summit of Trollstigen in Norway.

SUPER ROBOT Cubestormer III, a robot designed by David Gilday and Mike Dobson, solved a Rubik's Cube in just 3.253 seconds at a science fair in Birmingham, England. It took 18 months to build the robot, which is able to perform physical movements faster than the human eye can see.

Longest Moonwalk

At an event organized by the Ripley's Believe It or Not! museum in Pattaya, Thailand, on June 24, 2014, 16-year-old Niwat Otthon stepped backward in a continuous Michael Jackson-style moonwalk for a record-breaking distance of 0.75 mi (1.2 km).

TRICK SHOT American teen Sam Gove produced a near-impossible basketball trick shot—over the roof of a house! After a few unsuccessful attempts, his perseverance paid off when he threw the ball from the back of the house high over the single-story roof and straight through a hoop located in the front garden—a full court distance away.

BEE BODY On May 13, 2014, beekeeper Ruan Liangming sat covered in 100,000 bees for 53 minutes 34 seconds in Yichun City, China—and wasn't stung once. Ruan, who has also worn a suit of 137 lb (62.1 kg) of bees, says to avoid being stung the secret is to keep perfectly still so as not to agitate the insects.

MASTER OF BALANCE Doug McManaman of Amherst, Nova Scotia, can balance 56 golf balls for 1 minute on a tower resting on his chin. He has also balanced a snowboard on his thumb for 4 minutes 49 seconds and walked 1.73 mi (2.79 km) while balancing an egg on the back of his hand.

STILT WALKER Neil Sauter completed the 2013 Grand Rapids Marathon in Michigan in 5 hours 56 minutes 23 seconds—on 3-ft-high (0.9-m) stilts. As he has a mild case of cerebral palsy, Neil's feet turn inward making it difficult for him to walk normally, but when he wears stilts his feet are strapped in tight with the result that he is much more coordinated on a pair of stilts than on his own two feet!

DEADLY TRICK

Showman Li Peng from Jilin Province, China, entertains crowds by putting live poisonous snakes, scorpions and spiders into his mouth before pulling them back out again. He trained for the trick by being locked in a room with 30 deadly snakes. Although he has been bitten many times, he says he has learned to neutralize the snakes' venom.

Loop-the-LooP

Daredevil Scottish trials cyclist Danny MacAskill performed a gravity-defying loop-the-loop around a colossal 16-ft -high (5-m) loop erected on a barge floating on the River Thames, London, England in front of the London Eye ferris wheel.

After practicing the stunt for hours, he rode down a 60-ft (18-m) ramp to build up enough momentum to complete the terrifying loop, the biggest he had ever conquered.

NASAL TYPIST Mohammed Khursheed Hussain of Hyderabad, India, types amazingly fast with his nose. He does it with one eye closed to help to see and locate the keys more efficiently. He is even quicker with his fingers and can type the alphabet from A to Z on a keyboard in just 3.43 seconds.

REVERSE RIDE Australian Andrew Hellinga rode a bicycle backward for 209.77 mi (337.6 km) in 24 hours in October 2013 at an average speed of 8.75 mph (14 km/h). He first started riding backward to impress girls when he was a teenager!

WORLD CUP WALK In order to honor the England national soccer team that won the World Cup in 1966, four England fans walked 1,966 km (1,221.6 mi) to attend the 2014 World Cup in Brazil—a distance to reflect the numbers in the winning year. Adam Burns, David Bewick, Pete Johnston and Ben Olsen spent three months walking from Mendoza, Argentina, to the Brazilian city of Porto Alegre, hiking through swamps and a desert and even along a live train line. On the way they survived being charged by bulls and electrocuted by a farmer's fence. Their efforts raised more than £20,000 ($30,000) for a Brazilian poverty charity.

SUPER FANS In 2015, three avid football fans— Donald Crisman from Kennebunkport Beach, Maine, Larry Jacobson from San Francisco, California, and Tom Henschel from Natrone Heights, Pennsylvania—attended their 49th Super Bowl in a row. Their unbroken streak began on January 15, 1967, when they watched Green Bay beat Kansas City 35–10 at the Los Angeles Memorial Coliseum. Tickets for that first Super Bowl ranged in price from $6–$12, compared with $800–$1,900 in 2015.

BURNING DESIRE Ridip Saikia from Ratanpur, India, can swallow 30 pieces of burning charcoal in a minute—without suffering any injury.

SHARP SHUCKERS Using sharp knives, a team of ten Canadian oyster shuckers opened 8,840 oysters in one hour during the 2014 Tyne Valley Oyster Festival on Prince Edward Island.

STREET HOCKEY A street hockey game in Nanaimo, British Columbia, lasted for more than four days. Forty players took part in the game, which ran for 105 hours 44 minutes. The final score saw Team University Village Mall beat Team Coastal Community Credit Union by 1,728 to 1,381.

HIGH JUMP Wearing no safety gear, extreme trampolinist Greg Roe of Brampton, Ontario, can jump from a height of 180 ft (55 m)—equivalent to the 25th floor of an apartment building—and perform incredible twists and somersaults in midair before landing on a huge airbag.

ONE-ARMED WEIGHTLIFTER Within a year of losing her right arm in a car crash, Krystal Cantu of San Antonio, Texas, could lift 210 lb (95 kg) clear above her head with her remaining arm.

EGG BALANCING Cui Juguo from Changsha, China, can balance eggs on the points of needles—even ostrich eggs, the largest eggs in the world. He can also balance forks, toothpicks and eggs on a pin—all at the same time.

RHESUS NEGATIVE Tim Flock drove in eight NASCAR races in 1953 with a rhesus monkey, "Jocko Flocko," as co-driver. He retired the monkey after Jocko was hit by a pebble during a race and the resultant pit stop cost him a victory.

→ **A RECORD 1,161 RUNNERS DRESSED IN GORILLA COSTUMES IN OCTOBER 2013 TOOK PART IN THE 10TH ANNUAL DENVER, COLORADO, GORILLA RUN.**

TWO-DAY DIVE Scuba diver Sean McGahern from Brighton, England, spent nearly 50 hours at the bottom of the Mediterranean Sea off the coast of Malta. Despite strong winds and 3-ft-high (1-m) waves on the surface of the water, he remained submerged for more than two days, managing to eat and drink underwater and sleeping on a makeshift deck chair chained to the sea bed.

TEDDY TOSS In the 19th year of the annual Teddy Bear Toss, where Canadian hockey fans take stuffed toys to the game and throw them onto the ice when the home team scores its first goal, supporters of the Calgary Hitmen flung 25,921 toys onto the rink on December 1, 2013, after Pavel Padakin had opened the scoring against the Medicine Hat Tigers.

TRUCK PULL Lia Grimanis of Toronto, Ontario, can pull a transport truck weighing 17,000 lb (7,711 kg) a distance of 100 ft (30 m). She can also pull a 14,520-lb (6,586-kg) truck while wearing 3-in-high (7.5-cm) heels. She first realized she was able to pull heavy loads when she got a job as a rickshaw driver and found that she could pull up to eight people in the back of the rickshaw.

MARATHON GAME Two teams in the Philippines played a basketball game that lasted for 120 hours 1 minute 7 seconds—just over five days. The final score saw Team Bounce Back beat Team Walang Iwanan by 16,783 points to 16,732.

STRONG SHINS Martial arts expert Dr. Mak Yuree Vajramuni from Bangladesh has shins that are as strong as steel and he can use them to shatter a bundle of three baseball bats with a single shin kick. To break each bat requires 740 psi of force.

LONG SERVICE At age 100, Dolly Saville is still working as a barmaid three days a week at the Red Lion Hotel in the town of Wendover in Buckinghamshire, England. She reckons she has served two million pints of beer since she started working there in 1940, during which time she has looked after movie stars and Prime Ministers alike and has only ever had two weeks off sick.

MOTORBIKE YOGA

Gugulotu Lachiram performs death-defying yoga exercises on the back of a motorbike traveling at 40 mph (64 km/h) along roads in Telangana, India. The 40-year-old farmer can sit, stand or lie down on his moving bike for a distance of over 3 mi (4.8 km) and although disaster is just a slip away, he has never had an accident.

HOOKED UP

Russian BASE jumper Stanislav Aksenov leaped from a 1,300-ft-high (400-m) cliff near Bern, Switzerland, and glided to the ground with a parachute attached to metal piercings fixed into the flesh on his back.

Although his skin stretched under the strain of his body weight and he was left hanging by his flesh for more than two minutes, he still managed to land safely in a field.

TWO SPORTS Deion Sanders is the only athlete to play in both the Super Bowl, for the San Francisco 49ers (1995) and the Dallas Cowboys (1996), and the World Series, for the Atlanta Braves (1992).

YOUNG VOLUNTEER Jimmie Foxx (1907–67), "the right-handed Babe Ruth," who played Major League baseball from 1925 to 1945, was the only ten-year-old to volunteer during World War I. He tried to enlist in the U.S. military as a drummer boy, but the recruiting officer explained to him that drummer boys carried firearms.

KNITTING MARATHON David Babcock, design professor at the University of Central Missouri, ran the 2013 Kansas City Marathon in 5 hours 48 minutes—while knitting a scarf that became more than 12 ft (3.6 m) long.

GOLF SWING Law student Luke Bielawski from Fishers, Indiana, played golf all the way across the U.S.A. from the beach at Ventura, California, to Kiawah Island, South Carolina—a course that covered a 2,928 mi (4,712 km) area of land. The mammoth golf game took him 93 days and 46,805 strokes, and he lost 5,540 balls along the way.

DOMINO TOWER Graduate engineer Tom Holmes from Bristol, England, spent 7 ½ hours building a free-standing domino tower from 2,688 dominos. The tower stood 17 ft 4 in (5.3 m) tall—taller than a double-decker bus.

MARATHON EFFORT Doug Kurtis of Livonia, Michigan, ran his 200th sub-three-hour marathon when he finished the 2013 Detroit Free Press Marathon in 2 hours 59 minutes 03 seconds— at age 61. He broke the 3-hour barrier for the first time in 1974 and ran 12 of his record 76 sub-2-hour-20-minute marathons in a single calendar year, 1989.

ANTARCTIC TREK Explorer Ben Saunders from Devon, England, and former French international rugby player Tarka L'Herpiniere trekked 1,795 mi (2,889 km) from the Antarctic coast to the South Pole, following in the ill-fated footsteps of the 1912 expedition led by Captain Robert Falcon Scott. The pair set off on October 25, 2013 and took 105 days to complete the return journey, hauling 440-lb (200-kg) sleds in temperatures as low as −51°F (−46°C).

HEAVY GOING On October 5, 2013, 52-year-old Lloyd Scott from Essex, England, climbed 38 floors—1,037 steps—up London's Gherkin building in 2 hours 53 minutes—while wearing a 140-lb (63.5-kg) 1940s deep-sea diving suit. Back in 2002, he took over five days to complete the full London Marathon course of 26.2 miles (42 km) also while wearing an antique diving suit.

ACROBATIC SWORDSMAN Nick Penney of Augusta, Maine, can swallow three swords and then turn two consecutive cartwheels while keeping the swords in place. He has also swallowed three swords at once while suspended upside down.

MUSICAL GENIUS After receiving a blow to the head while playing lacrosse when he was 12 years old, Lachlan Connors of Denver, Colorado, became a musical genius. He had shown no interest or ability in music before the accident, but within a few years of the dramatic blow, he had taught himself to play 13 different instruments, including piano, guitar and bagpipes, entirely by ear.

HAPPY CLAPPER Bryan Bednarek clapped his hands 804 times in 1 minute at Arlington Heights, Illinois—over 13 claps per second.

PULLING POWER

Franz receives help for exhaustion after his amazing show of strength.

Extreme athlete Franz Muellner—the "Austrian Rock"—used sheer muscle power to pull a 156.5 ton Boeing 777 airplane by rope over a distance of 47 ft 6 in (14.5 m) at Vienna Airport on June 23, 2014.

He trained for five months for the feat and afterward described the effort of pulling the 210-ft-long (64-m) plane as "brutal."

175

CROSS COUNTRY In June 2013, U.S. Paralympian Ryan Chalmers from Churchville, New York, completed a 3,300-mi (5,311-km) journey from Los Angeles, California, to New York City in a wheelchair in just 71 days, pushing himself the equivalent distance of up to three marathons a day. He suffered 13 flat tires as well as calloused hands, sore shoulders and painful knees. He was born with spina bifida, leaving him with only partial use of his legs, but he began playing hockey, basketball and soccer at the age of eight with the help of crutches.

900-MILE SWIM Sean Conway from Gloucestershire, England, swam the length of Britain from Land's End, Cornwall, to John O'Groats, Scotland, in 135 days. Between June and November 2013, he swam 900 mi (1,448 km) up Britain's west coast, during which he made an estimated three million strokes and was stung ten times by jellyfish. Cold weather forced him to stay out of the water for 45 days overall, and, while swimming, his jaw became so numb he was unable to chew solid food and had to have his meals pureed.

TANDEM JUMP BASE jumpers Julie Wentz and Ramon Rojas pulled off a daring piggy-back tandem wingsuit jump in Kjerag, Norway. The pair leaped from a 3,000-ft-high (900-m) cliff with her perched on his back and flew through the air before gliding safely to the ground.

NORTH POLE MARATHON

Labeled the world's coolest marathon, the North Pole Marathon has been run since 2003 by intrepid athletes who have braved sub-zero temperatures, polar bears and a course that is constantly on the move beneath their feet.

The 26.2-mile (42.2-km) race is run in temperatures as low as −25°F (−32°C) across snow and thick ice covering the Arctic Ocean—and although the runners are unable to feel it, the ground beneath their feet is forever shifting with the ocean current.

The event is the brainchild of Irishman Richard Donovan, who won the inaugural South Pole Marathon in Antarctica in 2002. Before establishing the North Pole contest he ran a solo marathon there himself to see if it could be done and so became the first person to complete marathons at both poles.

Signposts indicate that this is a marathon far from civilization.

Ripley's Believe It or Not!®
www.ripleys.com/books
FEATS

TALL ORDER Kevin Schmidt, of Rapid City, South Dakota, climbed 1,500 ft (457 m) to the top of the KDLT-TV antenna near Salem just to change a light bulb. He has scaled hundreds of towers in his job as a communications company engineer, sometimes in 60 mph (96 km/h) winds.

HIGH CATCH In 1938, Henry Helf of the Cleveland Indians caught a baseball that was dropped 708 ft (215 m)—and thought to be traveling at 138 mph (222 km/h)—from the top of Cleveland's Terminal Tower.

STRONG BOY Fourteen-year-old Jake Schellenschlager of Glen Burnie, Maryland, can lift twice his own body weight. Standing 5 ft 3 in (1.6 m) tall and weighing 119 lb (54 kg), he deadlifted 300 lb (136 kg) at the 2013 Powerlifting Bench Press Championships in York, Pennsylvania.

MODERN MERMAID Wearing a mermaid-like monofin for greater speed, Rebecca Coales of Bristol, England, held her breath underwater for two-and-a-half minutes as she swam nearly four lengths of an Olympic-sized pool in July 2014. She swam the 587 ft (179 m) without a breathing device and without coming up for air at the pool in Stockport, Greater Manchester.

RIPLEY'S RESEARCH

A wind chill of −50°F (−45°C) can cause frostbite in just five minutes. As our bodies are designed to protect our heart, kidneys and lungs, in extreme cold all available blood is diverted to keep these vital organs warm and functioning. As a result our extremities—nose, fingertips and toes—lose their blood and become cold to safeguard the rest of the body and keep us alive. Shivering is another essential device for coping with the cold because it generates heat and warms the body.

Runners have to wrap up to survive freezing temperatures.

OLD REF Harry Hardy from Derbyshire, England, still referees local amateur soccer matches at age 87. He started refereeing in 1959 and says, "I can still run a bit."

HOOVER FAN Nine-year-old Harry Burrows from the West Midlands, England, has a collection of more than 40 vacuum cleaners. He has been fascinated by the vacuums ever since his parents used one to soothe him to sleep when he was a baby and he now spends his pocket money buying old or rare models.

BRIDGE RIDE On January 11, 2014, stunt rider Mat Olson rode his BMX bike over the top of the 24-ft-high (7.3-m) arches of the newly built West Seventh Street Bridge in Fort Worth, Texas. "It seemed like I was on top of a mountain," he said afterward. In his career the 25-year-old has suffered 13 concussions, a ruptured spleen, three knee surgeries and has had his front teeth (and replacement front teeth) knocked out several times.

MATCHBOX COLLECTION Steven Smith of Norfolk, England, has more than 20,500 matchboxes and over one million matchbox labels from 130 different countries.

HAPPY GRANDPA When 16-year-old Liverpool winger Harry Wilson made his debut for the Welsh national soccer team, against Belgium in 2013, he became the youngest-ever Welsh player and also won his grandfather a £125,000 ($200,000) bet. In 2000, Pete Edwards had placed a bet that Wilson would one day play for Wales at odds of 2,500 to one—when his grandson was only two years old.

LONG SCARF Helge Johansen from Oslo, Norway, has spent 30 years knitting a scarf that is 3.1 mi (5 km) long and weighs around 1,100 lb (500 kg). When he started work on the garment, at age 17, he did not know how to knit and had to be taught by his mother.

HIGH ACHIEVER With a parachute attached to his body acting as his only form of safety net, daredevil Andy Lewis from Moab, Utah, tiptoed along a 40-ft (12-m) slackline that was suspended in mid-air between two hot air balloons flying 4,000 ft (1,200 m) above the Nevada Desert. The high-rise walk took Andy 20 seconds, after which the 27-year-old skydived to the ground.

FREE CLIMB Without any ropes, safety equipment or even a helmet, rock climber Alex Honnold from Sacramento, California, scaled El Sendero Luminoso, a 1,500-ft-high (457-m) limestone wall at Nuevo León, Mexico, in less than 3 hours just by clinging with his hands to tiny crevices.

Floating Ramp

Brazilian-born professional skateboarder Bob Burnquist found a new setting to perform his stunts—a 7,300-lb (3,311-kg) floating ramp on Lake Tahoe, California. Designed by Jeff King and Jerry Blohm, the structure took 300 hours to build before being lowered into the lake. It consists of two wooden skateboard ramps, 8 ft (2.4 m) and 5 ft (1.5 m) high, resting on a 36-ft-long (11-m) platform.

SENTIMENTAL SKYDIVE In November 2013, 93-year-old Jack Hake from Dorset, England, carried out a tandem skydive from an altitude of 10,000 ft (3,000 m) while carrying the ashes of his late wife Veronica, to whom he had been married for 70 years.

HUGE HAMMOCK Bay Hammocks, a small company based in Seabright, Nova Scotia, created a giant handmade hammock, which measured 52 ft (16 m) long and 16 ft (5 m) wide, from 62 pieces of rope. It took more than 1 mi (1.6 km) of rope to make the hammock, which is 11 times the size of a regular hammock.

RIDING ON WATER Professional motorcycle racer Guy Martin from Lincolnshire, England, rode a distance of 208 ft (63.5 m)—over half the length of a football field—across water. Using a lightweight ski attached to the rear wheel and sitting as far back as possible, he rode down a shallow ramp across Bala Lake in North Wales—a body of water deep enough to submerge a ten-story building.

SPROUT PUSH Stuart Kettell from West Midlands, England, spent four days pushing a Brussels sprout up 3,560-ft-high (1,085-m) Mount Snowdon in North Wales—with his nose. Wearing a special faceguard to protect his skin, he deliberately chose a large sprout so that there would be less chance of it falling down a rock crevice, but he still went through 22 of the vegetables on his painstakingly slow ascent. He trained for the event by pushing a sprout around his garden.

FIN FUN

Wearing a snorkel and cumbersome swim fins that were more than twice the length of his foot, New Yorker Ashrita Furman has run 1 mile (1.6 km) in just under 8 minutes. Furman, who has been performing crazy athletic feats for 35 years, has also run 3.1 mi (5 km) in swim fins while juggling three objects in just over 32 minutes.

HANGING OUT

At the 2014 International Highline Meeting, 22 daredevils dozed in 16 hammocks suspended hundreds of feet in the air on Mount Piana in the Dolomites mountain range of northern Italy.

The thrillseekers attached their hammocks to a strengthened highline as they carefully walked along the 1-in-wide (2.5-cm) wire. Once nestled in their high-altitude sleeping quarters, some were so relaxed they even began playing the guitar.

Portuguese artist Bordalo II is turning the city of Lisbon into a giant trash zoo. He scours the streets in search of items of garbage, which he then builds into huge sculptures of brightly colored animals, birds and insects.

He tours dumpsters and dumps in search of discarded plastic sheeting, scrap metal, old tires, shingles, cardboard boxes and lengths of electrical cable. Once he has the basic materials for his artwork, he painstakingly positions the individual pieces in the shape of the creature before spray-painting it. His technique enables him to turn an urban environment into a fantasy wilderness populated with huge crocodiles, parrots and owls, and ladybugs the size of cars.

The grandson of an artist called the Real Bordalo, who also painted parts of Lisbon, Bordalo II says his aim is not only to promote recycling, but to show that we often have nice things that are based on junk without realizing it. He first had the idea for his urban zoo when he began gluing together some of the garbage that had collected in his studio to see if he could make anything from it.

Ripley's ask

Have you always been a graffiti artist? I've been a graffiti writer since the age of 11, painting illegal stuff in the street. However, the artwork I'm presenting now is different—it's more like street art, contemporary art or big-scale assemblage.

How did you come up with the idea to create art from junk? I had a lot of junk in my studio, so I started to glue small pieces to a canvas. I liked the effect, so I painted over the collages. Then, I started to explore various techniques using different materials.

What are some of the most unusual items you've used in your designs? I like to think there's nothing unusual about the objects I use, because they are just the city's waste—objects that we all use (and throw away) every day.

How long does each piece take and do you create the pieces on your own? I have two production assistants who help me with big-scale pieces, which might take three or four days, depending on the size and materials. I make my canvas pieces alone.

Which is your favorite piece? My favorite one is the Gift to Mother Nature, because the concept behind the piece is the basis of all my work—city waste, the fruit of consumerism.

LIFE IN A SARDINE CAN

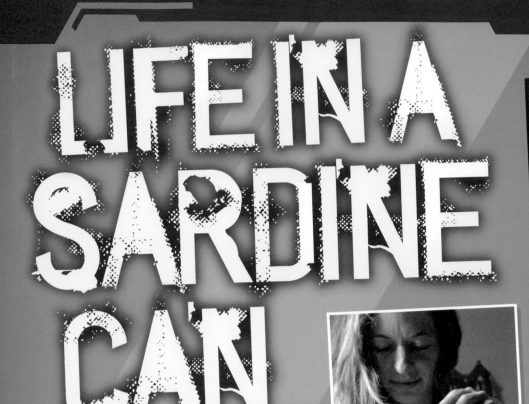

Nathalie Alony from Mantova, Italy, makes the most of small spaces, using clay to craft lots of tiny, everyday apartment scenes, which she then places within the confined space of empty sardine cans.

She has named the humorous series "Home Sweet Home" or "The Sardinas," and describes her cozy creations as being "all these different lives, different stories, different histories and futures, all that intimacy, condensed between four walls, one next to the other, in little apartments, little boxes that each of us calls home."

Nathalie started "The Sardinas" in 2006 after thinking about people "squeezed in like sardines" in apartment buildings, hearing their neighbors' lives in these enclosed spaces. She captures the scenes of people's daily lives within 2.4-x-4-in (6-x-10-cm) tins, despite the fact that the tins once housed small salty fish, which she feeds to her cats.

She has completed hundreds of sardine-can scenes, portraying a large array of scenarios. Most are inspired by her own life, but sometimes other people commission her to place their own stories within a can. Nathalie sees the cans as her own biography—in 3-D comic frames that reveal her life.

Ripley's ↓ ask

How long does it take to create one scene? It takes about three days—including molding, cooking, carving, sanding, painting and doing the interior.

Why in a sardine can specifically? When too many people are tightly sharing a small space we use the expression "squeezed in like sardines," so when the idea came up of making condo-buildings with cans, the medium served the metaphor.

What tools do you use to create the scenes? I use small cutters and professional modeling tools. I also have a kit bought in a dentist market in Delhi, India, which is extremely useful.

How do you come up with the ideas for each scene? I began with the most simple activities people do in their houses: have dinner, argue, go to the toilet and so on. Soon enough "The Sardinas" took me over and I started miniaturizing every situation I had in mind, everything I saw, heard, imagined or fantasized. It became an instinct, an impulse, a new and amusing communication form.

BOTTLE TREE Dalius Valukonis, a Lithuanian policeman, built a 13-ft (4-m)-tall Christmas tree from 1,100 empty bottles of champagne and sparkling water. A non-drinker, he spent three years obtaining the bottles from restaurants, bars, family and friends.

SAND DRAWINGS Using a device called a Focused Ion Beam, Brazilian artist Vik Muniz and researcher Marcelo Coelho etch detailed, microscopic drawings of sandcastles onto individual grains of sand.

3-D DRAWINGS

This may appear to be a three-dimensional object, but it is actually just a trick of the eye. The picture is the work of Italian artist Alessandro Diddi, who uses clever shading to create pencil drawings that, when viewed from a certain angle, seem to jump out of the page in 3-D. He often places his own hand or a pencil in his drawings to make them look even more lifelike.

JEDI TAPESTRY Sci-fi fan and artist Aled Lewis from London, England, has hand-stitched the entire *Star Wars* story onto a 30-ft (9-m) Bayeux-style tapestry. He watched and rewatched the movies and read up on the major plot lines and characters before creating his *Coruscant Tapestry*, the border of which features quotes from each film written in Aurebesh—the writing system used in the *Star Wars* universe.

MONEY BOAT Sergei Nikolayev Knurov, a chef from Mykolaiv, Ukraine, made a model of a ship from 17,000 coins and with banknotes for sails. The coins are held together by silicate glue and it took him six months to collect enough coins to build the 30-lb (13.6-kg) ship.

HUMAN HAMSTERS Performance artists Ward Shelley and Alex Schweder spent ten days living in a huge hamster wheel, 25 ft (8 m) high and 78.5 ft (23.9 m) in circumference, which was suspended from the ceiling at New York City's Pierogi Gallery. Alex, who is afraid of heights, lived on the inside of the wheel at the bottom, while Ward stayed on the outside of the wheel at the top. Each had a bed, desk, chair and bathroom. To reach different sections, the two men had to walk slowly along the wheel at the same time, but in opposite directions.

GOLDEN EGG A decade ago, an unnamed American scrap metal dealer paid $14,000 for a jewel-encrusted artifact at a Midwest flea market, thinking he could make a small profit by having it melted down for its gold content. Prospective buyers thought it was overvalued, so it languished in his kitchen until an online search revealed that it was one of the eight missing Fabergé Russian imperial eggs and was worth more than $20 million. The egg, which contains a luxury watch, sits on a jeweled gold stand and was originally given by Russian Emperor Alexander III to his wife, the Empress Maria, for Easter in 1887.

Zac Freeman of Jacksonville, Florida, has created a series of portraits of family members and friends from recycled garbage.

He incorporates up to 5,000 items of trash in each picture, including buttons, bottle tops, key caps and even old computer keyboards. He works from photographs of his subject, gluing the objects onto his canvas, and each portrait takes him up to two years to complete.

GARBAGE PORTRAIT

FAKE FOOD New York artist Roxy Paine spent six months building a replica of a fast-food restaurant entirely out of birch wood, maple and glass. It featured order screens, cash registers, soft-drink dispensers, a frozen yogurt machine, straw dispensers, coffee brewers, deep fryers and stacked-up containers for burgers and fries.

BEAR NECESSITIES For 13 days and 13 nights in April 2014, French performance artist Abraham Poincheval lived inside the hollowed-out carcass of a dead bear. He ate, drank, slept and lived inside the sterilized carcass while being filmed by two cameras at the Hunting and Wildlife Museum in Paris, France. He previously spent a week in an underground hole beneath a Marseille bookshop.

BLACK MAGIC Using the pseudonym "Roadsworth" (suggesting a poet of the roads), stencil artist Peter Gibson has transformed the streets, sidewalks and parking lots of Montréal, Quebec, into large-scale works of art. He creates huge paintings on black asphalt so that it looks as if flocks of geese are swooping along the city's streets and schools of sardines are swimming happily along busy roads.

BIZARRE BLAZERS

Dripping with irony, UK artist Anna Sternik's 2.3 in (6 cm) tall creepy candles feature faces so realistic and disturbing you might hesitate before you light them. From a red-lipstick mouth grinning from half a face, to two ears on either side of a faceless head, each of the artist's unique designs are made from a soybean vegetable wax called EcoSoya. As Stenik points out, "A melting face can be both creepy and entertaining."

ANTIQUE DOORSTOP A woman used an old wooden pot as a doorstop at her cottage in Hertfordshire, England, for more than 40 years before discovering it was a rare 18th-century Chinese ornament. She sold it an auction in 2014 for a staggering £150,000 ($250,000).

TWINKIE FAN Inspired by Andy Warhol, artist Nancy Peppin from Reno, Nevada, has created dozens of artworks featuring America's iconic, cream-filled Twinkie snack cakes. When makers Hostess Brands closed in 2012, she created *The Last Snack*, a nod to Leonardo Da Vinci's famous painting *The Last Supper*, featuring a Twinkie in place of Jesus.

PRISON MURAL While serving a 70-month jail sentence, artist Jesse Krimes created an impressive, 39-panel mural from prison bedsheets, newspapers and hair gel. He burnished thousands of high-quality images from *The New York Times* onto the bedsheets with just a plastic spoon and using hair gel as a transfer agent. He worked on one sheet at a time, and after he had finished each one, he shipped it to his home in New Jersey. It was only when he was eventually released that he saw the complete work.

PAPER SHIPS Since 1968, Peter Koppen from Munich, Germany, has folded more than 200,000 tiny paper ships to make colorful collages. To create his "microships," he makes 15 folds into pieces of paper that are about one-fifth the size of a postage stamp.

STRAW TWIST

Japanese artist TAO cuts and twists plastic drinking straws into sculptures of dragons, insects, animals and popular animé characters. He uses sharp scissors to cut into straws of different lengths and colors, then bends and knots the strands into shape. The leg of a beetle involves dozens of individual cuts into the straw.

Barbie

PARTS

For her "Plastic Body" series, Margaux Lange makes unique items of wearable jewelry from the parts of old Barbie dolls.

The New-York-born artist, who always loved Barbie as a child, has thousands of secondhand Barbies in her studio and uses their hands, arms, ears, mouths, breasts, eyes and legs to make necklaces, earrings, brooches and rings. One neckpiece is made up of 29 Barbie mouths; another contains 20 Barbie arms.

PENCIL TOWER Gandhavalla Umasankar from Andhra Predesh, India, took two months to build a model of the Eiffel Tower from 600 pencil leads.

RECYCLED HOMES Gregory Kloehn, a designer from Oakland, California, has turned recycled and reclaimed materials found on streets into mobile homes for homeless people, featuring washing machine doors for windows and minivan tops for roofs.

PUMPKIN DINOSAURS The 2013 Great Jack O'Lantern Blaze at Croton-on-Hudson, New York, featured sculptures made from 5,000 individually carved pumpkins. They included life-sized dinosaur skeletons made entirely from hundreds of pumpkins stacked together.

SOCCER NUT Using a scalpel and a magnifying glass, micro-artist Quentin Devine from Surrey, England, celebrated the 2014 World Cup by carving tiny sculptures of five England soccer legends from individual Brazil nuts.

189

PIXEL PAINTING

The body column on the left is largely illegible, but fragments can be read:

...his process involves... then injecting... bubble... each piece... with individual... palette...

...He has created other... pieces of work... including... Vincent van Gogh's self-portrait.

The New York-based artist was inspired to use bubble wrap after finding a roll left over from moving house. After exploration into the history of the product, he found that it was originally invented in 1957 as a modern form of wall covering. So he has taken it back in the direction as well as flipping it from its popular use as a protective covering for art into art itself.

He even manages to create a second collection of paintings from the actual injection process. As the bubbles are injected, the excess paint drips down the back of the piece. Upon completion, the drippings are peeled away to reveal an imprint of the work, which becomes part of his Impressions series.

Part of his Impressions series.

Completed Artwork

Ripley's ↧ ask

How did you start getting into bubble wrap art? That's a big question, and there were a bunch of ideas leading up to it. I was trying to find the quintessential dumb material, and to make something from everyday material. My first piece was a number of signs that said "Don't touch the art!" But as it was bubble wrap everyone wants to touch it! Then I spray painted over it saying "Touch me!" But if you did touch it, it is solid once the paint injected into the bubbles has dried, so I was playing with your senses. If you did work up the courage to touch the art you thought "Oh, I can't pop this."

What is the largest bubble piece you've created? The biggest piece I have done, which took me over 500 hours, is the old master, The Ladies, which is 7 x 6.5 ft (2.1 x 2 m) and contains more than 40,000 bubbles.

What do you do if you make a mistake? I invented a tool to remove damaged bubbles, a cylinder that can cut around the bubble remove it and replace it with a fixed bubble. The process is so seamless that even I cannot find the replaced bubble!

Your favorite piece? I couldn't answer it, it's really hard, I love them all. Although sometimes some do turn out better than I expected, but I love all my babies equally!

Made of **bubble wrap!**

TONGUE PAINTING

Artist Ani K from Kerala, India, has painted more than 1,000 artworks—including an 8-ft-wide (2.4-m) version of Leonardo da Vinci's *The Last Supper* and this portrait of Jesus—with his tongue. He uses his tongue as a palette on which to mix new colors and then licks the paint onto the canvas before twisting his head to form different strokes, even though the process often leaves him with headaches and jaw pain.

EGG CARTONS Charlotte Austen and Jack Munro used 6,500 egg cartons to create a life-size replica of a World War II Spitfire fighter plane at Duxford Imperial War Museum in Cambridgeshire, England. The egg cartons were attached to a wood and steel frame, which had to be broken down into 12 sections so that the replica could be transported by truck.

MINI LISA Scientists at Georgia Institute of Technology created a copy of Leonardo da Vinci's *Mona Lisa* that is just a third of the width of a human hair in size. They used an atomic force microscope and heat-based nanotechnology to make the tiny painting, and by varying the amount of heat applied at each pixel they were able to control the picture's shades to accurately replicate the original famous artwork.

CHEWED GUM Ukrainian artist Anna-Sofiya Matveeva creates portraits of celebrities such as Elton John and the late Steve Jobs from hundreds of pieces of gum chewed by her friends. After separating the gum into different colors and shades, she warms it up in a microwave. Each finished artwork can weigh up to 11 lb (5 kg).

MATCHSTICK MODELS Djordje Balac from Gospic, Croatia, has made a fully functional model of the world's largest crane—a Liebherr LTM 11200—from 175,518 matchsticks, 44 lb (20 kg) of glue and 17.6 lb (8 kg) of varnish. Working every day from 8 a.m. to midnight, it took him three months to make the crane, which, just like the real thing, has a moveable extending arm. He has also made amazingly detailed matchstick models of trucks, complete with detachable cabins.

EXPLOSIVE PICTURES Chemist and photographer Jon Smith from Fishers, Indiana, creates explosive artwork by taking pictures of lightbulbs, filled with brightly colored materials, shattering. He fills the glass bulbs with objects such as candies, sprinkles, chalk dust and beer caps, then fires at them with a pellet gun and captures the moment of impact on camera.

ROYAL TOAST Nathan Wyburn from Cardiff, Wales, created an image of the Duchess of Cambridge from 35 slices of toasted white bread and a pot of Marmite yeast extract.

GIANT DRAWING Working five hours a day for eight days, Singapore's Edmund Chen single-handedly created a drawing of koi fish and lotus flowers on a giant roll of paper that measured over 1,968 ft (600 m) long—that's six times the length of a soccer field.

UNDERWATER ARTIST Wearing full diving gear, Ukrainian artist Alexander Belozor paints landscapes underwater—at depths of up to 85 ft (26 m). He paints on canvases covered in an adhesive waterproof coating to prevent the colors running.

Lipstick Look-alikes

May Sum from Hong Kong, China, carves expensive lipsticks into small, lifelike 3-D busts of such fashion icons as Lady Gaga, Audrey Hepburn, Elizabeth Taylor and Madonna. Some of the lipstick sculptures take more than a week because she goes into great detail, even capturing English model Twiggy's individual eyelashes.

GLASS PLANTS

Glassblower Jason Gamrath of Seattle, Washington, makes 12-ft-tall (3.6-m) flowers from glass—even though it sometimes means him climbing inside a burning hot oven.

The biggest of his beautifully detailed flowers was made from one solid piece of molten glass, but his usual equipment was not big enough so he had to build a special 10 x 12 ft (3 x 3.6 m) oven heated to 1,832°F (1,000°C). Covered in flameproof Kevlar and a silver aluminum suit, he then climbed inside the red-hot oven and sculpted the flower, aware that he could remain inside only for so long. He still got a little burned—but reckons it was worth it.

11-Million Dollar
PAINTBRUSH

Instead of paint brushes, Princess Tarinan von Anhalt uses $11-million airplane jet engines to create one-of-a-kind artworks.

The New York-born artist hurls differently colored paints into the air flow of a Learjet engine, which then expels the paint at a force of 3,500 lb (15,569 N)—several times greater than a hurricane wind—onto an 8 sq ft (5.95 sq m) blank canvas positioned around 50 ft (15 m) away. The speed and heat from the engine combine to splatter the paint onto the canvas in unique, abstract designs.

Since 2006, she has made more than 30 jet paintings—after studying the work of her mentor and late husband, Prinz Jurgen von Anhalt of Germany, who pioneered the technique. Before creating each jet artwork, she carefully gauges the wind, the temperature, and the thickness of the paint.

Tarinan says that the blast from a Learjet airplane engine creates an amazing texture and structure that cannot be achieved by a conventional brush or palette knife, and she loves the experience. "When I'm in the midst of the creation, I don't think of the force, I don't think of the danger, I don't think of the heat. I'm caught up in the moment. It's addictive and you don't want to stop."

The air flow from the jet picks up the paint before splattering it on the canvas.

Princess Tarinan stands proudly beside a finished piece of her work.

BOTTLE MOSAIC A team of artists in Dubai, United Arab Emirates, created a mosaic from 12,844 plastic dishwasher liquid bottles. The mosaic, which took 30 hours to make and spelled out the brand name of the dishwasher liquid, was 38 ft (11.5 m) long and 22 ft (6.6 m) wide.

40 FRUITS By using pieces of tape to graft together different fruit-bearing trees, Sam Van Aken, an art professor at Syracuse University, New York, has created a single tree that produces 40 types of stone fruit—including peaches, plums, cherries, nectarines, almonds and apricots. The process took him over nine years to develop.

TO DIE FOR Adam Brown of Grandview, Missouri, incorporates his dead clients' ashes into beautiful prints. People send him a small amount of the cremated remains of their loved ones and he then mixes the ashes with paints, glues and resins to form a mixture used to create anything from the deceased's favorite place to a portrait of that person during life.

CANDY MAP Seventeen-year-old Jackson McKenzie of Nampa, Idaho, used more than 70,000 M&M candies to create a vast mosaic of Idaho and its state counties. The mosaic, which took ten months to plan and six days to complete, covered an area of 124 sq ft (11.5 sq m) on the bottom floor of the Idaho Statehouse.

Crocheted Creatures

At a glance, these may look as if they are the stuffed hides of real animals, but in fact they have been knitted from wool by Shauna Richardson of Leicester, England. Her "crochetdermy" collection features life-size replicas of monkeys, gazelles and buffalo, and for the 2012 London Olympics she spent two years hand-crocheting three 25-ft-long (8-m) lions out of 36 mi (58 km) of wool.

BEACH STENCILS To commemorate those who died during the World War II D-Day landings, sculptors Jamie Wardley and Andy Moss from Bradford, England, enlisted 200 volunteers to create 9,000 sand drawings on Arromanches beach in northern France. Sand was raked within stencilled outlines to form 9,000 individual silhouettes of civilians and Allied and German soldiers. The artwork, titled The Fallen, took two years to plan, but was erased a few hours after completion by the incoming tide.

REAL TEETH An 18th-century Mexican statue of Jesus Christ contains real human teeth. Restoration experts made the shocking discovery from X-rays, which showed that the teeth in the statue of the Lord of Patience in a church in San Bartolo Cuautlalpan once belonged to an adult human before being inserted into the mouth of the Christ figure. The teeth of statues are often made of animal bone, but rarely human teeth.

LOOKING UP Visitors to the Beaverbrook Art Gallery in Fredericton, New Brunswick, often view the large Salvador Dali painting Santiago El Grande by lying on the floor in the middle of the lobby. It is said that if you lie down and look at the painting from below, the horse appears to be jumping out of the canvas in 3-D.

RICE PORTRAITS For more than 20 years, artistic images the size of a football field have been created in a paddy field in Inakadate, Japan, using strains of red, purple, yellow, white and green rice. The pictures, which range from the likenesses of the Mona Lisa and Marilyn Monroe to Japanese anime characters and warriors, are first designed on a computer so that the farmers can work out where to plant the different types of rice. The finished landscape art is viewed from a specially constructed 72-ft-high (22-m) mock castle tower at the nearby town hall.

CHAIR TOWER

To mark the 125th anniversary of the completion of the Eiffel Tower, French company Fermob built a Paris art installation from 324 red Bistro chairs in recognition that the real tower stands 324 m (1,063 ft) tall. The 43-ft-high (13-m) model was held together by 5,184 rivets and contained 3,888 separate welding points.

STAPLE PORTRAITS

Made using **10,496** staples!

James Haggerty, an artist from New York, makes portraits of iconic Star Wars characters from tens of thousands of multi-colored staples. He has fashioned Darth Vader from 10,496 staples and C-3PO from 33,580 staples.

He punches each staple individually onto a painted board and can take six months to complete a work.

CANDY TRIBUTE

San Francisco, California, pop artist Jason Mecier spent over 30 hours creating a tribute to Robin Williams, shown as an amalgam of his most famous characters—Mork, Mrs. Doubtfire and Patch Adams—from pieces of candy, including jelly beans, gum balls, black licorice and Gummy Bears.

BLOOD SELFIE

Brooklyn-based artist Ted Lawson drew a life-size, nude self-portrait, titled *Ghost in the Machine*, from his own blood. Ted fed his blood, as if it were ink, intravenously into a pre-programed robotic arm attachment, which dispensed the blood onto a huge sheet of paper to form the illustration. He prepared for the three-hour blood selfie by eating a large cheeseburger as he says fatty foods improve his blood flow.

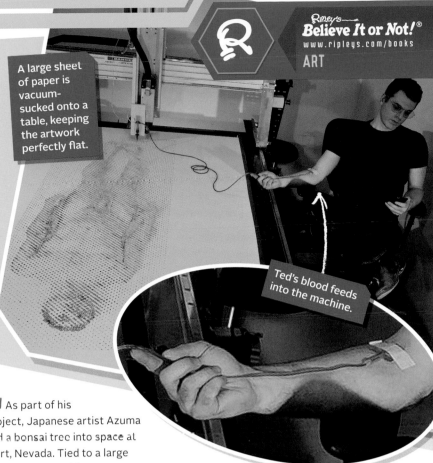

A large sheet of paper is vacuum-sucked onto a table, keeping the artwork perfectly flat.

Ted's blood feeds into the machine.

Blood flows as if it were ink, mapping out the illustration.

RIPLEY'S RESEARCH

Li bases his technique on traditional Chinese stretchable paper gourd decorations. He uses a brush to glue each sheet of paper individually at specific points to create a honeycomb effect. Once he has built enough layers to form a small block, he uses a woodworking saw to make the first cuts, removing any excess paper and reducing the area of the block into the desired shape. For the finer features, he uses an angle grinder, which allows him to achieve greater detail in the face. He then puts the finishing touches to the sculpture by shaping and smoothing it with sandpaper. The work is so painstaking that each design can take the former book editor several months to complete.

TO BOLDLY GROW As part of his Exobiotanica project, Japanese artist Azuma Makoto launched a bonsai tree into space at Black Rock Desert, Nevada. Tied to a large helium balloon, the tree soared for 100 minutes, reaching an altitude of 91,900 ft (28,000 m) before the balloon popped and the tree plummeted back to Earth. He also launched a bouquet of flowers 87,000 ft (26,500 m) into space.

SINGLE STROKE Using a 100-year-old technique called Hitofude Ryuu, the Sumie painters from the Kousyuuya Studio in Nikko, Japan, can paint the body of a dragon with a single stroke of the brush. Starting from the ornate head, it takes them just a matter of seconds to sweep a large brush across the canvas to paint the dragon's body, depicting all its scales and diverse shading.

COSTLY PRANK Pranksters painted cheap, red nail varnish on the white marble toes of the statue of Satyr Playing the Flute in the grounds of the Gatchina Palace Museum, Russia—but because of the way the varnish reacted with the marble, it cost the museum $70,000 to have it removed.

POWDERED MUMMY The paint color known as "mummy brown," which was popular with the Pre-Raphaelite artists of the 19th century, was made from powdered Egyptian mummies, both human and feline. Colormen could satisfy the demands of their artist customers for 20 years with the contents from a single mummy.

Paper Layers

Beijing-based Chinese artist Li Hongbo creates sculptures that look like Roman plaster busts but are really made from as many as 8,000 layers of thin paper, which are carefully glued together and then carved into shape. As these paper layers are flexible, the sculptures can be stretched and twisted in almost any direction like a giant slinky and then compressed back together into their original form.

CON-HORSE-TIONIST

Jockey Stefanie Hofer "rides" a team of ten painted acrobats contorted into the shape of a racehorse at the winning post at Ascot Racecourse in Berkshire, England, in July 2014. The unusual creature, which celebrated the Shergar Cup, was created in seven hours by the make-up artists Civilised Mess.

PAINTING PREMONITION Artist Chloe Mayo from Surrey, England, painted a near-perfect likeness of herself with her husband—months before she even met him! In 2009, she created the image of herself holding hands with her dream partner, a man with a dark beard. Weeks later, she joined an online dating website and spent two months messaging 30-year-old Michael Goeman before finally meeting him face to face. After they had been dating for six weeks, she thought his face looked familiar and remembered her oil painting. Seeing the similarity in the two men, she was so worried about being accused of stalking Michael that at first she hid the picture under her bed—but once they married in 2012 she could hang it proudly in their home.

MISSED OPPORTUNITY Original signed canvases by famous British street artist Banksy were sold from a stall in New York City's Central Park in October 2013 for just $60 each—despite being worth up to $30,000. Over a period of seven hours, only three people bought anything in the sale, the day's takings coming to just $420 with many valuable pieces remaining unsold.

MATCHSTICK GLOBE Over a period of almost two years, Andy Yoder of Falls Church, Virginia, built a 43-in (109.2-cm) diameter, 200-lb (90-kg) world globe from 300,000 matchsticks. He made his Earth's core from plywood, cardboard and expanding foam, then covered it in rice paper. Each colored match was carefully marked so he could replicate the image of 2012's Hurricane Sandy approaching the east coast of the U.S.A. He painstakingly hand-painted the matchsticks five at a time—blue for sea, green for land and white for clouds.

PLASTIC FANTASTIC Instead of using a brush, Sandy Byers paints beautiful landscapes with plastic credit cards. Her unusual technique started by accident when, on a 2013 painting trip to Marymere Falls in Olympic National Park, Washington, she realized that she had forgotten her brushes. Rather than go back, she took out her credit card and began painting with it. Since then, she has never used a brush, preferring to scrape the paint onto the canvas with her large array of cards.

Shell Skull

Artist Gregory Halili has carved delicate human skulls on black- and gold-lipped mother of pearl shells collected from his native Philippines. After the carving process is finished, he adds oil paint with such finesse that it is difficult to see where nature ends and the artist begins.
Also known as nacre, mother of pearl is a blend of minerals secreted by oysters and some other mollusks as an inner shell layer to protect them from parasites.

HANDMADE CAVES For over 25 years, sculptor Ra Paulette has used a pickaxe to scrape and shape New Mexico's sandstone cliffs into a series of 14 ornately decorated caves. One of his artistic caves, *Tree of Human Kindness*, located between Santa Fe and Taos, covers 208 acres (84 ha) and is valued at $795,000.

STRAW MOSAIC Fier, Albania artist Saimir Strati made a mosaic from over 150,000 plastic drinking straws The artwork, titled *Adam's Apple*, represents the bitten apple from the Garden of Eden and measures 325 sq ft (30 sq m).

BONE JEWELRY Kristin Bunyard of Austin, Texas, makes pieces of jewelry from old animal bones. She sources dead animals from farms or pet stores and after removing the organs and excess flesh, she slow boils the bones for a few hours. She then soaks the bare bones in a peroxide mixture until they are clean before turning them into elegant necklaces, bracelets and earrings.

SCRAP ROBOTS A scrap metal yard in Jinan, China, built and displayed more than 20 Transformer robots—including Optimus Prime, Bumblebee and Megatron—from leftover material. The tallest robot is over 52 ft (16 m) tall and weighs 5 tons.

21ST-CENTURY

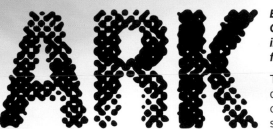

Evoking the spirit of Noah's Ark for his piece The Ninth Wave, *New York City-based Chinese artist Cai Guo-Qiang loaded 99 stuffed animals—including pandas, elephants and tigers—onto a fishing boat for a four-day voyage along China's waterways.*

The animals, which were deliberately arranged to appear close to death, were designed to highlight China's pollution problem in the light of 16,000 dead pigs being found floating in the Huangpu River, which supplies Shanghai's 24 million residents with most of their drinking water.

MAN ON LEASH For his performance art piece *Hipster on a Leash*, Chinese artist Guo O Dong rode a Segway while walking a bearded man on a leash around the streets and parks of the Williamsburg neighborhood of New York City. The artist had looked on Craigslist to find someone who would allow himself to be rented out for the day.

LEGO™ SANTA A team led by U.K. LEGO builder Duncan Titmarsh worked for 32 days to make a Santa Claus, complete with sleigh, sack of presents and nine reindeer, from 750,000 LEGO bricks for display in London's Covent Garden for Christmas 2014.

COIN MOSAIC Swedish company Sandvik Coromant unveiled a coin mosaic covering over 840 sq ft (78 sq m) in Chicago, Illinois. It used 214,000 dollars, quarters, dimes, nickels and pennies, worth over $65,000.

FILM COLLAGE Korean photographer Seung Hoon Park makes collages of famous buildings and landmarks from dozens of strips of 8-mm or 16-mm camera film. He takes hundreds of photos at a chosen location, places the film strips in rows and then weaves them together to give the impression of a single large print.

CARDBOARD DRAGON British artist Chris Gilmour has created a sculpture that retells the story of the patron saint of England, St. George, slaying the dragon. Measuring 10 ft (3 m) tall, the statue is made entirely from cardboard and glue using boxes and cigarette cartons found on the streets.

PUZZLE DESK Kagen Schaefer, a woodworker from Denver, Colorado, crafted a desk with an internal pipe organ and over 20 puzzles and secret compartments.

FINGER PAINTINGS Zaria Forman uses her fingers as a paintbrush to create incredibly realistic artworks of icebergs and Arctic seas. She took thousands of photographs on a 2012 expedition along the northwest coast of Greenland—retracing the 1869 journey of U.S. painter William Bradford—and once back in her Brooklyn, New York, studio, she used the pictures and her memory to compose large-scale images, smudging the colors with her hands for added realism.

WEEPING STATUE Thousands of worshipers descended on a house in the small Israeli town of Tarshiha in February 2014 after a statue of the Virgin Mary, bought by Osama and Amira Khoury a few months earlier, appeared to be weeping oil.

DIRTY WORK Parking attendant Rafael Veyisov uses just his fingers to draw amazing pictures of birds, buildings and landscapes in the layers of dust and dirt that collect on vehicles in the streets of Baku, Azerbaijan.

ICE HORSES Artists in Russia spent nearly two months sculpting 400 ice horses on Siberia's Lake Baikal—the world's deepest freshwater lake. Each horse was modeled from a 2-ton block of ice cut out of the lake's frozen surface.

Snake Bus

Forget *Snakes on a Plane*, this is a snake on a bus! Luckily it's not real, but is the work of a Danish advertising agency who, to promote Copenhagen Zoo, took pictures of an ordinary city bus and blended them with a picture of a very large boa constrictor. The result was so lifelike that some terrified passengers refused to board the snake bus.

FISHY BUSINESS French artist and photographer Anne-Catherine Becker-Echivard recreates scenes of everyday life using real fish heads. She obtains the open-mouthed fish heads from a market and, once she has come up with an idea, asks her mother to make the costumes. She then photographs the dressed fish as puppets. The whole creative process can take her three months per picture.

BONE CHINA Charles Krafft, from Seattle, Washington, makes fine bone china—out of human bones! He mixes cremation ash with clay to create unique mementoes of the dead.

STREET PAINTING A team of artists led by Yang Yongchun created a 3-D street painting on the campus of the Communication University of China in Nanjing that measured nearly a quarter of a mile long. The 1,200-ft-long (365-m) painting called *Rhythms of Youth* covered a total area of 29,466 sq ft (2,737.5 sq m) and took 20 days to complete.

SWEET ART Instead of using paint, Othman Toma of Baghdad, Iraq, creates colorful pictures from ice cream, including an impressive portrait of a lion from a chocolate ice cream bar. He places his chosen flavors of ice cream on a plate until they melt and then puts the sugary liquid onto a brush and applies it to the canvas. When the work is finished, he takes a photograph of it along with the ice creams used in the picture's making.

PIGEON POOP Frances Wadsworth-Jones makes £2,500 ($3,767) designer brooches that deliberately look like pigeon poop. The artist from London, England, took hundreds of pictures of bird poop to inspire the original design for "Heaven Sent," a line of jewelry consisting of black diamonds and sapphires arranged so that they replicate the shape, size and color of pigeon poop.

TREE LIKENESS The natural markings on a tree stump in Lillehammer, Norway, have formed a remarkable replica of artist Edvard Munch's famous painting *The Scream*.

TREE ILLUSION

It looks as if this tree is suspended in midair after having a section of its trunk removed, but in fact it is a clever optical illusion created by German graphic designers Daniel Siering and Mario Schuster. They wrapped the area of trunk in plastic sheet and then spray painted it with a landscape scene that perfectly matched the background. They had the idea after being commissioned to spray paint unsightly electricity transformer stations to make them blend in with the surrounding environment.

Ripley's Believe It or Not!®
www.ripleys.com/books
ART

BEAUTIFUL TRASH For his series *From the Street*, Louisville, Kentucky, artist Tom Pfannerstill turns pieces of wood into realistic-looking items of discarded trash— including a battered Budweiser can, a crushed Starbucks coffee cup, a flattened metal gasoline can and a squashed pack of cigarettes. He begins by choosing a real item of trash and tracing the outline onto a flat piece of wood. He then paints the wood in perfect detail, adding all the folds and creases to make it look like a 3-D object.

EXTREME EXHIBITIONS Abstract artist Edgy (real named Edward Fraser), from Alice Springs, Australia, staged his first exhibition at the Singing Sand Dunes of the Qatari Desert where the temperature was above 122°F (50°C). By contrast, his second exhibition was a cold one held at the base camp of Mount Everest at an altitude of 17,598 ft (5,364 m).

DUNG HEAPS *The Oriel of the Blue Horses*, a 2012 installation by Austrian artist Martin Gostner, consists only of four piles of fake dung. Each dung heap corresponds to one of the horses in Franz Marc's expressionist painting *The Tower of Blue Horses*, which the Nazis seized in 1937 for being "un-German" and has since vanished. It is not known whether or not the painting still exists.

BABY BELT 71-year-old Mary Jane François of Yellowknife, Canada, spent two years making a 21-ft-long (6.5-m) baby belt— the longest baby belt in the world. The belt—a traditional aboriginal garment which mothers use to carry their babies— consisted of 26 beaded flowers, each about the size of a person's hand, with a rainbow in the middle.

ARTISTIC LEAVES Iranian-born artist Omid Asadi from Manchester, England, uses a craft knife, needle and magnifying glass to turn dry, fallen leaves into intricate works of art. He carves beautiful silhouettes into the fragile brown leaves, including portraits of John Lennon, Bob Marley and Jimi Hendrix and an impression of Edvard Munch's painting *The Scream*. Each image can take him up to a month to create, after which he carefully presses the finished leaf onto a sheet of white paper with wood glue.

CARD MURAL Los Angeles-based artist Glenn Kaino made a large mural featuring a sculptural portrait of magician Ricky Jay from several decks of playing cards.

PLASTICINE PICTURES

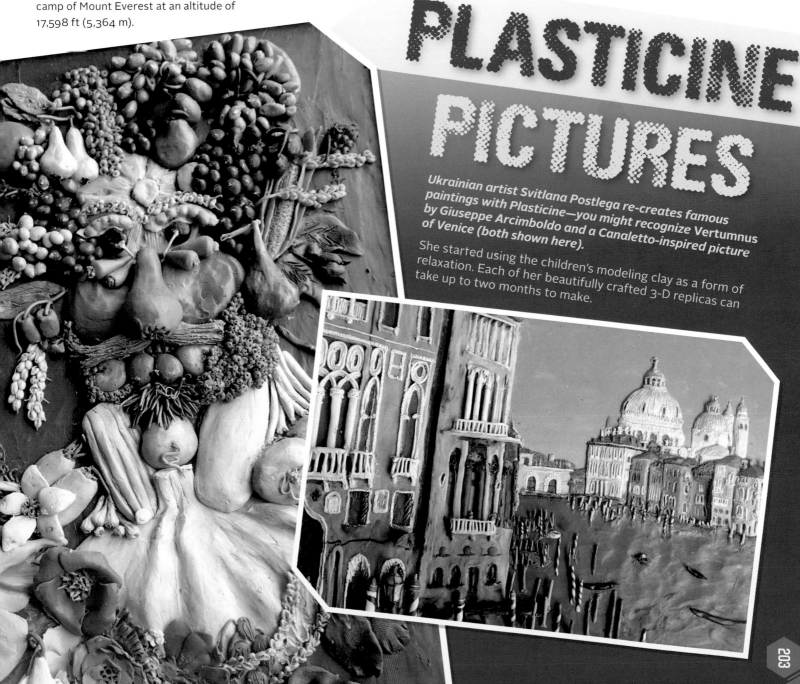

Ukrainian artist Svitlana Postlega re-creates famous paintings with Plasticine—you might recognize *Vertumnus* by Giuseppe Arcimboldo and a Canaletto-inspired picture *of Venice* (both shown here).

She started using the children's modeling clay as a form of relaxation. Each of her beautifully crafted 3-D replicas can take up to two months to make.

Tiny People

London, England-based artist Jonty Hurwitz creates nanosculptures of humans that are so tiny they can fit in the eye of a needle and can be viewed only through an electron microscope at 400x magnification. He uses over 200 cameras shooting simultaneously to scan life-size models and then prints his tiny sculptures using a special micro-sized 3-D printing technique. Then, over several hours, the sculptures are assembled, pixel by pixel and layer by layer.

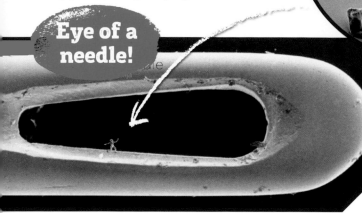

Eye of a needle!

FOUR SHOTS Gustavo Angel Tamayo, a student at Bryan College, Dayton, Tennessee, won $10,000 in October, 2014, by sinking four basketball shots in 30 seconds—a lay-up, a free throw, a three-pointer and a half-court shot. Amazingly, the college soccer player said he had never played basketball before and even managed to achieve the feat while he had a broken finger.

SEWER STUNTS Wakeboarders Matt Crowhurst, Lee Debuse, Christian Koester and Ollie Moore performed stunts in a sewer in Surrey, England. They swapped their boat for a rope attached to a portable petrol winch to show off their skills in the drain.

VICTORY CELEBRATION When the University of Mississippi football team, the Ole Miss Rebels, beat Alabama for the first time in 11 years in 2014, fans swarmed onto the field at the Vaught-Hemingway Stadium in Oxford, dismantled the goalposts and paraded them through the streets.

HUMAN COMPUTER Shakuntala Devi (1929–2013) of Bangalore, India, could instantly tell you the day of the week of any date in the last century. In 1977, she mentally calculated the 23rd root of a 201-digit number in 50 seconds—12 seconds faster than a computer at that time.

SCORCHING SCULPTURE A $500,000 public art sculpture, *Wishing Well*, in the shape of a giant, halved steel ball was removed from display in Calgary, Alberta, Canada, after the sun's rays bounced off its mirrored concave interior and burned a hole through a visitor's clothing. People had been encouraged to step inside the shiny object's 16-ft-high (5-m) hollow hemispheres and send text messages that would then be translated into a light display.

RECLAIMED TOYS Marlyn Pealane from Manila, Philippines, has a collection of hundreds of thousands of toys, many of which were found in local garbage.

1,000 BRICKS For more than two decades, 78-year-old Neil Brittlebank, from Leeds, England, has traveled the length and breadth of the U.K. collecting old and rare house bricks—and he now has more than 1,000 of them in his collection.

TOP MAN Bob Wheeler of Webster Groves, Missouri, reached the summit of Africa's 19,340-ft (5,895-m) -high Mount Kilimanjaro on October 2, 2014—at age 85.

HIGHLINE WALK Battling wind and rain, slackliner Alexander Schulz, from Rosenheim, Germany, after three days of trying and failing, finally managed to walk the incredible distance of 1,230 ft (375 m) along a highline in China. The line was anchored between two cliffs 330 ft (100 m) above the ground.

HIGH WIRE Dressed in his everyday clothes, Austrian daredevil Mich Kemeter walked across a tightrope 1,000 ft (300 m) above France's Grand Canyon du Verdon without any safety gear or ropes in two minutes.

GLASS KNITTING

This sculpture by Seattle-based artist Carol Milne makes it appear that she is able to knit with glass, but it is really the result of a painstaking four-week process. She begins by making a model of the sculpture in wax and encasing it in a mold material that can withstand very high temperatures. She melts the wax with hot steam to leave a cavity, which she fills with pieces of glass. The glass is then heated to 1,500°F (815°C) so that it too, melts into the shape of the artwork. After the piece is slowly cooled, over three to five days, she delicately chips away at it to create the remarkable wool-like effect.

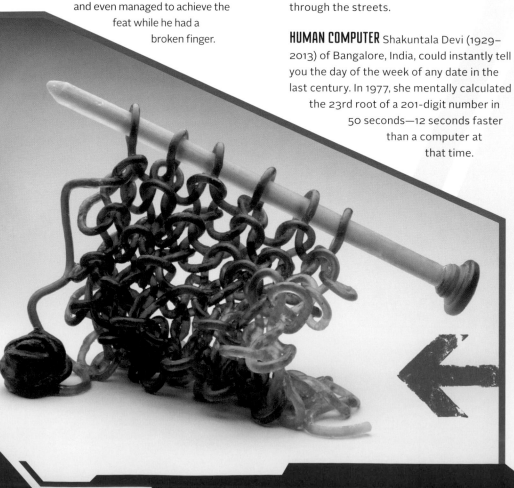

Dutch boxer and artist Bart van Polanen Petel paints with his fists.

Bart, who owns a gym in Tilburg, puts on boxing gloves, dips them in paint and throws punches at a blank canvas wrapped around a punching bag until it is daubed in a brightly colored abstract pattern. He says he just keeps punching until he is happy with what's in front of him, and sometimes adds finishing touches with his fingers. He needs to stay in peak physical fitness as each of his pieces take between one and three hours of boxing to complete.

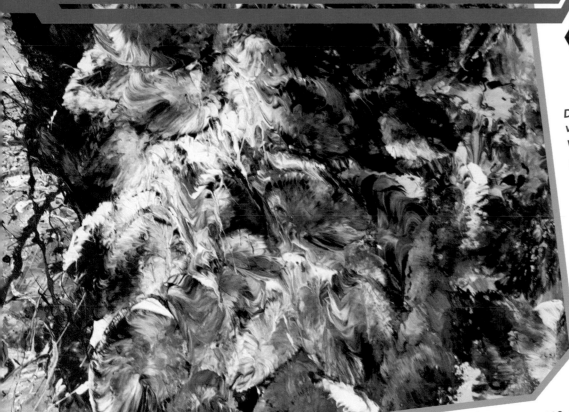

HAND PUNCHED ART

TAPE ARTIST

Emanuel Pavao shared with Ripley's these pictures of his artwork. The Toronto-based artist replicates photographs of storefronts, people and scenes of urban decay using different types of tape—including duct, electrical and masking—applied to paper or canvas board. He seals the final artwork with a clear resin for protection.

JUNK PORTRAIT For a 2014 installation in Paris, French artist Bernard Pras carefully arranged more than a dozen pieces of trash—including an old chair, a sofa and a guitar—in such a way that when viewed through a frame at the front, they miraculously formed an anamorphic 3-D image of a human face. His subject was Ferdinand Cheval, a French postman who, between 1879 and 1912, built his dream home out of materials that he found on his mail route.

HOLE PUNCHING Norwegian artist Anne-Karin Furunes makes black-and-white portraits by punching thousands of tiny perforations into large canvases. She covers the canvas with a layer of black acrylic paint and then punches the holes—making each one by hand and using 30 different sizes—to form an image.

PIANO BUTTONS Augusto Esquivel from Buenos Aires, Argentina, spent 2 ½ months making a life-size 3-D sculpture of an upright piano from 30,000 black and white buttons. He suspends hundreds of strings from the ceiling and then threads differently colored buttons onto those strings in the required order. When he brings the strings together, they form a pixelated image. The Miami-based artist has also used the technique to create monochrome portraits of movie stars including Audrey Hepburn, Marilyn Monroe and James Dean.

DUST DRAWINGS Using just one finger as his brush, artist Ben Long from London, England, draws beautiful pictures in the layers of dust that accumulate on the rear doors of commercial trucks. If the drivers don't wash their trucks, his artworks can last for six months.

IRON MAN Zhongkai Xiang, a young artist from Taiwan, spent 12 months of his spare time making an incredible full-size *Iron Man* suit out of cardboard. He has also created life-size sculptures of horses, dragons and birds from cardboard. As a break from working with cardboard, he made a sculpture of an alien out of drinking straws.

SPOON STATUE Sculptor Alfie Bradley built a 12-ft-high (3.6-m) statue of a gorilla from 40,000 metal spoons for spoon-bending entertainer Uri Geller. Hand-welding every spoon individually to the statue at the British Ironworks Centre in Shropshire, England, it took almost five months to finish the gorilla, using spoons donated from as far away as China, Kenya and India.

CLOUD SHAPER For his series titled *Shaping Clouds*, Argentinian artist Martin Feijoó took pictures of clouds on a visit to Mexico and drew on top of them what he imagined from their outline. The shapes of the clouds he photographed inspired him to create illustrations of a dinosaur, a dog, a turtle, a crocodile, a duck, a fish and even the "Father of Evolution," Charles Darwin.

CD PORTRAITS Italian artists Mirco Pagano and Moreno De Turco spent more than 200 hours lining up 6,500 compact disks to create portraits of seven world famous musicians—Michael Jackson, Bob Marley, Jim Morrison, Jimi Hendrix, James Brown, Freddie Mercury and Elvis Presley—from copies of their own CDs.

Made of feet!

BONE FLOWERS

Believe it or not, these delicate flowers are made from the bones of dead animals. Sculptor Hideki Tokushige from Tokyo, Japan, buys frozen rats and mice from pet stores, defrosts them, cuts away the flesh and spends over a month dissecting the skeleton. He then glues the individual bones together to create beautiful flowers, each one containing at least 100 rodent bones.

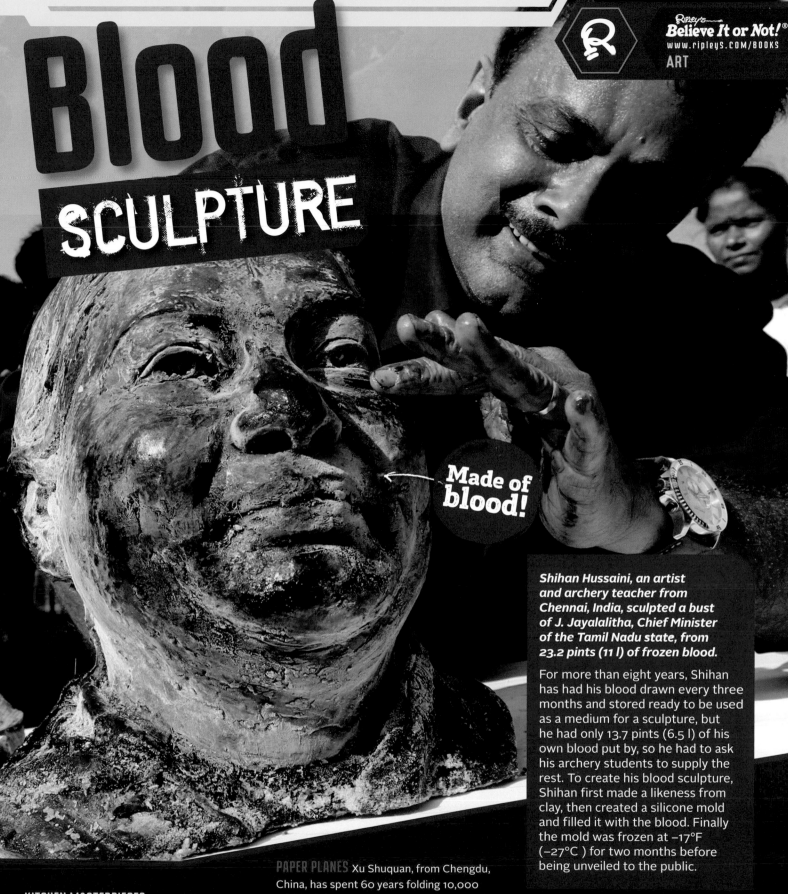

Blood SCULPTURE

Made of blood!

Shihan Hussaini, an artist and archery teacher from Chennai, India, sculpted a bust of J. Jayalalitha, Chief Minister of the Tamil Nadu state, from 23.2 pints (11 l) of frozen blood.

For more than eight years, Shihan has had his blood drawn every three months and stored ready to be used as a medium for a sculpture, but he had only 13.7 pints (6.5 l) of his own blood put by, so he had to ask his archery students to supply the rest. To create his blood sculpture, Shihan first made a likeness from clay, then created a silicone mold and filled it with the blood. Finally the mold was frozen at −17°F (−27°C) for two months before being unveiled to the public.

KITCHEN MASTERPIECES Two stolen paintings by French artists Paul Gauguin and Pierre Bonnard—worth $42 million—were found in 2014 hanging in the kitchen of a retired Sicilian autoworker. They had been stolen in London in 1970 and ended up five years later at auction in Italy where the Fiat factory worker, who was unaware of their value, bought them for just $30.

PAPER PLANES Xu Shuquan, from Chengdu, China, has spent 60 years folding 10,000 paper planes, using an origami technique called "Zhezhi."

TINY COMIC German artist Claudia Puhlfürst designed a comic strip, "Juana Knits the Planet," which Andrew Zonenberg etched onto a strand of human hair. He burned the dozen 25-micrometer frames into a single hair using focused ion beam etching.

ZOMBIE BALLS German spray-gun artist Oliver Paass designed a series of zombie bowling balls to promote *13th Street*, the country's popular horror TV channel. Oliver and his team snuck into bowling alleys all over Germany and swapped ordinary balls with ones depicting gruesome images of decapitated heads.

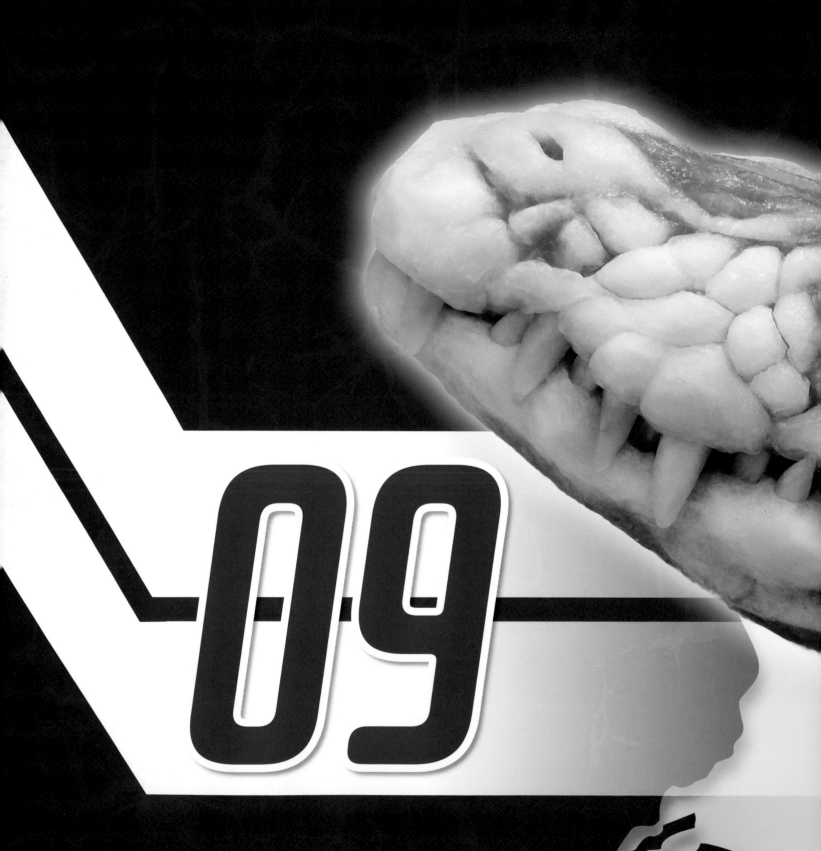

09

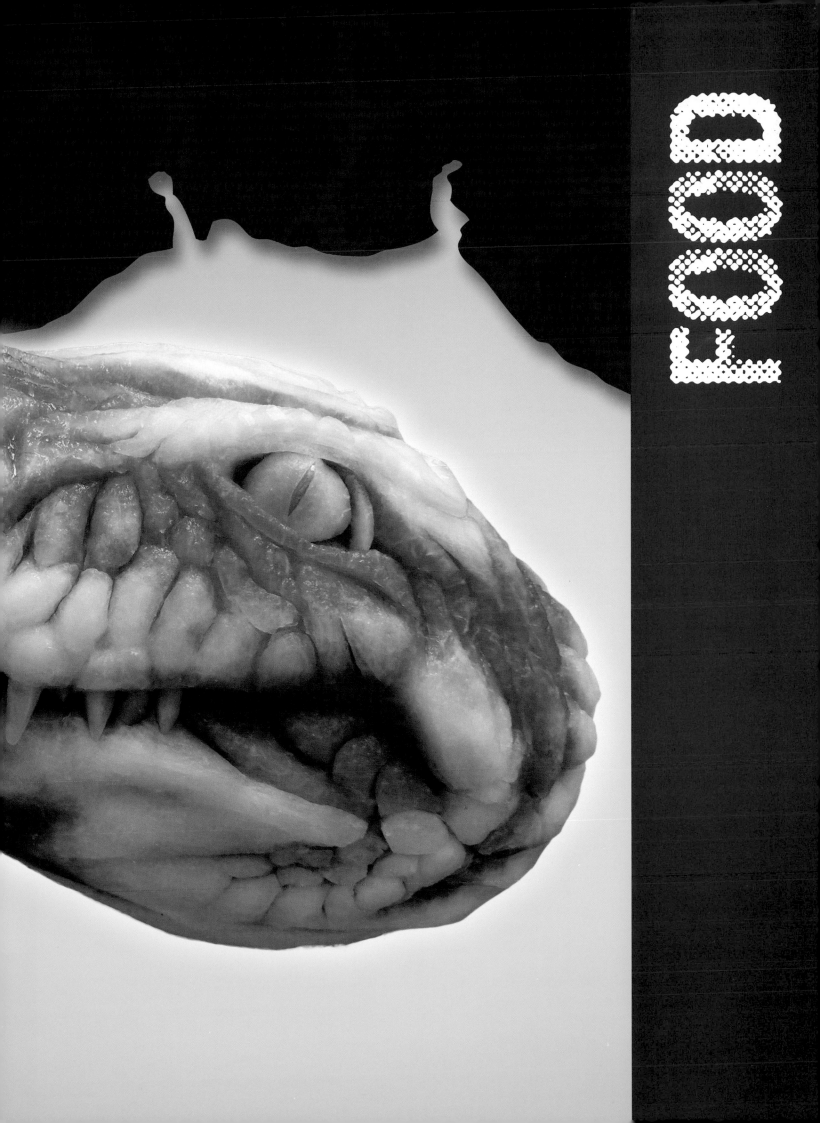

FOOD

PIE-SCRAPER

John Clarkson of Lancashire, England, created a burger that was 5 ft 4 in (1.6 m) tall—only 2 in (5 cm) shorter than himself. Called the "pie-scraper," it featured ten cheeseburgers, sausage rolls, a bacon sandwich, pizza, Spam, and pies, all encased in 18.7 lb (8.5 kg) of beef. Racking up 30,000 calories, it was enough to feed someone for nearly two weeks. It took John and his wife Corinne an hour and a half to assemble the burger on a specially made metal stand to make sure the tower did not topple.

SPROUT POWER An 8-ft-tall (2.4-m) Christmas tree in London, England, was lit up by a Brussels sprouts-powered battery. Copper and zinc electrodes were inserted into each sprout to create a chemical reaction that generated a current. The power was then stored in a capacitor and released through 100 LEDs.

SILENT SUPPER Jawdat Ibrahim, who owns the Abu Ghosh restaurant 6 mi (10 km) outside Jerusalem, Israel, offered customers a 50 percent discount if they turned off their cell phones during their meal.

KING NOODLE Zhao Mingxi, chef at a noodle restaurant in Chongqing, China, can make a noodle that is 1,000 ft (300 m) long—more than 12 times the length of a tennis court. He regularly makes 200-ft (60-m) noodles and spends up to ten hours preparing and swinging them.

SPECIAL TORTILLA In Vitoria-Gasteiz, Spain, chef Senen Gonzalez and his team cooked up a 3,300-lb (1,500-kg) tortilla that measured 16 ft (5 m) wide and was large enough to feed more than 10,000 people. An enormous pan and a complex heating mechanism were engineered specially for the event, allowing the gargantuan tortilla—made from eggs, potatoes, onions and 40 gal (150 l) of olive oil—to be cooked on both sides without needing flipping.

FOOD DROP Adam Grant, David McDonald and Huw Parkinson have founded a business in Melbourne, Australia, called Jafflechutes, which delivers toasted sandwiches by parachute from high-rise balconies to customers on the street below.

ZOMBIE BEER The Dock Street Brewing Company based in Philadelphia, Pennsylvania, created a zombie beer brewed with real smoked goats' brains. The company said of its zombie beer: "Don't be surprised if its head doesn't hang around forever!"

CABBAGE WINE Narusawa, a town in Japan's Yamanashi wine-making region, is famous for its cabbages, which it has used to make cabbage wine for 30 years.

FRUIT BABIES Farmer De He of Nanchang, China, grows fruit in the shape of babies. He was inspired to grow the fruit in little human-shaped molds by a Chinese fairy tale about a baby-shaped fruit that makes whoever eats it immortal.

JERKY MONUMENT To celebrate National Jerky Day (June 12, 2014), manufacturer Jack Link's built a 13-x-17-ft (4-x-5-m) meaty replica of Mount Rushmore. It took 1,400 hours to assemble "Meat Rushmore" by covering a foam sculpture with over 1,600 lb (726 kg) of beef, pork and turkey jerky. All the meat used laid out in a line would have stretched for almost 6¼ mi (10 km).

Black Tomato

By crossbreeding red and purple tomato plants, Professor Jim Myers of the University of Oregon created a black tomato. The Indigo Rose tomato starts green as normal but ripens to jet black, and apart from its unique color it is also believed to be beneficial in fighting obesity and diabetes.

HIP DINNER Norwegian artist Alexander Wengshoel boiled and ate his own hip. He took the body part home after undergoing a hip replacement operation, boiled it to loosen the meat and then ate it with potato gratin and a glass of wine. He said it tasted like "wild sheep." "First I just had a little taster, but since it tasted good, I made a full dinner of it. It was very exciting and stimulating. It was so personal."

VINE RIPE ROBOT

Developed in Japan by juice company Kagome and Japanese artist Nobumichi Tosa, the Tomachan robot will ride on the shoulders of marathon runners and feed them tomatoes during a race, as "tomatoes have lots of nutrition that combats fatigue," explained spokesperson Shigenori Suzuki. The hands-free feeding machine was created in time for use during the 2015 Tokyo Marathon, and is available in both an 8 kg (17 lb) and 3 kg (6.9 lb) size.

MEATBALL MUNCHERS

Vancouver, Canada, stages an annual contest in which competitors try to eat as many meatballs as they can in three minutes, the winner receiving the champion belt plus a year's supply of free spaghetti and meatballs. In 2014, Cody Jensen retained his title by devouring 15 meatballs in the allotted time. He says his secret is to eat the whole meatball in a single bite.

CAKE TWIN For his fourth birthday, Alfie Rose of Birmingham, England, was given a life-size replica of himself made from chocolate sponge cake. The 28-lb (13-kg) cake measured 47 in (1.2 m) from head to toe and was made by baker Lara Clarke from 20 sponge cakes, which were then coated in chocolate and buttercream icing and airbrushed with food coloring. The only part of the cake that was not edible was the polystyrene center of the head. Lara even made an edible replica of Alfie's favorite toy monkey.

IRON TEETH Chen Fengzhi, a 63-year-old Chinese woman, smashes lightbulbs and then chews the shards of glass with her "iron teeth." After swallowing the glass, she likes to bite down hard on a stone.

LARGE APPETITE In 1948, Sayler's Old Country Kitchen in Portland, Oregon, set up a challenge offering a free meal to anyone who can eat an entire 72-oz (2-kg) steak in under 1 hour—but on January 3, 2014, petite competitive eater Molly Schuyler of Bellevue, Nebraska, devoured one in just 2 minutes 44 seconds! Then on January 31, she won Wing Bowl 22 in Philadelphia, Pennsylvania, by consuming 363 wings— and the very next day she ate 5 lb (2.3 kg) of bacon in 3 minutes to win a contest in Des Moines, Iowa.

Chocolate Heart

This isn't any ordinary chocolate heart—it's an anatomically correct 1 lb (0.4 kg) solid chocolate heart, complete with tasty valves and ventricles. It is made by long-standing Illinois chocolate manufacturer, Morkes, who also produce chocolate skulls and a chocolate brain.

EDIBLE LANDMARKS Food artist Prudence Staite from Gloucestershire, England, re-created some of the U.K.'s most iconic landmarks—including the London Eye, Big Ben, Stonehenge and the White Cliffs of Dover—from French fries and mushy peas. Her version of the statue *The Angel of the North* required 240 fries and took 12 hours to make.

BUTTER CUP Nick Monte, owner of the Village Chocolate Shoppe in Bennington, Vermont, made a giant peanut butter cup that was almost 5 ft (1.5 m) wide and weighed nearly 230 lb (104 kg). It was made up of 70 lb (32 kg) of chocolate and 160 lb (72 kg) of peanut butter.

WHOSE TOOTH? Jane Betts of Cambridge, England, bit into a slice of cheese she had bought from a supermarket and discovered a piece of tooth. She frantically checked her own teeth to see where it had fallen from but, finding that they were all intact, she took it to her dentist who confirmed that it belonged to someone else.

NO MAC Montpelier, Vermont, is the only U.S. state capital without a McDonald's restaurant.

ALPHABET SANDWICH Nick Chipman from Milwaukee, Wisconsin, made a towering sandwich with 26 different fillings, one for each letter of the alphabet. His sandwich contained avocado, bacon, cheese, Doritos, egg, fish sticks, garlic bread, ham, Italian sausage patty, jalapeño peppers, a Krispy Kreme doughnut, lettuce, macaroni and cheese, noodles, onion rings, pepperoni, queso blanco dip, ramen noodles, spinach, a turkey burger, Usinger's bratwurst, veal parmesan, waffle, xylocarp (coconut), yams and zucchini.

CHRISTMAS TREAT A successful 1970s ad campaign led to it becoming popular in Japan to eat a bucket of KFC chicken on Christmas Eve—and orders are now taken months in advance.

NOODLE NIGHTMARE Jun Chia of China was knocked over by a scooter while snacking—lodging his chopsticks into his neck. Miraculously, there was no damage to any key organs!

WEIRD EATERS

Apple cofounder **Steve Jobs** once ate **only carrots** for so long that his skin turned orange.

Boxer **Joe Louis** drank **cow's blood** fresh from a Chicago slaughterhouse to toughen himself up.

Henry Ford used to eat sandwiches containing random **weeds** that he picked from his yard.

Russian–American novelist **Vladimir Nabokov** ate **butterflies.** He said they "tasted like almonds and perhaps a green cheese combination."

Angelina Jolie developed a taste for **cockroaches** in Cambodia, but disliked bee larvae.

Hollywood star **Gary Cooper** used to devour a whole can of **sauerkraut** every morning.

As a punishment for killing a **porcupine,** 13-year-old **Ernest Hemingway** was ordered by his father to cook and eat the animal.

COW → URINE

Hindu worshipers in Agra, India, believe that drinking fresh cow urine first thing in the morning can cure stomach problems, cancer and diabetes.

They also claim that cow pee is the only effective treatment for baldness. Hindus regard the cow as holy, and so dozens of people gather every day to drink the animals' urine, although apparently for the medicine to work the cow must not have given birth. Jairam Singhai has been drinking cow pee for more than ten years and says it has brought his diabetes levels under control.

213

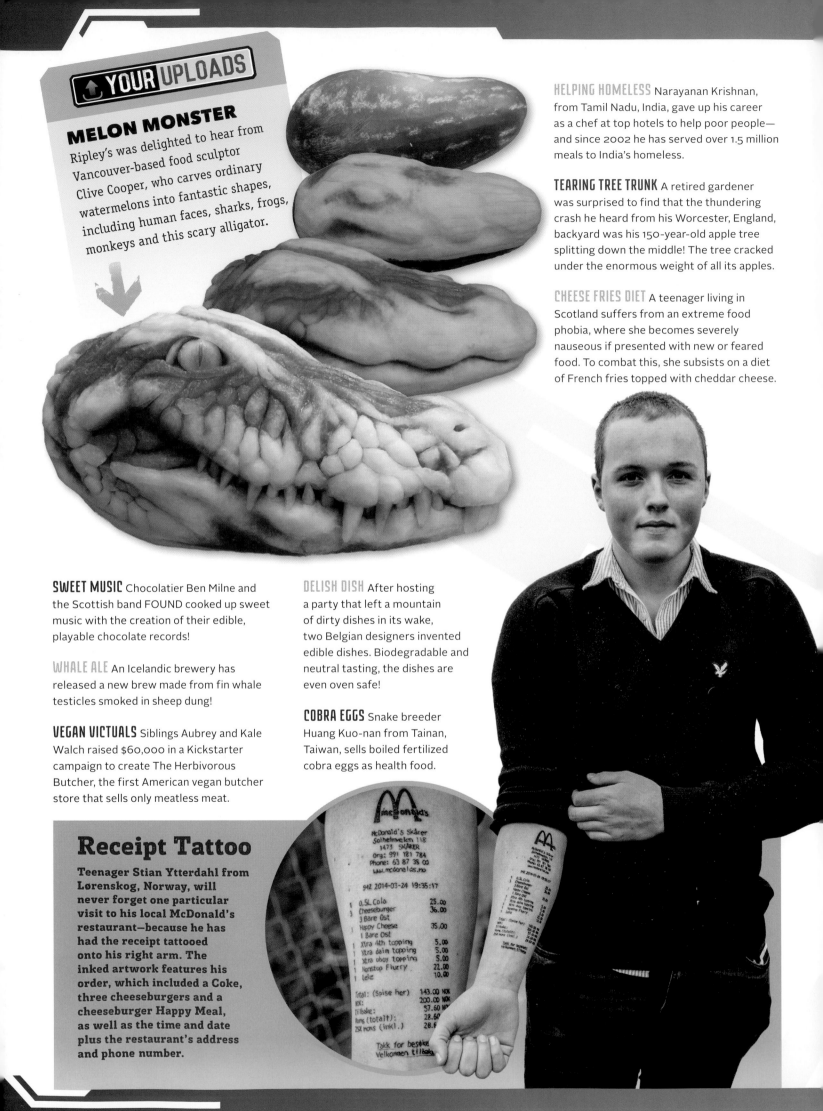

MELON MONSTER

Ripley's was delighted to hear from Vancouver-based food sculptor Clive Cooper, who carves ordinary watermelons into fantastic shapes, including human faces, sharks, frogs, monkeys and this scary alligator.

HELPING HOMELESS Narayanan Krishnan, from Tamil Nadu, India, gave up his career as a chef at top hotels to help poor people—and since 2002 he has served over 1.5 million meals to India's homeless.

TEARING TREE TRUNK A retired gardener was surprised to find that the thundering crash he heard from his Worcester, England, backyard was his 150-year-old apple tree splitting down the middle! The tree cracked under the enormous weight of all its apples.

CHEESE FRIES DIET A teenager living in Scotland suffers from an extreme food phobia, where she becomes severely nauseous if presented with new or feared food. To combat this, she subsists on a diet of French fries topped with cheddar cheese.

SWEET MUSIC Chocolatier Ben Milne and the Scottish band FOUND cooked up sweet music with the creation of their edible, playable chocolate records!

WHALE ALE An Icelandic brewery has released a new brew made from fin whale testicles smoked in sheep dung!

VEGAN VICTUALS Siblings Aubrey and Kale Walch raised $60,000 in a Kickstarter campaign to create The Herbivorous Butcher, the first American vegan butcher store that sells only meatless meat.

DELISH DISH After hosting a party that left a mountain of dirty dishes in its wake, two Belgian designers invented edible dishes. Biodegradable and neutral tasting, the dishes are even oven safe!

COBRA EGGS Snake breeder Huang Kuo-nan from Tainan, Taiwan, sells boiled fertilized cobra eggs as health food.

Receipt Tattoo

Teenager Stian Ytterdahl from Lørenskog, Norway, will never forget one particular visit to his local McDonald's restaurant—because he has had the receipt tattooed onto his right arm. The inked artwork features his order, which included a Coke, three cheeseburgers and a cheeseburger Happy Meal, as well as the time and date plus the restaurant's address and phone number.

SURPRISE STUFFING When Linda Hebditch from Dorset, England, opened a packet of supermarket-bought sage mix from Israel, a 3-in (7.6-cm) exotic praying mantis leaped out at her.

SILVER CARROTS German food company The Deli Garage has invented a tasteless edible spray paint called Food Finish to give meals an exciting splash of color—it comes in shades of gold, silver, red or blue.

7 UP In 2013, Joey "Jaws" Chestnut from San Jose, California, ate a record 69 hot dogs and buns in 10 minutes to win the Nathan's July 4th Hot Dog Eating Contest at Coney Island, New York, for the seventh consecutive year.

MASSIVE MUSHROOM A huge fungus found in Yunnan Province, China, was made up of as many as 100 individual caps attached at the base of their stems. It weighed over 33 lb (15 kg) and measured 36 in (90 cm) in diameter.

CHILI PIE At the State Fair of Texas in Dallas, cooks made a 1,325-lb (601-kg) Fritos chili pie, containing 635 bags of Fritos corn chips, 660 cans of chili and 580 bags of shredded cheese.

PITCH POTABLE Taking everyone's healthy zero-calorie drink to the next level, Blk is an electrolyte-infused mineral water that just happens to be completely—and naturally—black!

PASTA STRAND Lawson's Pasta Restaurant in Tokyo, Japan, created a single strand of pasta that measured an incredible 12,388 ft (3,776 m)–that's almost 2½ mi (4 km) long!

EDIBLE DRESS Donna Millington-Day, a baker from Staffordshire, England, created a cake in the shape of a stunning ivory wedding dress. The 6-ft (1.8-m) edible bridal gown weighed 55 lb (25 kg) and was made from 17 tiers of sponge cake and decorated with 48 lb (22 kg) of sugar-paste icing, 2 lb (0.9 kg) of royal icing, hundreds of sugar pearls and several hand-piped iced flowers. It was filled with 17 lb (7.7 kg) of vanilla butter cream and 7 lb (3 kg) of raspberry jam and could feed up to 2,000 wedding guests.

FLY BURGERS Villagers living near Lake Victoria in East Africa coat saucepans with honey to catch the trillions of flies that swarm around the area, they then make the trapped insects into nutritious flyburgers.

COOL CUBES

Japanese creative agency TBWA\Hakuhodo uses precision power tools to decorate cocktails with miniature ice sculptures, including a Buddhist temple, the Statue of Liberty, a shark, and a high-heeled shoe.

After receiving computer-generated designs, sharp tools and a CNC machine are used to whittle the ice cubes into 3-D shapes. As each sculpture can take up to six hours to make, the working environment has to be kept at a temperature of 19°F (–7°C) to keep the cubes from melting.

MILK VODKA Farmer Jason Barber from Dorset, England, produces vodka from pure cows' milk by fermenting the whey using a specialist yeast that turns milk sugar into alcohol. It took him three years to perfect the recipe for his Black Cow vodka.

LOST IN TRANSLATION When restaurant owner Fred Bennett of Nelson, New Zealand, began serving Thai food, he printed a Thai sign only to discover months later that it said "Go Away and Don't Come Back!"

→ AFTER BREAKING UP WITH HER BOYFRIEND, LOVESICK TAN SHEN STAYED AT A KFC RESTAURANT IN CHENGDU, CHINA, FOR A WEEK, EATING CHICKEN WINGS.

FRIED CAT At the now defunct Gastronomical Festival of the Cat in La Quebrada, Peru, townsfolk feasted on hundreds of specially bred domestic cats for two days. They believed that eating cat burgers, fried cat legs and fried cat tails could cure bronchial disease.

GOLDEN DELICIOUS Should you prefer some glitzy gluten, visit the Pan Piña bakery in Andalusia, Spain, where you can taste a loaf of bread sprinkled with 250 mg of gold dust. Loaves cost a sparkling $140.

MONSTER PIZZA A team of chefs headed by Dovilio Nardi baked a pizza in Rome, Italy, that measured 131 ft (40 m) in diameter and had a circumference of more than the length of a football field. Covering nearly a third of an acre and weighing over 25 tons—four times the weight of an adult African elephant—the giant pizza was made from 10 tons of flour, 5 tons of tomato sauce, 4½ tons of mozzarella cheese, 1,488 lb (675 kg) of margarine, 551 lb (250 kg) of rock salt, 220 lb (100 kg) of lettuce and 135 kg (298 lb) of yeast. Perhaps unsurprisingly, it took a full 48 hours to bake.

INFLIGHT TAKE-OUT Air Food One is a German food delivery service that exclusively caters to people who happen to love airline food and want to eat it at home as well as in the air. Created by a German grocery store in collaboration with the company that makes meals for the German airline Lufthansa, it includes weekly home delivery of meals that are "business-class quality." On the menu are such inflight delights as chicken in peppercorn sauce, beef tenderloin with caramelized onion sauce, filled ravioli, and bream with herb risotto. And just like on a real flight, there is always a vegetarian option, too.

GUMMY HUMANS

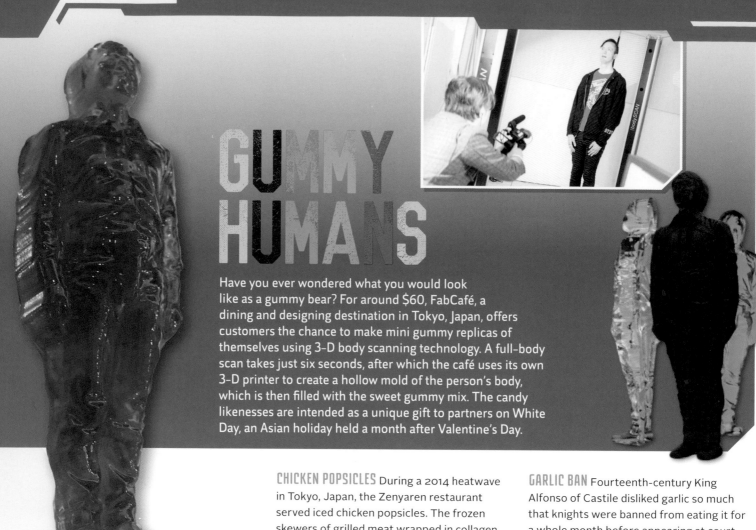

Have you ever wondered what you would look like as a gummy bear? For around $60, FabCafé, a dining and designing destination in Tokyo, Japan, offers customers the chance to make mini gummy replicas of themselves using 3-D body scanning technology. A full-body scan takes just six seconds, after which the café uses its own 3-D printer to create a hollow mold of the person's body, which is then filled with the sweet gummy mix. The candy likenesses are intended as a unique gift to partners on White Day, an Asian holiday held a month after Valentine's Day.

SEAGULL WINE Seagull wine is a traditional Inuit liquor made by fermenting a dead gull in a bottle of water.

GOLDEN CUPCAKE The Sweet Surrender candy store in Las Vegas, Nevada, sells a cupcake that costs $750. The "Decadence D'Or" is handcrafted from rare, expensive Venezuelan chocolate and Tahitian gold vanilla caviar, topped with Louis XIII Cognac—100 years in the making— and edible gold flakes.

ANCIENT CHEESE Cheese has been found on the bodies of mummies buried in China's Taklamakan Desert that is more than 3,500 years old, dating back to around 1615 BC The combination of dry desert air and salty soil prevented the cheese from decaying. It remains a mystery why the people were buried with pieces of cheese on their necks and chests, but the food may have been intended as food for the afterlife.

TASTY WORM The 12-inch-long (30-cm) Teredo worm, extracted from rotten mangrove trees, is considered a delicacy and is eaten raw by the Aboriginal people of Australia.

CHICKEN POPSICLES During a 2014 heatwave in Tokyo, Japan, the Zenyaren restaurant served iced chicken popsicles. The frozen skewers of grilled meat wrapped in collagen were snapped up by customers who said the ice pops not only kept them cool, but also improved their skin.

SWEET MEATS Grundhofer's Old Fashioned Meats of Hugo, Minnesota, makes more than 100 flavors of bratwurst, including Bloody Mary, Cherry Kool-Aid, Blueberry and even Gummy Bear.

GARLIC BAN Fourteenth-century King Alfonso of Castile disliked garlic so much that knights were banned from eating it for a whole month before appearing at court.

FREE FOOD At The Picture House, a pop-up restaurant in London, England, customers pay for their food with photographs. The restaurant belongs to frozen food company Birds Eye, and serves two-course meals that customers do not have to pay for if they take a picture of the meal and then share it online via the social media site Instagram.

COCKROACH TEA Tea made from cockroaches was a traditional remedy for tetanus in 19th-century Louisiana. Powdered roaches were also used to cure indigestion, while a crispy, fried cockroach tied tightly over a wound was said to relieve the pain of a bad cut.

Chocolate Room

This is every chocolate-lover's dream—a hotel room where nearly everything, including the book, lamp, candlestick and candles, vase of flowers, slippers, toothbrush, toothpaste and even the "Do Not Disturb" sign, is made of chocolate. The edible room was created by students from almost 220 lb (100 kg) of Callebaut chocolate and was installed for one night at London's Cavendish hotel. The room was kept at a constant temperature of 61°F (16°C) to prevent the contents from melting.

COFFEE CHAIN A woman started an act-of-kindness chain that lasted for 378 customers and 11 hours at a Starbucks drive-thru in St. Petersburg, Florida. She requested an iced coffee for herself and asked to pay for the order of the stranger in the car behind her. He did the same and the chain kept going throughout the day until customer number 379 pulled up at 6 p.m. and insisted that she wanted to pay for her own order and no one else's.

PET FOOD Dorothy Hunter, owner of pet stores in Richland and Kennewick, Washington, ate only dog, cat and bird food for a month to demonstrate their nutritional value. She had the idea when, not having time to go out for a snack, she grabbed a bag of pet treats from the counter and was surprised how good they tasted. One of her favorite pet foods was Tiki Cat brand chicken, which she ate straight from the can.

WARTIME RATIONS Carolyn Ekins of Nottingham, England, lost 80 lb (36 kg) over a 12-month period from 2013 to 2014 by following a ration-book diet from World War II. She weighed 350 lb (159 kg) at her heaviest, but saw the pounds fall off after sampling wartime favorites such as mock turkey and Spam fritters. Her food bill was also reduced by 80 percent, saving her nearly $5,000.

mouse KEBABS

Dried, salted and cooked field mice are strung on sticks in Malawi and sold as a tasty snack at markets or roadside stalls.

The mice are hunted in cornfields after the harvest when they are at their plumpest. Young boys either chase and catch them with their bare hands or lure them with food into water-filled clay pots where the rodents then drown. The most commonly eaten species is known locally as *kapuku* and is gray with a shorter tail than a rat.

FAST FOOD To promote the variety of restaurants in the small Philadelphia, Pennsylvania, suburb of Jenkintown, Mayor Ed Foley ate in all 24 of them in one day—April 19, 2014.

BEER ICE CREAM Atlanta, Georgia firm Frozen Pints has created beer-flavored ice cream. The strongest tub has an alcohol level of 3.2 percent, and so customers must be of legal drinking age to buy and eat it. The quirky concept came about by accident when someone spilled beer near an ice-cream maker.

DUMPSTER MISSION To protest against food waste, Baptiste Dubanchet of Tours, France, cycled 1,875 mi (3,000 km) from Paris, France, to Warsaw, Poland, eating only from dumpsters along the route.

PIZZA DRONE Francesco's Pizzeria in Mumbai, India, used a remote-controlled, four-rotor drone to deliver a pizza order to a customer in a skyscraper nearly a mile away. The restaurant hopes the drone will solve the problem of food getting cold as it is driven through the traffic-congested city, but at present the machine can fly for only around 5 mi (8 km) before its batteries run out.

Python Pizza

Evan Daniell, owner of Evan's Neighborhood Pizza in Fort Myers, Florida, sells snake pizza. Along with alligator sausage and frog legs, his "Everglades Pizza" has a topping of Burmese python meat to acknowledge the fact that the snakes, which can grow up to 20 ft (6 m) long, are widespread in the Everglades to the point that they are hunted to protect other species. The slabs of python are marinated for several hours to tenderize, before being sliced up. Customers say that python tastes a bit like chicken, but chewier.

DIET OF WORMS Three volunteers in Beijing, China, ate worms for over three months in a sealed laboratory to test whether astronauts could use them as their principal source of protein. The researchers fattened up the worms on plants grown inside the Moon Palace One biosphere and then ate them with a bean sauce.

CHEESY STREET As an alternative to salt, the city of Milwaukee, Wisconsin, has been experimenting with cheese brine—used in cheesemaking—to keep their streets from freezing in winter. Brine is particularly effective because it works at a lower temperature than normal salt.

COLESLAW WRESTLING

As part of Daytona Bike Week, Sopotnick's Cabbage Patch Bar in Samsula, Florida, stages an annual coleslaw-wrestling contest. Two competitors slug it out in a pit of vegetable oil and shredded cabbage until only one is left standing. Local girl and multi-champion Heather Spears, seen here fighting Laura Watts of Texas, says that although it's a fun contest, it can get rough. "I've had crater marks on me from all the girls digging in their nails and tearing my shirt and skin off."

SCORCHING SAUCE A sauce made by chef Muhammed Karim at the Bindi Restaurant in Lincolnshire, England, is so hot he has to wear a gas mask while preparing it. Called Atomic Kick Ass, the sauce scores 12 million units on the Scoville scale of hotness, making it nearly three times more fiery than police pepper spray.

GARLIC BEER Japanese company Aomori has created a garlic-flavored dark beer—Garlic Black Beer—with a spicy aftertaste. Black garlic is achieved by fermenting normal garlic in a hot room until it turns charcoal black in color.

SOUR TOE COCKTAIL Canada's Sour Toe Cocktail features an amputated human toe and the spirit of your choice. The drink's original digit was used more than 700 times before it was accidentally swallowed.

MARSHMALLOW ART Cake artist Michelle Wibowo of Sussex, England, made a life-sized reproduction of Michelangelo's famous Sistine Chapel fresco *The Creation of Adam* from 10,000 marshmallows and half a billion sprinkles.

SKUNK MEAT A Bolivian man who died in 2014 aged 107 said he owed his longevity to a diet of skunks. Carmelo Flores Laura, a herder from the mountain village of Frasquia, never ate pasta or sugar, preferring a wild grain crop called canahua, and skunk meat.

PIZZA ONLY Dan Janssen of Ellicott City, Maryland, has eaten nothing but cheese pizza for 25 years. He eats two 14-in (36-cm) pizzas a day, meaning that he has so far eaten more than 18,000 pizzas. He started his pizza-only diet as a teenager when he turned vegetarian, but realized he hated eating vegetables.

ROADKILL CRAVINGS

*Taxidermist Alison Brierley of Harrogate, England, usually turns the dead animals she finds on local roads into items of jewelry, but when she became pregnant she developed cravings for **eating** roadkill instead.*

She even hosted roadkill dinner parties, serving up pheasant, hare, rabbit, pigeon, deer and owl. She wanted to try fox and badger, but said they were always too squashed to go into the cooking pot.

Black Cheese

These may look like lumps of charcoal, but they are cheese! The cheese is made by British company Michael Lee Fine Cheeses and is called Char Coal Cheese because it is a mature cheddar that has been mixed with real charcoal. Despite its coal-like appearance it has a creamy cheddary taste.

DOUGH FEAST Employees at Rulli's Italian restaurant in Middlebury, Indiana, baked a calzone measuring 23 ft 7 in (7.2 m) long and weighing 212 lb (96 kg). It was made from 100 lb (45 kg) of pizza dough, 40 lb (18 kg) of cheese, 30 lb (13.6 kg) of pizza sauce and 25 lb (11.34 kg) of pepperoni.

STINKY CHEESE Limburger cheese from Belgium gets its color and pungent flavor from the same bacteria—*Brevibacterium linens*—that makes feet smell bad.

COKE CRAVING Jakki Ballan of Cheshire, England, loves Diet Coke so much she used to drink up to 50 cans a day. By consuming more than 34.87 pints daily, she was drinking the equivalent of double her body weight every week. Although she has since cut down to 30 cans a day, she estimates that she has spent $240,000 on her craving over the past 30 years.

FOOD WATCH Park Seo-Yeon of Seoul, South Korea, earns more than $9,000 a month by eating in front of a webcam and allowing thousands to watch her. People log in to watch "The Diva," as she is known professionally, eat for up to three hours a day in her apartment and they then donate money to keep her channel running.

PUB CRAWL In a 30-year pub crawl, Peter Hill, Joe Hill and John Drew from the West Midlands, England, had a drink in every county and region of Great Britain and Northern Ireland. The Blackcountry Ale Tairsters, as they were known, had visited around 18,000 pubs, including all 3,905 pubs in Wales, before founder Joe's 2014 death.

CENTURY-OLD SANDWICH The remains of a 118-year-old sandwich were discovered stuffed inside a church organ while the instrument was being dismantled. Kathy Yates, the organist at Padiham Road Methodist Church, Lancashire, England, found the sandwich wrapped in an 1896 copy of the *Stockport Advertiser* newspaper. Incredibly, the bread was still in good condition—a bit hard, but not moldy.

SLUGFEST Competitive eater Matt Stonie from San José, California, wolfed down 43 slugburgers—a traditional southern patty made of meat and soybeans served in a bun—in 10 minutes at the 2014 World Slugburger Eating Championships in Corinth, Mississippi.

TWIN DINER At the Twin Stars diner in Moscow, Russia, the waiters, bartenders and chefs are all identically dressed twins. Restaurant-owner Alexei Khodorkovsky was inspired to hire only twins by a 1964 Soviet film in which a schoolgirl crosses into a parallel world and finds her twin.

SPROUT CAPACITY Greengrocer Lawrence Jones of Berkshire, England, filled a Mini car to the brim with 38,182 Brussels sprouts. If laid out end to end, the sprouts would have stretched for a mile (1.6 km).

ROOF FARM Peng Quigen has created a farm on the roof of his four-story house in Shaoxing, China, growing rice, fruit and vegetables 40 ft (12 m) above ground. One year he harvested nearly 880 lb (400 kg) of watermelon—a 30 percent higher yield than when the crop is grown at ground level.

LOAF LIGHT

Yukiko Morita, a designer from Kyoto, Japan, makes artistic lampshades out of bread. Her Pampshades (which comes from the Japanese word for "bread") are made from real French baguettes, croissants and buns. After hollowing out the bread, she dries the shell, applies a resin coating to prevent mildew and uses LED bulbs so that the bread does not scorch.

Ripley's Believe It or Not!®
www.ripleys.com/books
FOOD

WORM TACO

The restaurant La Cocinita de San Juan in Mexico City sells tacos filled with Maguey worms, a species of edible caterpillar.

Highly nutritious—a 3.5-oz (100-g) portion contains calories equal to two plates of rice—the worms can be eaten alive and raw, or braised and served with a spicy sauce. The moth larvae are also used in bottles of the Mexican liquor *mezcal* to give added flavor to the drink.

PINEAPPLE FALL A 39-year-old warehouse worker from Jersey City, New Jersey, was taken to a hospital in May 2013 after 1,500 lb (680 kg) of pineapples fell on him.

FRENCH FRIES Chef Daan Vernaillen cooked French fries continuously for 125 hours—more than five days—at Sint-Katherina-Lombeek, Belgium, serving up around 2,000 portions to customers.

RAW MEAT For health reasons, Derek Nance, a butcher from Lexington, Kentucky, has eaten nothing but raw meat since 2008. He began by slaughtering two goats that he had kept for milk and now refuses to eat cooked meat because he thinks it tastes burned. To cure his digestion problems, he also eats rotten meat because it contains probiotic bacteria and even brushes his teeth with animal fat. Ironically, his girlfriend is vegetarian.

FRUIT NAUSEA Faye Campbell, 23, from Suffolk, England, has never eaten a fruit or vegetable. She even avoids thinking about these foods, as the prospect of eating them makes her feel nauseous. Instead, Faye eats only junk food—yet weighs a remarkably healthy 138 lb (62.5 kg).

EXPLOSIVE FISH Oilfish and escolar are popular seafood dishes in many Asian countries, but if you eat more than 6 oz (170 g) of them at a single sitting, they cause explosive, oily, orange diarrhea between 30 minutes and 36 hours later.

CANNIBAL RESTAURANT Health authorities closed a restaurant in Anambra, Nigeria, in 2014 after they discovered it had been serving dishes made with human flesh. Police officers said they recovered two fresh, bloodied and severed heads wrapped in cellophane sheets from the restaurant amid claims that roasted human head had even been an item on the menu.

PICNIC TABLE To celebrate its centenary, Hellmann's mayonnaise built a 320-ft-long (98-m) wooden picnic table weighing 8,000 lb (3,629 kg) at Hudson River Park in New York City. The accompanying picnic in September 2013 served burgers, potato and macaroni salads, corn on the cob and cupcakes—all prepared with mayo.

Bug Satay →
Among the tasty dishes on sale at the Shenyang Summer Food Festival in China was centipede satay served on a skewer.

BARBECUE MARATHON Lee De Villiers and Simon Clarke kept a barbecue going for more than 29 hours at the Old Sergeant pub in the Wandsworth borough of London, England, during which time they cooked 500 pieces of meat.

RICH DIET Tests on the body of King Richard III of England, who died in 1485 and whose remains were discovered under a parking lot in 2012, show that he drank up to a bottle of wine a day in the last years of his life. Samples taken from a femur, rib and tooth also reveal that he ate exotic bird meat including swan, crane, heron and egret.

SUBWAY MEAL To demonstrate that a new model of vacuum cleaner kills bacteria and germs, brand manager Ravi Dalchand ate a meal off the floor of a subway station used for filming in Toronto, Ontario. After cleaning the floor area with the Bissell Symphony, he tipped pasta onto the platform, pulled out a fork and ate his meal, even mopping up the sauce with bread.

LONG LIFE

English-born American chemist Robert Chesebrough, the inventor of Vaseline®, attributed his longevity to eating a spoonful of the petroleum jelly every day right up until his death in 1933 at the age of 96.

GLOWING TREAT Food inventor Charlie Harry Francis of Bristol, England, has created an ice cream that gives off a neon green glow when it is licked. Made out of jellyfish protein that glows in the dark, it incorporates calcium-activated proteins that react when they are agitated by the tongue, but each scoop costs £140 ($230)!

FLYING WAITERS The Royal Dragon restaurant in Bangkok, Thailand, has 1,000 staff, including 540 waiters on roller skates, to serve its menu of more than 1,000 dishes. It can seat up to 5,000 customers who are entertained by martial arts demonstrations and by waiters flying through the air on zip lines.

COFFEE CRAZY French writer and philosopher Voltaire (1694–1778) got his regular caffeine fix by drinking 50 cups of coffee a day.

GARLIC COLA The city of Aomori, known as the garlic capital of Japan, has produced such novelties as garlic beer, garlic ice cream and Jats Takkola, a garlic cola.

COSTLY COCKTAIL In honor of former British Prime Minister Winston Churchill, Club 23 in Melbourne, Australia, has created the Winston—a cocktail made with 156-year-old brandy that takes 16 hours to prepare and has a $10,027.69 price tag.

FIERY BURGER The XXX Hot Chili Burger sold at a takeout restaurant in Hove, England, measures 9 million units on the Scoville heat scale—that's more than 2,000 times hotter than Tabasco sauce and so potent that it has put at least seven people in the hospital. Of the first 3,000 people who tried to eat it, only 59 were able to finish it. Owner Nick Gambardella refuses to sell the red-hot burger, which is made with a special spicy sauce based on a piri-piri chili concentrate, to people under 18 and insists that anyone brave enough to try it must sign a waiver releasing the restaurant from any responsibility.

Ripley's Believe It or Not!®
www.ripleys.com/books
FOOD

JESUS PANCAKE A pancake served up on Good Friday at Cowgirl Cafe, Norco, California, bore what looked like the face of Jesus Christ. Manager Karen Hendrickson was so moved by the religious image, she would not allow it to be eaten and instead preserved it in a freezer.

BEST CUSTOMER The late North Korean leader Kim Jong-il spent a reported $650,000 a year on Hennessey brandy—and was their largest single customer.

KING CAULI Peter Glazebrook of Nottinghamshire, England, grew a cauliflower that measured 6 ft (1.8 m) wide and weighed a whopping 60 lb (27 kg), making it 30 times bigger than a regular cauliflower. The vast vegetable would make 120 portions of cauliflower cheese, but would require 6 lb (2.7 kg) of cheese as an accompaniment.

COLOR CHANGE Physicist Manuel Linares of Barcelona, Spain, has invented an ice cream that slowly changes color from blue to pink as it melts. Called Xamaleon, its exact recipe is secret, but it is made with strawberries, cocoa, almonds, banana, pistachio, vanilla and caramel, and it tastes like tutti-frutti.

➔ IN KOREA, A SUNDAE IS NOT AN ICE CREAM BUT A FOOD MADE FROM COW OR PIG INTESTINES STUFFED WITH NOODLES AND BLOOD.

PURRFECT PERK In Indonesia, palm civet cats—also known as toddy cats—that prowl around coffee plantations ingest only the ripest beans, and their excretions are used to create a smooth, uniquely flavored $75 cup of coffee!

GINGERBREAD VILLAGE New-York-City chef Jon Lovitch spent a year making a 300-sq-ft (28-sq-m) gingerbread village, which featured 135 gingerbread houses and 22 commercial buildings, including a town hall, train terminal, hot-chocolate brewery, pie bakery and fire station. He also made 65 candy trees, five gingerbread train cars and four gingerbread cable cars. To build the village, he used 500 lb (227 kg) of gingerbread dough, 400 lb (182 kg) of M&Ms and 2,240 lb (1,017 kg) of royal icing.

CRUNCHY CASTLE A 4-ft-sq (0.37-m sq) replica of Carlisle Castle in Cumbria, England was created from 5,000 custard cream cookies. It took three days to build.

MUSHROOM FEVER The edible ink cap mushroom causes vomiting and fever if eaten within three days of drinking alcohol, and for that reason it has been used to treat recovering alcoholics.

CHEESE SHOES

Lisa Dillon, a fashion student from Bath Spa University, England, designed and made this tasty-looking pair of shoes from cheese!

She sculpted a block of cheddar to form the heel of her "Jimmy Cheese" shoes, incorporated a stale cheese sandwich into part of the platform sole and melted more cheese to create the pretty embellishments on the top.

FLY EATER Daniel Dudzsisz, a 26-year-old German tourist who went missing for almost three weeks in 2014 while walking in the Australian outback, survived by eating flies. He left Windorah, Queensland, with some baked beans and cereal, but supplies quickly ran out and he was forced to eat any protein-rich insects he could catch.

BLOODY SUNDAE Washington, D.C., eatery The Pig serves a chocolate ice-cream sundae made with real pig's blood. The dessert, called "Sundae Bloody Sundae," uses blood instead of egg yolks in the ice-cream-making process to give a subtle mineral taste to the dark chocolate.

DONKEY SANDWICH A popular cough remedy in 19th-century England was for the patient to eat a sandwich filled with donkey hair.

DOG HAIR DIET Dog lover Wang Jing of Heilongjiang Province, China, eats dog hairballs every day as a snack. She has eaten 1,000 hairballs over the last two years and says they taste especially nice—"sweet, like chocolates"—after she has given her pet poodle Kuku a bath. She began eating dog hair when Kuku shed some fur while she was washing it. Out of curiosity she put it in her mouth and immediately fell in love with the taste. Wang's obsession with dog hair has actually improved her health because it led her to quit her stressful job as a graphic designer and start designing clothes for dogs.

Fried Leaves

The symbol of Canada, the maple leaf is also a tasty delicacy in Japan, where it is served deep-fried. When the leaves turn red in the fall, they are preserved in salt barrels for more than a year before being dipped in sweetened tempura batter and fried in hot vegetable oil.

SELFIE TOAST The Danville-based Vermont Novelty Toaster Corporation has invented the Toaster Selfie, an electric toaster that burns a picture of customers onto every slice. Customers upload a picture of themselves to the company's Burnt Impressions website and then a plasma cutter transfers the image onto a metal plate, which in turn is fitted to a toaster. The bread is grilled to light brown, except for the image, which is burnt darker.

BANNED FRUIT The ackee fruit, which is popular in Jamaica, can induce a deadly vomiting sickness if eaten when unripe. Its raw form is restricted in the U.S.A.

COFFEE WINE Florida beverage company Fun Friends Wine has created a new drink that combines coffee and wine in the same can. The company sells flavors such as Cabernet Coffee Espresso and Chardonnay Coffee Cappuccino.

FRIED WEEVIL The larvae of the 4-in-long (10-cm) palm weevil grub is harvested by many South American tribes as an excellent source of essential nutrients, and is usually eaten pan-fried.

BEER FOR LIFE The Danish Nobel Prize-winning physicist Niels Bohr (1885–1962) lived on the grounds of the Carlsberg Brewery in Copenhagen and received a lifetime supply of beer from them.

COOL SHORTS To keep his five-year-old son cool in summer, Ruifeng Fan from Taipei, Taiwan, made him a pair of shorts out of a watermelon. Fan initially gave him the melon to eat, but after cutting out the inside, he thought the rind would make a good pair of shorts, so he cut two holes for the legs and fitted it with a pair of braces to hold it up. The boy loved the outfit so much that Fan later made him a watermelon hat and watermelon boxing gloves.

ANTIQUE BUN A hot cross bun owned by Andrew and Dot Munson and kept in a cardboard box at their home in Essex, England, is over 200 years old. They were given the bun 30 years ago by a neighbor along with paperwork stating that it was baked in 1807. A traditional Easter food, hot cross buns were often stored for luck instead of eaten.

Made from chocolate!

CHOCOLATE TEAPOT

Scientists in York, England, made a chocolate teapot that was able to hold boiling water for two minutes without falling apart. They used dark chocolate with a high melting point that was built up in thick layers inside a silicon mold. As a result, the teapot did not leak, although a slight melting on the interior meant that the cup of tea poured from it was described as possessing a "hint of chocolate."

Ripley's Believe It or Not!®
www.ripleys.com/books
FOOD

CHILI POT Volunteers in Minto, North Dakota, cooked a pot containing 2,420 lb (1,098 kg) of chili—made up of 900 lb (408 kg) of diced tomatoes, 700 lb (318 kg) of ground beef, 500 lb (227 kg) of kidney beans, 250 lb (113 kg) of onions and green peppers and 70 lb (32 kg) of spices. They used a specially made cooking pot, which weighed 1,480 lb (671 kg) and had a volume of 348 gal (1,317 l).

FRUIT PRINTER A design studio in Cambridge, England, has invented a 3-D printer that can create edible fruit. The device uses a molecular gastronomy process called spherification that mixes liquid droplets and different flavors to create fresh, organic 3-D fruits.

INSECT PASTA

Absente, an Italian-style café in Kinshicho, Japan, serves a spaghetti dish topped with a generous helping of cooked locusts!

Although they may look disgusting, locusts are packed with protein, calcium and vitamin A, and were widely eaten in Japan during World War II to help combat malnutrition.

BEYOND BELIEF

SCARY SELFIES

Self-taught mother-of-three Nikki Shelley uses face paint to transform herself into scary monsters, zombies and ghouls that look as if they have stepped straight out of a horror movie. Her creepy characters have proved so popular that her pictures have gone viral on Facebook, winning her thousands of likes, and also impressing Neill Gorton, the acclaimed prosthetics designer on Doctor Who.

The 34-year-old care-home worker from Warwickshire, England, started by painting the faces of her children—Taylor, Leah and Kaiden—for Halloween and was soon able to paint as many as 12 children's faces in an hour. She also painted her husband Craig, but realized that she could not rely on her family to be human canvases all the time, so she began experimenting with designs on her own face.

"I didn't think anything would come of it, but the reaction to my work has been incredible," she says. "I don't really have an idea in mind when I start to paint. I just start and see what happens."

Turn over to read more about Nikki and how she transforms herself!

Ripley's ask

How did you discover your incredible talent for face painting? I first started as most moms do, with a small set of Snazaroo face paints, painting the kids' faces for Halloween. Then once, while I was painting children's faces at my nephew's birthday party, the other parents were asking me if I had any business cards for their kids' parties! I started practicing more and more on my own children, but they soon got bored with being my canvas, so I started to paint my own face!

How do you come up with your ideas? There are so many talented face/body artists out there, and I wanted to find a way to make my work stand out. I am a HUGE fan of horror movies, so took my inspiration from movie characters and from masks that I found on the Internet, taking ideas from a number of different characters and making them my own. Each time I started something new, I was pushing my skills to try something a little harder, a little more unusual.

What's your process for creating a painting? I start by outlining any major shapes such as eyes or mouth, but I use my own facial structure to do this, it just makes it look that bit more natural. Then, once I know where everything is going, and I'm happy with the placement, I start with the base layer. Once the base layer is on, and any blending is done, I can go in with the detail and shading to complete the look.

How long can it take for you to complete a painting? It's time-consuming, with an average painting taking around an hour and a half, depending on the detail.

YOUR UPLOADS

CLIP ART

New Yorker Mike Drake sent Ripley's this paperweight he made containing a year's worth of his fingernail—and toenail clippings (nearly 500 in total) encased in acrylic. He had hoped to build up a collection of nail paperweights, but his wife was so disgusted by the idea she threw out a lot of the clippings that he had been carefully keeping since 2001.

When the 164-ft-high (50-m) SAT Telefontornet, or Phone Tower, opened in Stockholm, Sweden, in 1887, 4,000 separate wires led from it to homes across the city, creating such darkness in the sky that locals complained that the sun was blocked.

At the time Stockholm had more telephones (5,500) than any city in the world and these required 3,107 mi (5,000 km) of overhead wire. The tower was demolished in 1953 following a fire.

HIGH WIRES

ROOF TRACK

With space on the ground in short supply, an elementary school in Taizhou, China, decided to build its running track on the roof. The 200-meter track fits perfectly on the roof of the oval-shaped, four-story building at the TianTai No. 2 school.

HERE COMES THE PUN The George Harrison memorial tree in Griffith Park, Los Angeles, California, has been killed by—beetles! Planted in 2004, the pine tree had grown to a height of 10 ft (3 m) until an infestation of tree beetles killed it in 2014.

ACCIDENTAL CALL A man in Tennessee was arrested on a drug charge after he accidentally "pocket-dialed" 911. Dispatchers heard him talking about going to a drug dealer's house and managed to trace the call to a Mexican restaurant in the town of Mount Pleasant, where he was enjoying dinner with a female friend. A search of the caller's car revealed a small bag of drugs.

DOWN THE DRAIN Fire crews had to rescue 16-year-old Ella Birchenough when she became stuck in a storm drain while trying to retrieve her cell phone. She jumped into the drain in Dover, England, after accidentally dropping her phone down it, but then became wedged up to her waist.

MISHEARD CALL A dog walker sparked a major search-and-rescue operation in Stirlingshire, Scotland, because her pet was called Yelp. A fellow walker mistook her calls for cries of "Help," prompting 20 police officers, many with dogs, and three mountain rescue workers to scour the area for hours fearing that the woman may have fallen down an old copper mine.

DELAYED DEATH A Swedish man, Johan Johansson, was finally declared dead in 2013—more than a century after he probably died. His family requested that the National Tax Agency should pronounce him dead as he had not been heard from for 102 years.

DISSATISFIED CUSTOMER Tonya Ann Fowler of Commerce, Georgia, was arrested for wasting police time after calling 911 to complain about the quality of the mugshot of her that was issued following a previous arrest.

LEG MISSILE A flight from Tunisia to Edinburgh, Scotland, was diverted after a female passenger threw her prosthetic leg at the cabin crew. She also demanded cigarettes and a parachute so that she could jump off the plane.

BOTTLE COFFIN Anto Wickham, a 48-year-old former soldier, has spent $5,000 on a 10-ft-long (3-m), custom-made casket shaped like a bottle of Jack Daniel's whiskey, which he wants to be buried in when he dies.

DOZY SUSPECT Burglary suspect Dion Davis was found fast asleep on a bed next to a bag of stolen jewelry after allegedly breaking into a house in Nokomis, Florida. A cleaning lady who discovered him called the police, and Davis remained asleep even while deputies took pictures of him lying on the bed.

CLEAN RACE Before the 2014 Fredagsbirken, a major cycle race held in Rena, Norway, a liquid detergent company handed out free samples of its product to all the competitors so that they could wash their outfits in it afterward. However, during the race six thirsty cyclists mistook their sample for an energy drink, gulped it down and had to be rushed to hospital.

LOST GOLD French athlete Mahiedine Mekhissi-Benabbad was stripped of his gold medal for the 3,000 meters steeplechase at the 2014 European Championships in Zurich, Switzerland, because he ripped off his running vest 100 meters from the finish. In doing so, he violated the rule that athletes' bibs must be visible throughout the race.

TWISTED HEAD Claudio Vieira de Oliveira from Monte Santo, Brazil, was born with his neck completely folded back on itself so that it appears to be upside-down, but he has defied his condition to graduate as an accountant and become an inspirational public speaker. He has badly deformed legs and little use of his arms and hands, yet he has taught himself to type on a computer using a pen held in his mouth and to operate a cell phone and a computer mouse with his lips. He has been diagnosed with a rare condition called congenital arthrogryposis that causes joint contractions. Until the age of eight years old, he had to be carried everywhere, but then learned to walk on his knees. Owing to his unusual shape he cannot use a wheelchair. When he was born nearly four decades ago, doctors told his mother not to bother feeding him because they believed he would not survive.

CABBAGE WALKERS

In an art performance at a Beijing music festival, dozens of Chinese teenagers treated cabbages as pets by taking them for walks on lengths of string. The stunt was arranged by artist Han Bing, who has been walking humble cabbages across the world for over 14 years as a reflection upon materialistic society. The walkers said that cabbages are more suitable for walking than dogs because they don't bark, need feeding or leave a mess on the sidewalk and they don't start fights with other cabbages.

POETIC JUSTICE When a horse thief in 17th-century Scotland was sentenced to decapitation by the Scottish Maiden (an early form of guillotine), the stolen animal was used to pull the cord that brought the blade down on the criminal's neck.

ACCIDENTAL DISPLAY Pensioner Hung Feng inadvertently started a spectacular blaze in a fireworks factory in Wuhan, China, by cooking sausages in the building. The explosion destroyed the building as well as hundreds of thousands of fireworks, but it gave locals a dazzling display.

BACK TO LIFE Several hours after being pronounced dead, 78-year-old Walter Williams of Lexington, Mississippi, woke up in a body bag. Workers at a funeral home opened his body bag in preparation for embalming him—but stopped in their tracks when he suddenly began kicking. It is thought his pacemaker had stopped working and then started again.

WEEPY PAPER Notebook manufacturer Magnus Ferreus has launched the Onion Note, a pad that makes you cry whenever you write on it. The pages are treated with compounds found in onion oil and the heat caused by the friction of pen on paper evaporates these compounds, releasing tear-inducing gas into the writer's face.

ZOMBIE WEDDING Abby Riggs married Thomas Ehmer in a zombie-themed wedding at Muncie, Indiana, the bride walking down the aisle with artificial blood dripping down her chin and her white dress covered in grime. Even the priest wore fake blood and grey skin.

TOILET TALK The Miraikan science museum in Tokyo, Japan, staged a three-month exhibition devoted to toilets—including a choir of singing toilet seats, poop jokes, and explanations about how feces are made. Visitors could also flush themselves down a 16-ft (5-m) toilet slide.

FACEBOOK BLUNDER A burglar who broke into a house in St. Paul, Minnesota, was easily apprehended after checking his Facebook profile on the homeowner's computer, but forgetting to log out.

Edible Cards

Believe it or not, this business card is made out of meat! Chris Thompson, head of Philadelphia, Pennsylvania, company MeatCards, creates the distinctive name cards by laser-etching the customer's details into 2-x-4-in (5-x-10-cm) pieces of dried beef jerky. Not only are the cards impressively different, they remain edible for up to a year.

SKIN THEFT A man was charged with stealing more than $350,000 worth of human skin from Mercy Philadelphia Hospital, Pennsylvania. Prosecutors say he repeatedly stole skin grafts from the hospital between November 2011 and July 2013.

CRAZED LAWYER Angry at the way an inheritance case was going for his client, Evgeniy Tankov, a lawyer from Karaganda, Kazakhstan, suddenly pulled out a flyswatter in court and started hitting the judge with it in a fit of rage. After the lawyer had delivered the third blow, the judge jumped up from behind his desk and wrestled with Tankov, who was immediately barred from practicing law and faced a ten-year prison sentence for assault.

Teddy

This looks like a normal butcher's shop except that all the "meats" are teddy bears and other soft toys.

Vegetarian Miroslav Menschenkind, an artist from Hamburg, Germany, beheaded the toys and displayed them in a mock-up butcher's shop as a protest against animal slaughter. Menschenkind hung the decapitated teddies on meat hooks and made sausages out of the head fillings. His exhibit also featured a row of eyeless Teletubbies hanging by their feet and even his own childhood toy dog was put through the meat grinder. Other cuddly toys were vacuum packed just like joints of meat ready for the oven.

Kuscheltier-Schlachterei seit 1886

GOOSE PULLING Goose pulling—a man on horseback attempting to pull the greased head of a live goose from its body—was a traditional European and North American sport from the 17th to 19th centuries. It is still practised today, using a dead goose, in parts of Belgium, Germany and the Netherlands.

RAT BOUNTY Businessman Gareth Morgan has introduced a plan to offer students at the Victoria University of Wellington, New Zealand, a reward of free beer for every rat they catch—dead or alive.

HOLLYWOOD HERO Danielle Davies of Ocean City, New Jersey, lives with a full-size cardboard cutout of Hollywood star Bradley Cooper. She shops with him, cooks, eats and mows the lawn with him, and takes him to bed—even though she is happily married with children. Danielle, who has her own website, "My Life With Bradley Cooper," where she documents her adventures, actually met her hero during her sophomore year at Villanova University when they appeared in a play together.

CROCODILE BRIDE Joel Vasquez Rojas, mayor of San Pedro Huamelula, Mexico, "married" a small crocodile in a special ceremony. According to tradition, the crocodile is a princess and the wedding ritual guarantees plenty of seafood for fishermen to catch along the Pacific coast. Before the nuptials, the wedding party walked through the town with the crocodile bride dressed in white with its jaws wired shut, and afterward the guests danced with the reptile.

KISSED PIG To fulfil a promise he made to his young students if they stopped dropping litter, Hong Yaoming, deputy head teacher of Xianning Experimental Elementary School in China, kissed a 44-lb (20-kg) pig.

HUMPTY'S FALL When two men climbed onto a wall in 2014 to pose for a photograph at the Enchanted Forest theme park in Salem, Oregon, they accidentally knocked Humpty Dumpty off his perch. The cement Humpty crashed to the ground where he smashed into pieces, leaving his creator, artist Roger Tofte, with the task of putting him back together again. Humpty had sat on the wall ever since the park opened in 1971.

SATANIC CHEESE Polish exorcist Elzbieta Gas warned shoppers at her local supermarket to avoid buying packets of goat's cheese priced at 6.66 zlotys ($2.24) as she pointed out that 666 is the sign of the devil. Her fears were fueled further by the goat horns, which, not unreasonably, appear on the packaging.

Flying Car

This white SUV somehow ended up stuck in a tree several feet above ground in a hillside forest close to a zoo in Wenzhou, China.

MASH SPILL A busy highway in North Yorkshire, England, was completely blocked for more than four hours in June 2014 after a truck spilled its load of instant mashed potatoes. Cars skidded dangerously on the liquid mash, which was eventually removed by plowing it with a tractor to make it easier to clear and then washing it away with freezing chemicals and high-powered hoses.

CARTWHEEL BAN 65-year-old Dianne Barker, of Phoenix, Arizona, has been banned from doing cartwheels at public meetings held by the Maricopa Association of Governments. A former college cheerleader, she says the cartwheels are her way of expressing passion, but the association claimed they were disruptive and a danger to public safety.

SCHOOL DRAG When floods made it impossible to use a nearby suspension bridge in 2014, young students in Sam Lang, Vietnam, had to get to school by crossing a swollen river inside giant plastic bags. Adults put the children inside the bags to keep their uniforms dry, and then pulled them through the raging torrent before unwrapping them on the other bank.

LUCKY TOILET The Kalamazoo Christian prep baseball team from Michigan carries a portable toilet to every game to bring the players good luck. The toilet is said to symbolically represent the team flushing away its past losses in order to move onto future victories.

BITE BET Norwegian soccer fan Thomas Syverson won almost $900 after placing a $5 bet that Uruguayan international soccer player Luis Suarez would bite an opponent during the 2014 World Cup.

BAT BOMB During World War II, the U.S. Army tested incendiary bombs attached to 6,000 Mexican free-tailed bats.

RHEUMATIC CURE

Believe it or not, this man at Eden, New South Wales, Australia, was standing inside a dead whale in the hope of curing his rheumatism. In early 20th-century Australia, some people believed that rheumatic pain could be eased for up to a year if the patient spent 30 hours inside the carcass of a slaughtered whale where the heat and gases caused by putrefaction were thought to possess soothing properties.

Ripley's Believe It or Not!®
www.ripleys.com/books
BEYOND BELIEF

BELOVED PLANT Ronna Scoratow of Pittsburgh, Pennsylvania, is leaving $5,000 in her will to a friend on condition that Phil, her 7-ft-tall (2.1-m) philodendron house plant that she has kept for more than 40 years, is lovingly fed and watered for the rest of its life.

DUMMY MUMMY A skeleton found in 2013 in an attic in Diepholz, Germany, that was originally declared by scientists to be a 2,000-year-old mummy has instead been exposed as a worthless plastic dummy. "The Mummy of Diepholz" had been sprayed with a chemical that made the bones appear real to experts.

➔ A MAN WAS ARRESTED WHEN HE RETURNED TO THE SCENE OF HIS CRIME TO TRY TO BUY BACK THE GUN HE HAD DROPPED DURING A FAILED ROBBERY ATTEMPT AT A MOTEL IN BRADENTON, FLORIDA.

LAME EXCUSE A 67-year-old Canadian man who was stopped while driving at 112 mph (180 km/h) near Black Diamond, Alberta, told Mounties he was speeding so that he could dry his newly washed car. He was fined $800 and suspended from driving for 45 days.

DEATH SCENT Raychelle Burks, a chemist at Doane College, Crete, Nebraska, has developed a perfume to help people survive a zombie apocalypse. Eau de Death features putrescine, cadaverine and methanethiol to create a scent that stinks of rotten eggs and boiled cabbage but works on the principle that zombies are attracted by the smell of the living.

FLY KILLER Eighty-year-old Ruan Tang of Hangzhou, China, devotes her life to exterminating flies and estimates that she kills up to 1,000 of the disease-carrying insects every day. She has been a one-woman pest control operation for 15 years and spends eight hours a day prowling the city with her swatter.

OWN GOAL During a tense overtime clash, Phoenix Coyotes' hockey goalie Mike Smith unfortunately decided the game in favor of the Buffalo Sabres with a freak goal against himself after the puck lodged in the back of his pants. When the puck looped up into the air and disappeared from view, confused players skated around searching for it and Smith retreated into his goal—a fatal move as a replay showed he had unknowingly carried the puck with him. The goal was awarded to the Sabres, marking the end of the game.

elf ears

BEFORE

Convinced that she was an elf in a past life, Melynda Moon, a 24-year-old model from Guelph, Ontario, had surgery to give herself pointed ears.

The tops of her ear cartilages were skinned and pieces were cut from the tips to form points. She often dresses like an elf, too.

CRAZY NAME After losing a bet at a poker game, a 22-year-old man from Dunedin, New Zealand, has legally changed his name to Full Metal Havok More Sexy N Intelligent Than Spock And All The Superheroes Combined With Frostnova. The name had been chosen for him by his fellow card players.

FRESH AIR As a protest against pollution in his home country, artist Liang Kegang gathered a jar of French fresh air in Provence during a trip and sold it for $860 in Beijing, China.

BARBIE WANNABE Blondie Bennett of California has spent more than $40,000 on surgery in an attempt to replicate her heroine Barbie's physique.

RESTORATION GOES BADLY WRONG

In 2012, 80-year-old local artist Cecilia Giménez made a disastrous attempt to restore *Ecce Homo*, a 19th-century fresco depicting Jesus Christ that was originally painted by Elias Garcia Martinez on the walls of the Sanctuary of Mercy church in Borja, Spain. Her handiwork (on the right) was described by one critic as resembling "a crayon sketch of a very hairy monkey in an ill-fitting tunic." Ironically, so many people wanted to see the botched fresco that the church began charging visitors to view it.

SPACE PASTRY A team of amateur scientists on the island of Sicily, Italy, launched a model pastry into space. The clay replica of a *cannolo* (a local cream-filled delicacy) was placed inside a spacecraft made from an ice-cream box and attached to a large helium-filled balloon that soared to an altitude of 97,664 ft (29,768 m). Two cameras fitted to the *Cannolo Transporter* captured pictures of the voyage before the balloon burst and the craft parachuted back to the ground.

MUMMIFIED BODY A dead woman lay undiscovered in her Pontiac, Michigan, home for six years—while bills continued to be paid from her bank account and a kindly neighbor regularly mowed her lawn. A worker sent to repair a hole in the house roof eventually found her mummified body seated in her car in the garage.

LAST POST On the run for two months in Freeland, Pennsylvania, Anthony Lescowitch Jr. was finally captured by police after making the mistake of posting a wanted picture of himself on his own Facebook page. Posing as a woman, a policeman began chatting online about the post with the fugitive, who readily agreed to a meeting at which he was arrested.

Box Set

Scott Wiener from New York City has spent 15 years building up a collection of more than 750 pizza boxes from over 45 different countries—including some that turn into puzzles and model airplanes. He paid $200 for a 54-in (137-cm) box from Big Mama's and Papa's Pizzeria in Los Angeles, California—the largest commercially available pizza box in the world. Although Scott eats pizza every day, he limits himself to 15 slices a week.

IRON SHOES

For over seven years, 53-year-old Zhang Fuxing from Tangshan, China, has walked 50 ft (15 m) a day in a pair of homemade iron shoes, each weighing over 440 lb (200 kg)—to cure his back pain. It takes him over one minute just to walk ten paces with the blocks strapped to his shoes.

HANGING AROUND

BEE STINGS Michael Smith, a scientist at Cornell University, New York, forced bees to sting him from head to toe over a five-week period so that he could find out which part of the body would hurt most from the stings. He got the bees to sting him three times in 25 different areas of the body and then rated the pain factor, concluding that the nose was the worst, followed by the top lip. He did not encourage the bees to sting him on his eyes because it would have been too dangerous.

PERMANENT BRIDE When Xiang Junfeng of Shandong Province, China, married Zhu Zhengliang in 2004, it made her so happy that she has refused to wear anything but her wedding dress ever since. To ensure that she could wear one all year round, she had three more wedding dresses made, and she even wears her bridal gown while working in the fields.

EXTRAVAGANT GIFT As a gift to his future bride, Meng Huang hired 18 drivers and a fleet of luxury cars to deliver bamboo baskets filled with $1.5 million in cash to her home in Zhejiang, China.

PERFECT MATCH Married couple Mel and Joey Schwanke, from Fremont, Nebraska, have worn matching clothes every day for more than 35 years. They own around 150 custom-made matching outfits, which they wear whenever they go out together—ensuring that his tie always matches her dress.

FREAK INJURY While celebrating England's goal against Italy at the 2014 World Cup, national soccer team physiotherapist Gary Lewin fractured and dislocated his ankle—an injury that ruled him out of the rest of the tournament because he had to fly back to the U.K. for surgery.

LONG WILL The last will and testament of Frederica Evelyn Stilwell Cook, who died in London, England, on January 9, 1925, at age 68, was 1,066 pages (95,940 words) long and occupied four leather-bound volumes.

SECURITY CHECK At the 2014 Commonwealth Games in Glasgow, Scotland, Olympic cycling champion Sir Chris Hoy was denied access by a security guard to the building named in his honor, the Sir Chris Hoy Velodrome. The guard demanded to see his I.D. before finally admitting him.

DEEP POOL The Deep Joy, a swimming pool at the Hotel Terme Millepini in Montegrotto Terme, Italy, reaches a depth of 130 ft (40 m)—equivalent to the height of nine double-decker buses stacked on top of each other.

SOLDIER'S FATE British soldier Gordon Heaton was killed in World War II, but his family were never told of his death because the official telegram and his last will and testament remained undiscovered for 67 years after a delivery boy left them on a bus. They were found in November 2011 in a lost property box at a bus depot in Birmingham, England.

For pre-wedding pictures that neither of them will ever forget, groom Zheng Feng, an amateur rock climber, took his brave bride-to-be 65 ft (20 m) up the side of a vertical cliff in Jinhua, China.

FOUR MANAGERS The Boston Red Sox baseball team used four different managers during their game with the Tampa Bay Rays on May 30, 2014. John Farrell, Torey Lovullo and Brian Butterfield were all ejected by umpires after arguing over pitchers targeting batters, leaving Greg Colbrunn to coach the Red Sox to a 3–2 victory.

ASH ADDICT When her husband died suddenly, a 26-year-old woman from Fayetteville, Tennessee, found comfort by eating his cremated ashes. At first she just carried his remains with her wherever she went, but one day some of the ashes spilled onto her hand and instead of wiping them away, she licked them off her finger. After that, she became addicted to eating the death dust, and within a year had devoured 1 lb (0.45 kg) of her late husband's ashes with another 5 lb (2.3 kg) remaining. She describes the taste as resembling "rotten eggs, sand and sandpaper."

BORN SURVIVOR Bill Hillman, a Chicago-based co-author of the book *Fiesta: How to Survive the Bulls of Pamplona*, was hospitalized in Spain after being seriously gored during the 2014 Pamplona bull run. When he tripped and fell, the horn of a 1,320-lb (600-kg) bull sliced through his thigh, just missing his femoral artery. If the artery had been severed, he could have bled to death in seconds.

Knee Shrapnel

World War II veteran Ronald Brown lived with 6 oz (170 g) of metal shrapnel in his left knee for 68 years. His family only learned the extent of his injury after he died in 2012 at age 94 and a pile of metal was found among his cremated ashes. He had stepped on a booby-trap device while serving with the British Army in France in 1944.

STRAY BULLET A moose hunter on the Norwegian island of Vesteroy shot at a moose, but accidentally hit an elderly man sitting on the toilet in a nearby wooden cabin. The wayward bullet hit the senior in the abdomen, but his injury was not serious. The moose escaped unharmed.

POISON PLOT During World War II, the British Secret Service attempted to "poison" German leader Adolf Hitler with female hormones—a side effect of which would be his mustache hair falling out.

HUMAN PUNCHBAG Forty-eight-year-old Xie Shuiping earns $3,500 a month by letting strangers punch him. He tours the bars and clubs of Wuhan City, China, charging people to hit him hard in the stomach three times. Any challenger who manages to hurt him receives free drinks.

ALWAYS THE BRIDESMAID New Yorker Jen Glantz is a professional bridesmaid. After being a bridesmaid at four of her friends' weddings, she posted an advertisement on Craigslist offering her services to brides all over the world. For a fee, she will write a speech, encourage the wedding guests to dance and even lift the bride's dress when she needs to go to the bathroom.

MUDDY MARRIAGE Jared Baylor and Taylor Ratcliff got married in a giant sloppy mud pit at the 2014 Toronto Days Mud Run in Kansas. The bride's white dress was spattered in mud after the groom drove his pick-up truck into the center of the competition bog for the ceremony. Both are fans of the filthy sport of mud bogging, which challenges drivers to plow through a deep mud pit in the fastest possible time.

KISSED TO DEATH

A gravestone in New York City's Woodlawn Cemetery recounts the sad demise of George Spencer Millet who died in 1909 on his 15th birthday while trying to escape six young women intent on giving him a birthday kiss. The women did not realize that he was carrying an ink eraser—a sharp, 6-in-long (15-cm) metal tool—in his pocket, and as they moved in for their kisses, he fell forward and the point of the eraser drove into his heart, killing him.

UNHAPPY ENDINGS

Hans Steininger died in Braunau, Austria, in 1567 by **tripping over his beard.** He was in such a hurry to escape a fire that he forgot to roll up his 4.5-ft-long (1.4-m) whiskers!

Sir Arthur Aston, a Royalist leader during the English Civil War, was **beaten to death with his own wooden leg** by Oliver Cromwell's soldiers at the siege of Drogheda, Ireland, in 1649.

Acting as a pallbearer at a cemetery in London, England, in 1872, Henry Taylor stumbled on a stone, fell and was **crushed to death by the coffin** he had been carrying.

Czech housewife Vera Czermak was so distraught to learn of her husband Franz's infidelity that she **jumped out of the window** of her third-story Prague apartment in 1978—just as Mr. Czermak happened to be walking along the street below.

Wesley Parsons, a farmer from Laurel, Indiana, died laughing in 1893. After being told a joke, he was seized by **fits of uncontrollable laughter** for nearly an hour, and when he was finally able to stop, he began hiccupping. Two hours later he died of exhaustion.

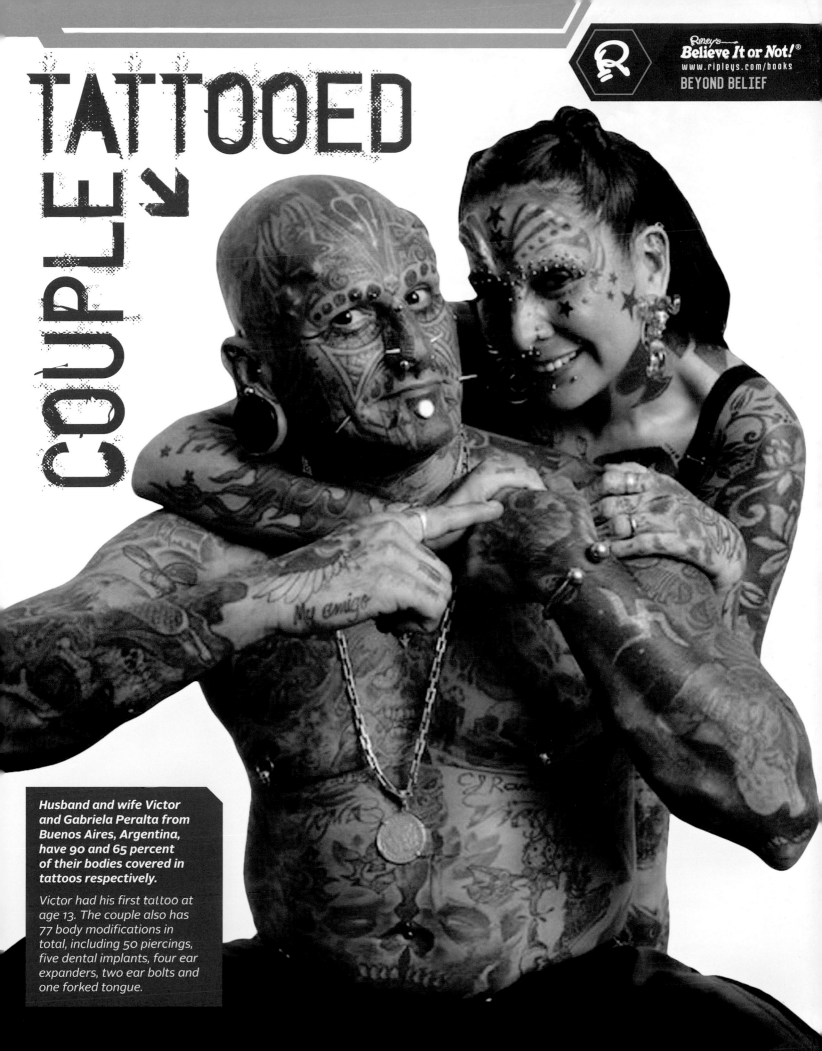

TATTOOED
COUPLE

Husband and wife Victor and Gabriela Peralta from Buenos Aires, Argentina, have 90 and 65 percent of their bodies covered in tattoos respectively.

Victor had his first tattoo at age 13. The couple also has 77 body modifications in total, including 50 piercings, five dental implants, four ear expanders, two ear bolts and one forked tongue.

239

Normal toilet roll!

Big Roll

This giant toilet roll made by Charmin measures 9.73 ft (3 m) in diameter and contains more than 1,000,000 sq ft (92,903 sq m) of toilet tissue—enough to make 95,000 standard-sized rolls.

RUNNING OF THE BALLS A new festival in the Spanish town of Mataelpino features runners racing downhill trying to outpace giant 275-lb (125-kg) polystyrene balls. The balls have replaced traditional live bulls following complaints that the event was cruel.

CARDBOARD COMPANION After her father died in 2012, Jinna Yang of Norfolk, Virginia, traveled the world with a life-size cardboard cut-out of him to show him the places he had always wanted to visit. She took photos of herself with the cardboard replica at such locations as Iceland's Blue Lagoon, The Louvre in Paris and the Leaning Tower of Pisa in Italy.

CLUB BADGE Bulgarian builder Zdravkov Levidzhov is such a big fan of English soccer club Manchester United that he has officially changed his name to "Manchester United" and has had the club's red-and-yellow badge tattooed onto the center of his forehead as a permanent reminder of his allegiance.

NO DYING! In 2012, Giulio Cesare Fava, mayor of Falciano de Massico, near Naples, Italy, banned its 4,000 residents from dying because of a dispute with a neighbouring town over how to expand the local cemetery. The mayor asked the residents to keep living until he had built them a new cemetery elsewhere.

ANIMAL COSTUMES When a drunk man started threatening women in the street in Coventry, England, he was arrested by two off-duty policewomen dressed as a monkey and a zebra. Officers Terri Cave and Tracy Griffin were on their way to a costume party.

LIZARD MIMICS The Australian sport of goanna pulling gets its name because the rival competitors adopt the pose of goanna lizards. A strap is tied around the necks of the two fighters, who get down on all fours opposite each other with their stomachs touching the ground and their heads held high. The game is like tug-of-war, but instead of their hands, the competitors use their heads to pull each other over a line and win the fight. The National Goanna Pulling Championships have been held in Wooli, New South Wales, since 1985.

SECRET MMUSEUMM

Hidden behind heavy, unmarked metal doors on the edge of the Tribeca district of Manhattan lies New York's most secret museum—a one-room space of quirky, random objects packed into an abandoned elevator shaft. Founded by Alex Kalman and brothers Benny and Josh Safdie, the museum contains such diverse items as a facsimile of the shoe thrown at George W. Bush during a 2008 press conference, a homemade antenna, an assortment of tip jars, papers accidentally left behind in copy machines, newsstand paperweights and a collection of plastic vomit from around the world. It is open to visitors only on weekends, but passers-by can peer through a series of small viewing windows 24/7.

5 OTHER CRAZY EXHIBITS IN THE MUSEUM

- *Potato chips from around the world*
- *Homemade weapons of defense*
- *Misspelled food-container labels*
- *Disney bullet-proof backpacks*
- *Objects made for prisoners or by prisoners*

DEATH STRUGGLE

A 10-ft-long (3-m) water python swallowed a crocodile whole after a five-hour struggle in front of startled onlookers at Lake Moondarra in Queensland, Australia.

After slowly constricting the 3.3-ft-long (1-m) freshwater croc to death, the snake dragged it ashore before devouring it headfirst in just 15 minutes. Afterward, the exhausted and overstuffed snake lay still, while it digested its dinner, with the crocodile's ridges and legs clearly visible inside its belly.

MEASURE FOR MEASURE Founded by New Yorker Scott Griffin, the Drunk Shakespeare Society puts on performances of Shakespeare's plays in the city's bars—and each night a different member of the cast is genuinely drunk.

EYE GOUGING Gouging was an 18th-century North American backwoods sport that was used to settle arguments, the aim being to gouge out your opponent's eyes. Fighters would grow their fingernails extra long for this purpose.

ALL CHANGE The Mexican national soccer team had four different coaches in 41 days in 2013 because three were fired following poor results in the team's World Cup qualifying campaign. After Jose Manuel de la Torre was dismissed in early September, Luis Fernando Tena lasted just one match—a 2–0 defeat to the U.S.A. Tena's successor, Victor Manuel Vucetich, fared little better—a defeat to Costa Rica saw him replaced by Miguel Herrera in mid-October.

241

SHOWER SIREN

Nineteen-year-old Kiyuu Oikawa, of Japan, has converted his showerhead into a creepy "girlfriend" in which the water flows from her mouth. To create the doll, he taped a human mask with wig onto the showerhead, attached clothing stuffed with a balloon for the body, and made spindly arms out of packing tape and wire.

SMALL DEMAND A month after Alastair King emigrated from the U.K. to New Zealand, he received a tax demand from his former council—South Somerset District Council—for just 2 pence, which they said he could pay in installments.

Rooftop Grazing

Passersby in Bern, Switzerland, did a double-take when they looked up and saw a cow standing precariously on the steep roof of a farmhouse. The inquisitive animal had climbed on to the roof in search of new pastures but, not finding any, calmly made her way back unharmed to her field, leaving her owner Dieter Mueller to pay for the tiles she had smashed.

CHOCOLATE BATHROOM U.K. chocolatiers Choccywoccydoodah teamed up with bathrooms.com to create an £80,000 ($133,000) chocolate bathroom containing 9.4 million calories—the equivalent of 12 years' worth of recommended calorie consumption. Made entirely of Belgian chocolate, it featured a £50,000 ($83,600) bathtub, a £7,000 ($11,700) bidet, a £9,000 ($15,000) sink and a £14,000 ($23,000) toilet. Kept at room temperature, it would apparently last for six months before spoiling.

FLYING TOILET A creative group of rocket enthusiasts launched a portable toilet 2,000 ft (600 m) into the sky from a field in Three Oaks, Michigan, and watched it land safely by parachute. The Michiana Rocketry club's aluminum-frame rocket stood 10 ft (3 m) tall and had seven motors and a portable toilet bolted on to it. The contraption weighed a total of 450 lb (204 kg) and was lifted with 2,865 lb (12,744 N) of thrust, compared to a NASA space shuttle's 7.8 million lb (34.7 million N).

NATURAL GAS French inventor Christian Poincheval has come up with a range of pills that make human gas smell like roses, violets or chocolate. The capsules, which are made from natural ingredients such as fennel, seaweed, vegetable coal, and blueberries, also ease indigestion and reduce the amount of flatulence.

DANGER KIT The Gilbert Atomic Energy Lab, a 1950s science kit for children, included genuine radioactive uranium and polonium, and a Geiger counter!

DEAD HEAD Students at the Puchenii Mosneni elementary school in Romania's Prahova county learn human anatomy by studying the real-life skeleton of a former school principal. Alexandru Grigore Popescu worked at the school for half a century until his death in the 1960s. Since then his skeleton has been put on display for biology lessons.

SNEEZE LOG Since 2007, Peter Fletcher from Birmingham, England, has carefully logged every one of his sneezes—more than 4,000 in total. Whenever he sneezes, he makes a note of the time and date, where he is, and what he is doing. Looking back through his records, he realizes that he has never sneezed while on the toilet and is particularly proud of sneeze number 42, which, although powerful, he managed to avoid getting on a quiche.

PREHISTORIC MONSTER Seventy-seven-million-year-old bones found in Argentina reveal the existence of probably the largest animal ever to have walked the Earth, *Dreadnoughtus schrani*, a dinosaur that weighed a colossal 65 tons—as heavy as an entire herd of elephants and seven times heavier than *Tyrannosaurus rex*. It measured 85 ft (26 m) long, making it nearly the length of a passenger jet airplane. Despite its fearsome size, it was a plant eater, but would have had to spend almost all its time eating just to maintain its body weight.

UNLUCKY SHOT U.S. sea captain John Kendrick was killed in Hawaii in 1794 while having dinner on board his ship, *Lady Washington*, when a British vessel accidentally used a live shot to fire a cannon salute in his honor.

TROLL SEARCH Lars Christian Kofoed Rømer, an anthropology student at the University of Copenhagen, was awarded $430,000 in 2014 to carry out research that includes investigating the existence of underground trolls (small mythical creatures) on the Danish island of Bornholm.

GLACIER WEDDING Landon Woods and Tara Coultish, from Alberta, Canada, got married in June 2014 on top of Iceland's 4,200-ft-high (1,280-m) Myrdalsjokull glacier, which sits on an active volcano. The bride wore a wedding gown and snow boots.

SNAIL CARPET

Untreated snail poop.

Snail poop made into thread.

Woven snail poop.

Snail eating colored paper.

Snail poop floor tiles.

Made of snail poop!

Believe it or not, these brightly colored floor tiles are made from snail poop!

Dutch artist Lieske Schreuder discovered that when snails eat colored paper their feces retain that color because the snail's digestive system does not absorb the pigments. So she set up a small laboratory where the malleable excrement from 1,000 snails was collected and fed into a machine that mixed and ground it into a 5-mm-thick (0.2-in) thread. She then wove the thread to form speckled floor tiles. The process moves at a snail's pace because it takes nine snails five days to produce enough poop for just 3.3 ft (1 m) of thread.

WHO LOO

Customers wanting to use the toilet at the Warmley Waiting Room Café near Bristol, England, must step into a replica of the TARDIS, Doctor Who's time machine. Justin and Claire Hoggans paid £1,800 ($3,000) for the TARDIS on eBay and spent almost as much again converting it into a functioning "Who Loo" fitted with toilet, sink and hand dryer. Whenever anyone enters or leaves the cubicle, lights flash courtesy of a motion sensor, while TARDIS sound effects are operated via a doorbell in the café.

INDOOR SLIDE Trisha Cleveland from Minneapolis, Minnesota, has come up with a device that entertains children by converting a staircase into an indoor slide in just a few minutes. The SlideRider consists of a series of foldable mats with safety rails.

IDIOT SIGN After impatient driver Shena Hardin mounted the curb in Cleveland, Ohio, because she did not want to wait behind a school bus, a judge fined her and ordered her to stand at an intersection for two days with a sign saying, "Only an idiot would drive on the sidewalk to avoid a school bus."

ESCAPE ARTIST Wayne Carlson of Canada has escaped from different North American prisons 13 times since the 1960s.

GOOD TIMING Nicollette Brynn Anders was born in Missoula, Montana, at 2.15 p.m. on November 12, 2013, meaning that she was born on 11-12-13 at 14:15.

IDENTITY CRISIS Xu Fei, a teacher at a primary school in Wuhan, China, was alarmed to discover that 20 of the 22 children in her new class were twins. Nine of the 10 sets of twins were identical, and because they all wore school uniform, she had to resort to memorizing minor differences such as facial moles and different hand sizes to distinguish them.

QUICK SALE The flawless, 59.6-carat Pink Star diamond—at 0.8 x 1 in (2.69 x 2.06 cm) the world's largest cut diamond—sold for $83 million at an auction in Geneva, Switzerland, in 2013—but the sale never went through.

RARE QUADS Sharon Turner of Berkshire, England, gave birth to amazing quadruplets—a pair of identical twin boys and identical twin girls—at odds of 70-million-to-one.

THIRD TWINS Karen Rodger from Renfrewshire, Scotland, defied odds of 500,000 to 1 by giving birth to three sets of twins. Daughters Isla and Rowan arrived in 2013 to join four boys, 14-year-olds Lewis and Kyle and 12-year-olds Finn and Jude.

LEAP YEAR Betty Flemming, of Springfield, Virginia, celebrated her 22nd birthday in 2012—even though she was born in 1924. Her birthday is February 29, so she has a "real" birthday only every four years—on which basis she became legally old enough to buy alcohol only in 2008, at age 84!

RING RETURNED When Brenda Caunter lost her wedding ring while pulling cabbages in a muddy field in Cornwall, England, in 1972 and an extensive search failed to find it, she thought she would never see it again. However, 41 years later an amateur metal detector scouring the field found the ring—and although the ground had been plowed regularly in the intervening period, the gold band was in perfect condition.

LUCKY COUPLE Calvin and Zatera Spencer of Portsmouth, Virginia, won the state lottery three times in March 2014—including two $1 million prizes.

FLASH MOB Tim Bonnano, a student at Aptos High School, California, enlisted a flash mob consisting of hundreds of fellow students to persuade Gabriella DeNike to accompany him to the school prom. While he played the guitar, his accomplices held up signs begging Gabriella to be his date.

LONG HAIR

Tom Wilson of Lino Lakes, Minnesota, sent Ripley's this image featuring his one gray chest hair, which measures an incredible 9 in (22.5 cm) long.

OLDEST DIVORCEES An Italian couple who had been married for 77 years announced they were divorcing in 2012 after the 99-year-old husband learned that his 96-year-old wife had had an affair in the 1940s.

SINKING FEELING Just hours before Stan Bennett was buried in July 2012, his shrimp boat mysteriously sank to the bottom of St. John's Harbour, Newfoundland, Canada. The boat had survived at sea in storms and hurricanes, only to sink while tied up at the wharf in the middle of summer on the very day its owner was laid to rest.

DOUBLE TRAGEDY A farmer and his sister were killed in separate car crashes at the same spot on the same road just six hours apart. Emanuel Davidescu died when he lost control of his car on the highway in Caras Severin, Romania, on June 7, 2012. A few hours later his sister, Maria Patrascu, died when the trailer she was riding in was rear-ended on the same stretch of road.

TATTOOED SANTA

Vitor Martins, who has been dressing as Santa for more than 15 years in the Brazilian city of São Caetano do Sul, has 94 percent of his body covered in tattoos, many with a Christmas theme, including Santa himself, a reindeer, an elf helper and a Christmas tree.

245

INDEX

Page numbers in *italic* refer to the illustrations

ACKNOWLEDGMENTS

Cover © Markus Gann - Shutterstock.com, © DLA - Shutterstock.com; Contents 21 Brett Kern; 134 Maor Zabar Hats moarzabarhats.etsy.com; 137 Angela Rossi; 152 Hubcap Creatures; 184 NaTalica www.natalica.com; 192 http://www.wahahafactory.com/; 228 Nikki Shelley - The Painting Lady

11 (tr) Courtesy of Ugly Models: 13 Angus James Tackle Tactics; 14–15 www.burghleyimages.com; 16 (t) Eric J. Eakin, (b) Adam Pacitti, (r) William Rice; 17 Caters News Agency; 18 Bournemouth News/Rex; 19 (t) AP/Press Association Images, (b) Circus World; 20 (t) Hari Punjabi/Barcroft India, (b) Paul, Andrew & Sophia Hung; 21 Brett Kern; 22–23 Collection of the John and Mable Ringling Museum of Art Tibbals Digital Collection; 24 Kirstin Mercer; 24–25 (t) Newsflare.com; 25 (c) Patrick Page-Sutter; 26 (t) Solent News/Rex; 26–27 (t/r) Mikeal/Rex; 27 (b) © Europics; 28 (t) Geoff Robinson Photography, (b) Stefan Siverud/Wenn.com; 29 Angus James Tackle Tactics; 31 Irene Becker/Contributor/Getty Images; 32 (t) Sameer Ashraf/Barcroft India; 33 Reuters; 34 (t) Bruce Black, (b) Villa Escudero Plantations & Resort, Inc.; 35 Michael Nichols, National Geographic Creative; 36 (t) © Andy Marshall/Alamy, (b/l, b/c) SWNS.com, (b/cr, b) Rex; 37 (t) Rex, (c) AP, (b) Michael McGurk/Rex, (r, t/r) © Eddie Linssen/Alamy; 38 AFP/Getty Images; 39 (t) Reuters, (b) ChinaFotoPress via Getty Images; 40 (t) Reuters/Damir Sagolj; 40–41 (b) Sergey Krasnoshchekov; 41 (t) Imagine China/Rex; 42 (t) Arkaprva Ghosh/Barcroft Media; 43 Getty Images; 44 (t) Rex/HAP/Quirky China News, (b) David McQuinn/Janet Potter; 45 Caters News Agency; 46 Public Domain; 47 (t) EPA, (b) Getty Images; 48 (c) Alfredo Barsuglia/Hotspot Media, (b) EPA; 49 (t, c) Craig Robertson/Rex Features, (b) © Eric Murphy/Alamy; 50 (t) AFP/Getty Images, (b) Cedric Favero/Solent News/Rex; 51 Caters News Agency; 52 (t) Reuters, (b) PA Wire/Press Association Images; 53 Supplied by Wenn.com; 54 Janae Copelin/Barcroft USA; 55 (t) Imagine China/Rex, (b) Photograph by Barcroft India; 56 (t) Photograph by Luca Zanetti/Laif, Camera Press London, (b) © Chaiwat Subprasom/Reuters; 57 © Miguel Vidal/Reuters; 58 (t) "Wieliczka" Salt Mine archives/Rafal Stachurski, Wieliczka Salt Mine, (b) Irene Becker/Contributor/Getty Images; 59 Zafer Kizilkaya; 61 Sherry Lemcke Photography; 62–63 © Florian Schulz/visionsofthewild.com; 64 (t) Don Cooke/Cuddle Clones; 65 (t) Goodman, Brett A.; Johnson, Pieter T. J. (2011): Effects of limbs malformations on the locomotory performance of Pacific chorus frogs (P. regilla) in laboratory trials. Figure_1.tif. PLOS ONE. 10.1371/journal.pone.0020193.g001., (b) Cats Protection/SWNS.com; 66 © 2004 MBARI; 67 (t) Gianfranco Gómez, (b) Exclusivepix media; 68 Caters News Agency; 68-69 (b) Caters News Agency; 69 (t) ChinaFotoPress /Stringer/Getty; 70 (t) Reuters/Oscar Martinez; 70–71 (b) I.M. Chait/Rex; 71 (t) Getty Images; 72 (b) AP/Press Association Images; 73 Well Animal Clinic/Bournemouth/Rex; 74 (t) John Birkett/Solent News/Rex, (b) Shivan Chanana/Barcroft India; 75 Stephen Hopkins/Rex; 76 (t) © Enrique Marcarian/Reuters, (b) © David A. Northcott/Corbis; 77 © Reuters Photographer/Reuters; 78 (b) Matt Rudge/SWNS.com; 78–79 (t) Getty Images; 79 (b) Caters News Agency; 80 (t) AndreeSiwadi/BNPS, (b) Ingo Arndt/Minden Pictures/FLPA; 81 National News & Pictures; 82 (t) Sherry Lemcke Photography, (b) The LIFE Picture Collection/Getty; 83 Emir Ozsahin/Rex; 84 (t) Photo courtesy of Monica Beckner and Roy Beckner, (b) Debra Mayrhofer/Lort Smith; 85 Caters News Agency; 86 (t) AP/Press Association Images, (b) Caters News Agency; 87 Robertus Pudyanto/Stringer/Getty; 88 (t) © Alex Mustard/naturepl.com, (b) Peter Roosenschoon & Dubai Desert Conservation Reserve; 89 Barry Bland/Rex; 91 Richie the Barber; 92–93 John Robertson/Barcroft Media; 94 (t) Caters News Agency, (b) Sam Ireland; 95 (c) Supplied by Wenn.com, (sp) Rex/Braun Shavers; 96 AFP/Getty Images; 97 (sp) Library of Congress, (b/r) Snap Stills/Rex; 98 Caters News Agency; 99 Barcroft Media; 100–101 Caters News Agency; 102–103 © The Natural History Museum/Alamy; 104 Circus World; 105 (t) Getty Images, (b) Circus World; 106 (t) Matt Writtle/Barcroft Media, (b/l) AP/Press Association Images; 107 Macchina anatomica – Donna (Giuseppe Salerno, 1763–64) © Massimo Velo; 109 (t/l) Sipa Press/Rex, (t/r, c, b) AP/Press Association Images; 110 (t/r) Meredith Cahill, Cherryhill NJ, (b) National Archives of Australia: A1336, 4890; 111 AP/Press Association Images; 113 (c) Alinari Archives/Contributor, (l) TT News Agency/Press Association Images; 114–115 AP/Press Association Images; 118 (t) HAP/Quirky China News/Rex, (b) ©Europics; 119 Richie the Barber; 121 Angela Rossi; 122–123 Leon + Lilly Mackie/cardboardboxoffice.com; 124 (t/l) Alex Dodson/Solent News/Rex, (r) Getty Images; 125 Reuters; 126 (t/l) Kim Kowalski of Clever Kim's Curios, (b) © Medavia; 127 Reuters/Sergei Karpukhin; 128–131 Courtesy of Derin Bray American Art & Antiques; 132 (t) Ruaridh Connellan/Barcroft USA, (b) Rex/Imagine China; 133 Tom McShane/Solent News; 134 (t) Hoang Tran, (b) Maor Zabar Hats moarzabarhats.etsy.com; 135 Supplied by Wenn.com; 136 (t/l, c/r) Rex, (b) Ji Tan www.wildlifemalaysia.com www.pixelsdimension.com; 137 Angela Rossi; 138 (t) © Hulton-Deutsch Collection/Corbis, (b) Mary Evans/SZ Photo/Scherl, (l) © Bettmann/Corbis; 139 © Pictorial Press Ltd/Alamy; 140 Marutaro/Rex, (b/l) Imagine China/Rex; 141 (t) Vin Los; 142-143 AFP/Getty Images; 144 Supplied by Wenn.com; 145 (t) Wessex Water/Julian James Photography/Rex Features, (b) ChinaFotoPress via Getty Images; 146 (t) Caters News Agency, (b) Imagine China/Rex; 147 (tl) EPA/CHING BIN, (tr) AP/Press Association Images; 148 (t) SAPOL, (b) AP/Press Association Images; 149 Supplied by Wenn.com; 150 (t) Wang jiayu - Imagine China, (b) David McHugh/Rex; 151 Science & Society Picture Library/Contributor/Getty Images; 152 (t) AP/Press Association Images, (b) Caters News Agency; 153 Austral Int./Rex; 154 (t) Laurent La Gamba/Solent News/Rex; 154-155 (b) Getty Images; 155 AFP/Getty Images; 156-157 © KIMMO BRANDT/epa/Corbis; 158-159 Andy Farrington/Red Bull Content Pool; 160 (t) Andy Farrington/Red Bull Content Pool, (c) Dean Treml/Red Bull Content Pool, (b) Brian Nevins/Red Bull Content Pool; 161 (t) Reuters/Jason Lee, (b) SWNS.com; 162 (t) Caters News Agency, (b) © Europics; 163 Hou wei zk – Imaginechina; 164 (t) Caters News Agency, (b) facebook.com/ITTFWorld/Remy Gros; 165 To Mane/Barcroft Media; 166 Cornell Capa/Contributor/Getty Images; 167 (t) © Bettmann/Corbis, (c) Underwood Archives/Contributor/Getty Images, (b) Collection of the John and Mable Ringling Museum of Art Tibbals Digital Collection; 168-169 (t) © KIMMO BRANDT/epa/Corbis, (b) © Darren Staples/Reuters; 169 Nathan Edwards/Newspix/Rex; 170 (b) Quirky China News/Rex; 171 Rex/Tom Dymond; 172 Barcroft India; 173 © Europics; 174–175 Action Press/Rex; 176–177 Mike King/Rex; 178 (t) Supplied by Wenn.com, (b) James Cheadle/Solent News/Rex; 179 Caters News Agency; 181 Jason Mecier; 182–183 Bordalo II; 184–185 NaTalica www.natalica.com; 186 Alessandro Diddi/HotSpot Media; 187 Woolff Gallery, London; 188 (t) BODILY CANDLES BY ANNA STERNIK, PHOTO COURTESY OF THE PHOTOGRAPHER, ANNA STERNIK; (b) Tao/Rex; 189 www.margauxlange.com © Margaux Lange; 190–191 Bradley Hart bradley@bradleyhart.ca; 192 (t) Barcroft India, (b) http://www.wahahafactory.com/; 193 Supplied by Wenn.com; 194 (t) AP/Press Association Images, (sp) Joe Raedle/Staff/Getty Images; 195 AP/Press Association Images; 196 (t) Caters News Agency, (b) Véronique Vedrenne; 197 Caters News Agency; 198 Jason Mecier; 199 (t) Ted Lawson/Rex, (b) Reuters; 200 (t) Getty Images for Ascot Racecours, (c) Nancy Hoffman Gallery, New Y/Rex; 201 (t) Xiao junwei sh- Imagine China, (l, r) Shdaily - Imagine China; 202 (t) Supplied by Wenn.com, (l, c/l, b) Art-EFX/Rex; 203 Svitlana Postelga/Rex; 204 (t) Jonty Hurwitz/Rex, (b) www.carolmilne.com/Rex; 205 Caters News Agency; 206 (t) Emanuel Pavao, (b) BNPS.co.uk; 207 Reuters; 208-209 Clive Cooper - www.sparksflydesign.com; 210 (t, l) © Cavendish Press, (r) Sutton Seeds/Bournemouth News/Rex; 211 YOSHIKAZU TSUNO/AFP/Getty Images; 212 (t) Landov/Press Association Images, (b) Morkes Chocolates; 213 Arkaprava Ghosh/Barcroft India; 214 (t) Clive Cooper - www.sparksflydesign.com, (b) Solum, Stian Lysberg/Scanpix Norway/Press Association Images; 215 Suntory Holdings Limited/Rex; 216 (t) Mayumi Ishikawa, (b) Jonathan Hordle/Rex; 217 AP/Press Association Images; 218 (t) Caters News Agency, (l) KeystoneUSA-Zuma/Rex; 219 Caters News Agency; 220 (t) Michael Lee and Fine Cheeses Ltd., (b) Pampshade/Yukiko Morita/Rex; 221 (t) Reuters, (b) ChinaFotoPress via Getty Images; 222 (t) Reuters/Kim Kyung-Hoon, (b) © Europics; 223 SWNS.com; 224 (t) Exclusivepix media, (b) Supplied by Wenn.com; 225 Absente Semba; 227–229 Nikki Shelley - The Painting Lady; 230 (t) Mike Drake, (b/l) Nikki Shelley - The Painting Lady, (b/r) Tekniska museet, Stockholm; 231 Sun jinbiao - Imagine China; 232 (t) © Europics, (b) meatcards.com; 233 Supplied by Wenn.com; 234 (t) HAP/Quirky China News/Rex, (b) National Library of Australia; 235 Laurie Cadman Creative (http://www.lauriecadman.com); 236 (t) ABACA/Press Association Images, (r) AFP/Getty Images, (b) Caters News Agency; 237 Imagine China/Rex; 238 (t) Matt Austin/Rex, (b) Allison C. Meier; 239 SWNS.com; 240 (t) Haney Inc. - www.haneyprc.com, (b) Mmuseumm; 241 Marvin Muller/Barcroft India; 242 © Europics; 243 Lieske Schreuder; 244 Jon Kent/swns.com, (b) Thomas F. Wilson; 245 Reuters/Nacho Doce

Key: t = top, b = bottom, c = center, l = left, r = right, sp = single page, dp = double page, bg = background
All other photos are from Ripley Entertainment Inc. Every attempt has been made to acknowledge correctly and contact copyright holders and we apologize in advance for any unintentional errors or omissions, which will be corrected in future editions.

CONNECT WITH *Ripley's* ONLINE OR IN PERSON

There are **31** Ripley's Believe It or Not! Odditoriums spread across the globe for you to visit, each jam-packed with weird and wonderful exhibits from the Ripley collection. Bookmark our website for exclusive Ripley's Believe It or Not! stories, photos, contests, and more! And don't forget to connect with us on Facebook, Twitter, Pinterest and Instagram for a daily dose of eye-popping Ripley's fun!

31 ZANY ODDITORIUMS

ripleys.com
/RipleysBelieveItorNot
/ripleys
/ripleysodditorium
/RipleysBION

Atlantic City **NEW JERSEY**
Baltimore **MARYLAND**
Blackpool **ENGLAND**
Branson **MISSOURI**
Cavendish **CANADA**
Copenhagen **DENMARK**
Gatlinburg **TENNESSEE**

Genting Highlands **MALAYSIA**
Grand Prairie **TEXAS**
Guadalajara **MEXICO**
Hollywood **CALIFORNIA**
Jackson Hole **WYOMING**
Jeju Island **SOUTH KOREA**

Key West **FLORIDA**
London **ENGLAND**
Mexico City **MEXICO**
Myrtle Beach **SOUTH CAROLINA**
New York City **NEW YORK**
Newport **OREGON**

Niagara Falls **CANADA**
Ocean City **MARYLAND**
Orlando **FLORIDA**
Panama City Beach **FLORIDA**
Pattaya **THAILAND**
San Antonio **TEXAS**

San Francisco **CALIFORNIA**
St. Augustine **FLORIDA**
Surfers Paradise **AUSTRALIA**
Veracruz **MEXICO**
Williamsburg **VIRGINIA**
Wisconsin Dells **WISCONSIN**

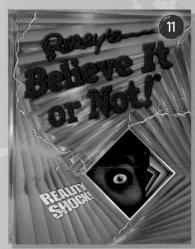
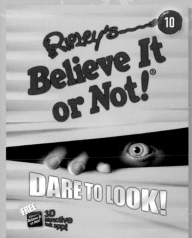

FUN FACTS & SILLY STORIES

Filled with wacky stories and colorful images of crazy animals, incredible talents, amazing people and goofy events, readers will have a hard time putting these books down!

ONE ZANY DAY!

In the tradition of *The Big One*, *One Zany Day* is filled with all-new hilarious true stories, incredible photos, and interactive games and puzzles to keep readers busy from sunup to sundown! With this book, every day is *One Zany Day*!

TWISTS

Ripley's award-winning TWISTS books combine fascinating facts and unbelievable stories to make learning fun! These books are filled with amazing Ripley's stories, exclusive artwork, and a number of additional features to give readers hours of enjoyment.

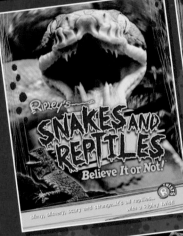